Front-End Tooling wi
Gulp, Bower, and Yeoman

Front-End Tooling with Gulp, Bower, and Yeoman

STEFAN BAUMGARTNER

MANNING
SHELTER ISLAND

For online information and ordering of this and other Manning books, please visit
www.manning.com. The publisher offers discounts on this book when ordered in quantity.
For more information, please contact

    Special Sales Department
    Manning Publications Co.
    20 Baldwin Road
    PO Box 761
    Shelter Island, NY 11964
    Email: orders@manning.com

Manning Publications Co.
20 Baldwin Road
PO Box 761
Shelter Island, NY 11964

Development editor:	Leslie Trites
Review editor:	Aleksandar Dragosavljević
Technical development editors:	Nick Watts, Michael Williams
Project editor:	Kevin Sullivan
Copyeditor:	Linda Recktenwald
Proofreader:	Melody Dolab
Technical proofreader:	Johan Pretorius
Typesetter:	Dottie Marsico
Cover designer:	Marija Tudor

ISBN 9781617292743
Printed in the United States of America
1 2 3 4 5 6 7 8 9 10 – EBM – 21 20 19 18 17 16

brief contents

contents

preface

I fell in love with the web way back in my teenage years. And like every teenage love, this one had an enduring impact on me. The idea of having the web as this almost anarchic way of publishing, carrying open thoughts and free speech and allowing everybody to raise their voice (for good and for bad) fascinated me. And it allowed me to transform from a consumer into a producer.

Digging the video game series "Dragon Quest" led me to spend around 11 years publishing over 1,500 pages of strategy guides online. A passion for literature and films prompted me to publish my thoughts in podcasts over the course of four years. And rumor has it that there are prototypes of unfinished video projects somewhere on my hard disk backups that thankfully never saw the light of day. Any hobby, any obsession of mine found a way onto the web. And the web was always kind enough to show great acceptance of my work.

It was not until 2010—"the day Nintendo called" (literally)—that I realized my biggest hobby was actually not one of the several topics I had created content for. I was offered the chance to extend my writing on video games for a variety of products. While I was flattered, honored, and highly motivated to do so, I quickly realized that I would never be able to provide the same quality for projects that I didn't care as much about. But I could enable others by focusing on the common denominator for all the projects I'd worked on: the technologies running these websites—HTML, CSS, and JavaScript.

I quit my day job as a scientist in the field of image processing—which I never actually liked—and called myself a web developer from that day on. I was lucky enough to get hired by a local web agency and finally get paid for the work I loved so much. That was by far the best decision I've ever made. Shortly after, I had the opportunity to lead some of the best front-end development teams you can find on the planet. The thing that I found the most challenging with all of them was bringing code conventions, project structure, and automation to every team member in the most efficient and unobtrusive manner. These technologies should be a joy to use, not a chore. We tried many things, but had the first real breakthrough when tools like Yeoman came on the scene. From then on, every new project needed a good setup with a JavaScript build tool, a dependency manager, and a scaffolding tool.

With this book, my long relationship with the web has come full circle. It takes my love for publishing on the web to a meta level by publishing about web technologies—not only on the web, but in print, a thing that was unimaginable for me years ago.

The web's impact on me continues to this day. Through it, I've found friends all over the world. It has given me the chance to travel to other cities and countries. And it was even the way I found my wife. I look forward to the things to come.

acknowledgments

You might think that writing a book is one of the loneliest occupations possible. The reality is quite the opposite.

Of all the persons involved, Lesley Trites deserves first mention. As my development editor at Manning, she provided invaluable feedback and proved to be the perfect companion on my writing endeavors. She single-handedly taught me how to write. If it weren't for her, this book would not be in the shape it is right now.

Speaking of people at Manning, my technical editors Johan Pretorious and Nick Watts were a joy to work with! Thank you for sanity-checking my ideas.

Thanks also to the reviewers who contributed valuable feedback throughout the writing process: Andy Knight, David DiMaria, Giancarlo Massari, Harinath Mallepally, Jason Gretz, Jeroen Benckhuijsen, Johan Pretorius, Mario Ruiz, Nikander and Margriet Bruggeman, Palak Mathur, Tanya Wilke, Unnikrishnan Kumar, and Zorodzayi Mukuya.

Alexander Zaytsev, Lars Johansen, and Jens Klinger held the spirit of open source high and kept improving my Gulp examples on GitHub as the book progressed.

Addy Osmani taught me everything I know about front-end workflows. I learned open source through the guidance of Sebastian Gierlinger and Blaine Bublitz.

Thomas Pink and Thomas Heller are not only the best colleagues imaginable, but also kept improving my build tool skills by asking the right questions. Their urge for improvement and their concrete real-world examples provided context and a solid foundation for this book.

Cheers to my "Working Draft" podcast friends Christian Schaefer, Peter Kröner, Rodney Rehm, Anselm Hannemann, and Hans-Christian Reinl, who are always up for fun and challenging discussions and gave me necessary looks over the rim of the teacup. The same goes for the rest of the "Klassenfahrt" gang: Fabian Beiner, Sven Wolfermann,

Sebastian Golasch, Der Pepo, Robert Weber, Marc Hinse, Bianca Kastl, Joschi Kuphal, Marc Thiele, Khalil Lechelt, Frederic Hemberger, Tobias Baldauf, Tom Arnold, and Maik Wagner. Without you, I would have never come this far.

People imagine that writers of romance spend weeks and weeks writing in a chalet in the French Provence. To satisfy the cliché, I was glad to be hosted by my parents-in-law, Hans and Marianne, every other weekend at their house in the Austrian Innviertel. I also want to thank my parents, Hans and Rosi, for taking care of me on the weekends in between. Thank you all for your support!

Last, but not least, I want to thank my wonderful wife, Doris. Her patience, love, and care are second to none. Doris, I owe you a lot.

about this book

Front-end Tooling with Gulp, Bower, and Yeoman was written with a strong focus on a broad concept of development workflows. The book ties together three phases that a developer enters when working on new and existing web projects: initialization, development, and deployment. For each phase, this book details the requirements and take-aways and introduces a tool suited to this job.

In modern web development, tools tend to have a short lifespan, and seem to come and go as often as a new day dawns. A writing time of over a year might as well be a decade in JavaScript land. This provided quite a challenge, but was also a reason to not make the tools themselves the center of attention. Instead, each technology in this book can be easily exchanged with a well-suited counterpart, with all the key concepts still intact. On the other hand, the covered tools were picked not with an eye on trends, but for a touch of sustainability. These tools have a broad reach, an established user base, and a general-purpose application area. These characteristics should help keep this book relevant in the years to come.

Who should read this book

Front-end Tooling with Gulp, Bower, and Yeoman is for front-end web developers who want to introduce process automation and tooling into their daily workflows. This book establishes a workflow pattern suited for both beginners and experienced front-end developers. While there are plenty of tutorials and blog articles out there for every one of the mentioned tools, this book ties all the tools together into one workflow and goes far beyond the surface of the tools' functionalities.

Roadmap

The book is divided two parts with five chapters in each.

The first part deals with a new workflow for front-end developers and their dedicated tools. While this part describes how to set up the workflow with three distinct tools, it also deals with the overall concepts of front-end development workflows. Reading this part in order is recommended.

- Chapter 1 shows the day-to-day challenges for a front-end developer and establishes a workflow built upon three types of tools to overcome these challenges.
- Chapter 2 gives insights into the first kind of tool, the build tool, which helps to automate low-level code modification tasks and provides a high-level interface. The build tool Gulp provides the basis for this chapter.
- Chapter 3 introduces dependency and execution chains. Here the tasks from the previous chapter get combined into a series of executions that allow you to set up a local development environment.
- In chapter 4, dependency management is introduced. The chapter shows the difference between flat and nested dependency trees and their pros and cons for front-end development. Bower is the selected dependency management tool for this chapter.
- The first iteration of the front-end workflow comes to an end in chapter 5, where the processes established in chapters 2 through 4 are made reusable through the scaffolding tool Yeoman.

After reading part 1, you should be able to use the three aforementioned tools to adapt the proposed workflow for your own needs. (All described tools use Node.js as their runtime. An appendix is provided for developers new to Node.js who want to take a peek under the hood.)

Whereas in part 1 the tools Gulp, Bower, and Yeoman are easily exchangeable with respective counterparts, part 2 dives deep into the inner workings of these three tools specifically. Each chapter is meant to boost productivity of the established workflow and showcase why the selected tools are so unique and helpful.

- In chapter 6, Gulp features such as incremental builds and pipeline switches are used to create output for different deployment environments.
- Chapter 7 goes deep into the underlying technology of Gulp—file object streams—to make similar pipelines reusable for different input and output scenarios.
- Chapter 8 gives insight into Gulp's plugin ecosystem and how redundancy and loss of quality can be avoided when selecting new pieces for build pipelines. It also shows how tools outside the plugin space can be integrated with Gulp's task and streaming APIs.

- Chapter 9 swings back to dependency managers. It introduces the concept of modules and shows different module definition systems. Modules provide an easy way to integrate dependencies into the main application.
- Chapter 10 concludes the book with another look at the scaffolding tool Yeoman. With the use of Yeoman's sub-generators, scaffolding becomes a useful process not only for the ignition of a new project, but throughout development.

Part 2 is meant to make you an expert in each one of the tools. The examples build on each other, but the concepts and details can be consumed on their own.

Code conventions and downloads

This book contains many examples of source code, both in numbered listings and inline with normal text. In both cases, source code is formatted in a `fixed-width font` `like this` to separate it from ordinary text. Sometimes code is also **in bold** to highlight elements that have changed from previous steps in the chapter, such as when a new feature adds to an existing line of code.

In many cases, the original source code has been reformatted; we've added line breaks and reworked indentation to accommodate the available page space in the book. In rare cases, even this was not enough, and listings include line-continuation markers (➥). Additionally, comments in the source code have often been removed from the listings when the code is described in the text. Code annotations accompany many of the listings, highlighting important concepts.

Source code for the examples in this book is available for download from the publisher's website at www.manning.com/books/front-end-tooling-with-gulp-bower-and-yeoman.

The examples are also available on GitHub at https://github.com/frontend-tooling. The project "sample-project-gulp" has solutions for each chapter inside a branch.

Author Online

Purchase of *Front-End Tooling with Gulp, Bower, and Yeoman* includes free access to a private web forum run by Manning Publications where you can make comments about the book, ask technical questions, and receive help from the author and from other users. To access the forum and subscribe to it, point your web browser to www.manning.com/books/front-end-tooling-with-gulp-bower-and-yeoman. This page provides information on how to get on the forum once you're registered, what kind of help is available, and the rules of conduct on the forum.

Manning's commitment to our readers is to provide a venue where a meaningful dialog between individual readers and between readers and the author can take place. It is not a commitment to any specific amount of participation on the part of the author, whose contributions to the AO remain voluntary (and unpaid). We suggest you ask the author challenging questions, lest his interest stray!

Online resources

Need additional help?

- The Gulp.js tag on Stack Overflow (http://stackoverflow.com/questions/tagged /gulp) provides a great resource of questions and answers. The audience is friendly and knowledgeable and provides good solutions to special cases.
- The Yeoman website (http://yeoman.io/) is not only the hub page for the Yeoman tool itself, but also a good resource with links to tutorials and guides for all of the workflow's tools.
- There are a lot of Gulp and Yeoman tutorials on my blog: https://fettblog.eu. They are concise and to the point, and tackle more-specific challenges.

about the author

STEFAN BAUMGARTNER lives and works in Linz, Austria. He is a passionate web developer and speaker and organizes tech meetups and conferences in his hometown. His research areas include web performance, automation, architectures, and progressive enhancement. He loves Italian cuisine and enjoys the occasional Belgian beer after work.

about the cover illustration

The figure on the cover of *Front-End Tooling with Bower, Gulp, and Yeoman* is captioned "Man in Medieval Dress." The illustration by Paolo Mercuri (1804–1884) is taken from "Costumes Historiques," a multivolume compendium of historical costumes from the twelfth, thirteenth, fourteenth, and fifteenth centuries assembled and edited by Camille Bonnard and published in Paris in the 1850s or 1860s. The nineteenth century saw an increased interest in exotic locales and in times gone by, and people were drawn to collections such as this one to explore the world they lived in—as well as the world of the distant past.

The colorful variety of Mercuri's illustrations in this historical collection reminds us vividly of how culturally apart the world's towns and regions were a few hundred years ago. In the streets or in the countryside people were easy to place—sometimes with an error of no more than a dozen miles—just by their dress. Their station in life, as well as their trade or profession, could be easily identified. Dress codes have changed over the centuries, and the diversity by region, so rich at one time, has faded away. Today, it is hard to tell apart the inhabitants of one continent from another, let alone the towns or countries they come from, or their social status or profession. Perhaps we have traded cultural diversity for a more varied personal life—certainly a more varied and faster-paced technological life.

At a time when it is hard to tell one computer book from another, Manning celebrates the inventiveness and initiative of the computer business with book covers based on the rich diversity of regional life of many centuries ago, brought back to life by Mercuri's pictures.

Part 1

A modern workflow for web applications

This first part is dedicated to front-end development workflows and tooling. In these chapters, you'll learn about the daily challenges a front-end developer has to face, and will implement a workflow to overcome those challenges by using three tools.

Chapter 1 introduces the proposed workflow and details which types of tools are necessary to manage all the tasks ahead.

Chapter 2 starts with the first tool: the build tool, Gulp. With Gulp, you'll set up automation for testing as well as compilation for JavaScript and CSS files.

Chapter 3 builds on the tasks from chapter 2 and organizes them in execution chains. Additionally, you'll set up a live-reloading development server, which updates the build files to a full-fledged local development environment.

Chapter 4 introduces the second tool: the dependency-management tool, Bower. You'll learn about components and dependency trees and will use Bower to keep third-party software at ease.

In Chapter 5, all the efforts from the previous chapters are combined and packaged with the third tool: the scaffolding tool, Yeoman. With Yeoman, you'll be able to roll out development-ready project templates for your future projects.

Tooling in a modern
front-end workflow

This is a great time to be a front-end developer. Browsers are more advanced than ever, and with the new technologies of the HTML5 era come numerous new possibilities. JavaScript isn't a toy language anymore and is used for a large variety of applications. The fat client—running the majority of an application's code directly in the browser, and thus the front end—is embraced and considered a good development strategy for web applications.

With JavaScript being taken seriously, developers face challenges in delivering the best possible code for their platforms—running authoring tools, bundling files,

2

minifying applications, optimizing images...the list goes on. To meet all those expectations you need proper tooling.

In this chapter, we look at which non-coding tasks you have to tackle in your day-to-day workflow and how tools can help you as front-end developers. We divide those tasks into three categories and look at three tools to conquer them all:

- A build system, such as Gulp, allows you to run a multitude of file-transforming processes at the click of a button.
- A dependency manager, such as Bower, helps you keep an eye on versions of different libraries you use frequently, notifying you of conflicts and, in some cases, solving them on their own.
- A scaffolding tool, such as Yeoman, provides you with the essential project files to get things going. Yeoman allows you to create new applications and modules by entering a single command in your command prompt.

These three tools encompass the idea of front-end tooling: a set of software providing the necessary tools to get your application up, running, and deployed. In this book, you'll learn how to set up these tools for you and your coworkers. You'll dive deep into each of those technologies and see how they can be combined to create a tailored workflow for your needs.

1.1 A software developer's workflow and task list

Taking a look at the typical software development workflow, you can easily identify three phases developers go through when coding (see figure 1.1):

- *Initializing*—In any software development process, this is the starting point. It's where you set up your project or add new files to an existing project.
- *Development*—This is the phase where you write code. Should you need more modules or want to refactor some code into a new file, you have to go back to the initializing phase. If everything is well, you move on to the next phase.
- *Deployment*—Your code is ready. It's time to create an executable bundle and deploy it. For web development, this means deploying HTML, JavaScript, and CSS to your web server. From there you can return to the development phase (fixing bugs or adding new features to existing code) or to the initialization phase (creating new modules).

Although every software development process has those phases in common, the tasks a developer performs during those phases differ from technology to technology. Also, the most tedious of those tasks are those that are not directly related to the coding part but are mostly concerned with setup, structure, and optimized output. Figure 1.2 shows typical tasks for a JavaScript project.

The initializing phase has to do with setting up folders and applying boilerplate code. You also download and add third-party libraries. Development is about authoring tools like preprocessors (LESS) or JavaScript tools. Many tasks are done in the deployment phase.

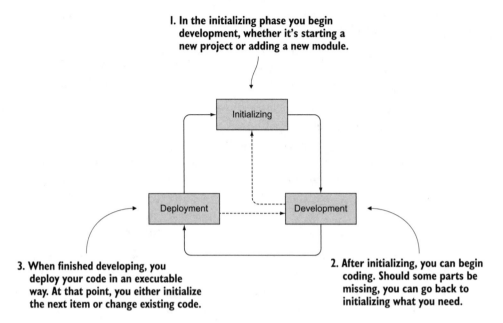

I. In the initializing phase you begin development, whether it's starting a new project or adding a new module.

3. When finished developing, you deploy your code in an executable way. At that point, you either initialize the next item or change existing code.

2. After initializing, you can begin coding. Should some parts be missing, you can go back to initializing what you need.

Figure 1.1   The three phases of development workflow

Figure 1.2 depicts numerous tasks, and we'll explore them in detail in the following section. Don't feel overwhelmed by the numbers of duties you'll face on the next few pages. You're here to find a pleasant and easy solution for them via automation. To see what you're dealing with, let's examine those tasks in detail.

1.1.1   *Initialization phase tasks*

During initialization, the tasks aren't necessarily JavaScript-specific but are more generic to be suitable for any programming language. To get things started, you create a project structure and the first files to start coding.

SET UP A KNOWN AND RELIABLE PROJECT STRUCTURE

Based on your experience with other projects, you know how you like to structure your code and your files. You'll most likely use the same structure in the next project, maybe with some little improvements here and there. If you're familiar with the way your folders and files are organized, you'll easily find your way through the territory of your new project.

APPLY REUSABLE PATTERNS/BOILERPLATE CODE

Boilerplate code is code that can be included in a project with little or no alteration. As a developer you're just filling in the blanks. Boilerplate code not only saves you time in writing code, it also ensures that certain often-used, standard code is included and in the right place. Boilerplate code prevents you from starting with a blank page and helps you get started more easily.

The initializing phase is all about tasks that create something for you, such as folders for your structure, files containing boilerplate code, or downloads from third-party libraries.

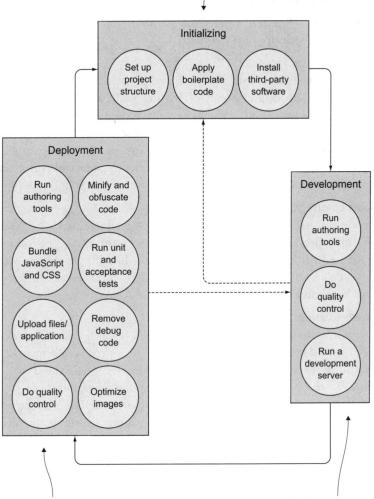

The deployment phase contains all tasks where heavy computing and manipulation happen. You run your authoring tools, again, with different settings, test your code, remove unnecessary development annotations, and bundle and deploy everything into an executable application.

In the development phase you mostly run your authoring tools like LESS and CoffeeScript and refresh the browser to see the results. This phase is where you create your application.

Figure 1.2   Tasks for each development phase

INSTALL THIRD-PARTY SOFTWARE/LIBRARIES

Libraries like jQuery provide you with basic functionality and a good framework on which to set your projects. We often call those libraries *dependencies*, which means that an application's successful execution depends on using those libraries.

1.1.2   Development phase tasks

Entering the development phase, the scope of your tasks gets more specific toward front-end and JavaScript development.

USE CODE-AUTHORING TOOLS

One trend that hit front-end development pretty hard in recent years was the many ways of code authoring. Instead of writing with the native languages of the web (JavaScript, CSS, and HTML), you write your code in a different language, which provides new syntax or features not available in the original, helping you to write more sophisticated code. But the browser can't interpret all of those languages directly, so you have to compile your program into understandable and runnable code. You run code-authoring tools in the development phase as well as in the deployment phase.

PERFORM QUALITY CONTROL

The code you write should be of high quality: readable, understandable, of low complexity, and without code smells.[1] You can ensure this quality by following coding conventions and using code style checkers. Tools like JSLint and JSCS check your code against a ruleset of different indicators and alert you if your code doesn't pass. Quality control happens in both the development and deployment phases.

RUN A DEVELOPMENT SERVER

Web applications are run best on a web server. Booting up a development server during coding and mimicking the conditions of your production environment are essential if your application calls to back ends and retrieves data via AJAX.

Tasks in the development phase should offer quick iterations so you can see the results from your coding efforts with minimal wasted time. Saving a source code file should trigger the respective authoring tool, doing a code quality check and displaying the results directly in the browser window.

1.1.3   Deployment phase tasks

As figure 1.2 depicts, this phase has the most tasks, because you want to create the best output for your deployed application. Besides two tasks from the previous phase, you also have to do the following.

BUNDLE AND MINIFY JAVASCRIPT AND CSS FILES

Every file you refer to in your HTML document causes the browser to open a new HTTP connection to download it, and every connection needs time to get established

---

[1] Code that's okay in terms of syntax and functionality but poorly styled is a source of possible problems in the future.

before contents can be transferred. When deploying your code, it's better to combine the files into one file, thus reducing the number of requests made to the server.

HTML, CSS, and JavaScript are basically plain text. Compared to other programming languages, they don't have things such as compiled binary code. With every character written resulting in a byte transferred, you need to optimize your deployed code by removing whitespace, truncating function and variable names, and applying every optimization trick in the book. Tools like UglifyJS and MinifyCSS help in doing so.

REMOVE UNUSED CODE

During development, developers tend to add extra code to their software for logging and additional debug output. You might end up with code that isn't referenced anywhere, resulting in dead bytes you carry over into production. Your end users will never experience the results of those lines, so you might as well remove them.

OPTIMIZE IMAGES

Images make up a good chunk of a website's page weight. Depending on the image format, a lot of metadata is stored in the file that can't be interpreted by browsers and will result in extra, unnecessary weight. Tools like ImageOptim and ImageMagick deal with that information and remove it. They also apply optimized compression algorithms, reducing the size of JPEGs by about 10% and PNGs by 40%.

RUN UNIT AND ACCEPTANCE TESTS

Unit tests allow you to validate the functionality of your modules, whereas acceptance tests check if your results meet certain requirements. Those tests ensure that your application won't fail regarding basic conditions. Only if those tests are passed can the application be deployed.

UPLOAD APPLICATION

Finally, you deploy your files on your web server, making it accessible from the outside.

As you can see, there's a lot for you to do. Not only do you have to keep so many things in mind, but you also have to deal with an added complexity: the human factor.

1.1.4   *The human factor*

You can accomplish many tasks by using the right tool for the job. Authoring abstractions provide tools to compile your code, and you can perform quality control with a few calls on the command line. Developers not only have to know those tools, but they also must know how to operate and access them.

This process can be tedious and confusing. It's also error-prone: you might forget to execute a task or might omit a parameter when starting your command-line tool. This complexity even occurs when you're working in teams. Can you be sure that your co-worker remembers to run the minification process after finishing their JavaScript work?

With this added complexity, you're more likely to make mistakes. You can easily lose track of running roughly 10 tools that are operated on different levels while taking care of all the intermediate results and passing them on to the next process. In reality, you just want to run a single command: `deploy`. And you don't want this just for yourself; you also want your coworkers to be able to run this command without alteration. Even a machine should be able to do so.

Taking this thought further, you want to execute all the tasks from the deployment phase by issuing one `deploy` command. Why not initialize your application with one `init` command or run all the tasks you need while developing with a `develop` command? As it turns out, you can easily do this.

1.2 JavaScript tools and a new workflow

To get rid of the possible errors, you need to greatly reduce the possible points of failure. If you look back at the tasks you're doing besides coding in a project, you'll see that they all deal with code in different stages. Let's get back to our workflow diagram, but instead of focusing on the different phases, we're going to check what happens to your written code. The boundaries are shifting a little, as shown in figure 1.3.

You end up with three types of code: code you want to adapt (boilerplate code), code you want to use (libraries, dependencies), and code you want to process (self-written CSS, JavaScript, HTML). You can define three types of tooling out of those categories: a scaffolding tool, a dependency manager, and a build tool. Let's look at those types of code in detail.

1.2.1 Three types of code and their tools

As shown in figure 1.3, you can categorize the tasks you have to do by looking at the type of code you're dealing with. It turns out that for each code type, you have a certain type of tool that allows you to deal with that code.

SCAFFOLDING TOOLS: CODE YOU WANT TO ADAPT

Typical boilerplate code provides good defaults and structure, and you fill in the blanks. Boilerplate code can range from simple module definitions to large chunks of almost-finished program code that just lacks the necessary parameters to be complete. This code is defined somewhere and is meant to be duplicated multiple times with different parameters, creating the files where you insert your own code (see "Build tools: code you want to process" on page 10).

Scaffolding tools take care of this type of code. They initialize boilerplate code and kick-start your application. They also create folder structure and add new modules to your existing project, thus taking care of two tasks in the initialization phase. Additionally, scaffolding tools can provide you with the necessary setup for your other tools: the build tool and the dependency manager.

DEPENDENCY MANAGERS: CODE YOU WANT TO USE

The code you want to use is more commonly known as library code. It's either modules that you've written some time before and that are now usable as a self-contained component, which you call from your new code, or it's third-party code from frameworks like jQuery. The most important part is that you don't touch this code when you're writing your own programs. This is stuff you use, not something you have to change.

Code you want to adapt:
Boilerplate code is meant to be extended with your own ideas. Folder structure is a good starting point but will eventually be extended with new folders and files. Your scaffolding tool will help you here.

Code you want to use:
You don't want to alter third-party code at all. Also known as packages, dependencies, or libraries, this code provides functionality to your projects. jQuery is a prominent example. You use package managers for this stage.

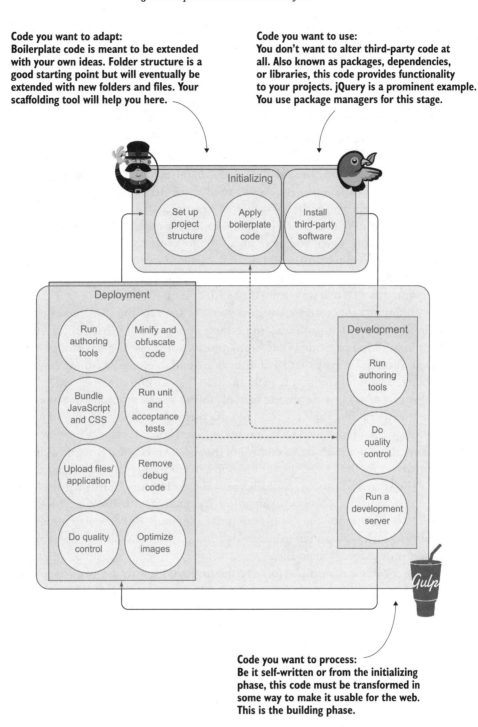

Code you want to process:
Be it self-written or from the initializing phase, this code must be transformed in some way to make it usable for the web. This is the building phase.

Figure 1.3   The tasks categorized in types of code

Dependency managers take care of the self-contained modules, or *packages*. You don't touch the packages' internals; you just wire them up to your existing project. Dependency managers also take care of conflicts between packages. If a developer wants to install a module that doesn't meet certain requirements of existing modules (a carousel needing a newer version of jQuery, for instance), the dependency manager takes care of updating older dependencies or at least alerting the user.

BUILD TOOLS: CODE YOU WANT TO PROCESS

The code you want to process or transform is your self-written software. You spend most of your time on this part because it features the tailored implementation that you need for a certain project. As you've likely heard many times, the code you deploy is not the code you write: you use abstractions like LESS and bundle JavaScript through concatenation. Also, you need to keep a close eye on your coding style and run linting tools. Once you're ready to deploy, you crush your images to the lowest possible size, remove all the debug and development code you don't need, remove unused CSS, and create the lowest number of files possible. In the end, you upload everything via FTP to a server or content delivery network.

A building tool creates a layer on which to steer all the file-processing tasks, transforming your source code into something deployable. Code quality, authoring, and bundling all happen here. The configuration of those tools is stored in build files, which should be easily adaptable and extendable. In addition, build tools take installed dependencies and wire them up to the existing project.

Instead of using a multitude of tools for all your development tasks, you concentrate on automating the execution of tasks through three different tool types: scaffolding tool, dependency manager, and build tool. Figure 1.4 shows how they interact.

You, the developer, are in control of three tools. You start the scaffolding tool (Yeoman) to set up the project, search and install components with the dependency manager (Bower), and process your files with the build tool (Gulp). Figure 1.4 also shows the interconnection between your tools. Yeoman, as a scaffolding tool, can scaffold initial configurations for Gulp (the build file) and Bower (basic dependencies for your projects). Gulp can use the information provided by Bower to wire up dependencies in your project's main files.

The project is the central focus of the three tools, with the developer adding to the project via interfaces provided by the tools. You create scaffolding for a new project—the bare essentials—with the scaffolding tool. You search for dependencies via the dependency manager and add them to the project. At the very bottom lies the build tool. You execute a command that integrates your files and the files created by the scaffolding tool and dependency manager into your project. You have three easy-to-use interfaces that hide the complexity. The tools take care of the complex parts. Up until now, many different runtimes and environments provided you with those tools. With the advent of Node.js, you have a new environment that's much more tailored to the skills of the everyday JavaScript developer.

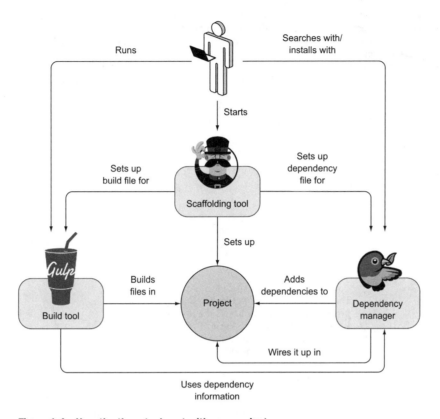

Figure 1.4 How the three tools act with your project

1.2.2 Node.js for JavaScript tools

Because you have so many alternatives for the three types of tools, you have to focus and decide on one tool for each type. In the past, although almost all tools for the smaller tasks were written in JavaScript (with some notable Ruby or native exceptions), the integration tools were written in languages that had nothing to do with JavaScript. This has changed. In recent years, a programming platform has come up that is specifically designed for JavaScript developers: Node.js.

According to its website, Node.js brings the power of the Chrome browser's JavaScript engine to a platform suitable for fast network applications. But the true power of Node.js and the reason for its huge popularity lie in something completely different: JavaScript, the very language web developers use to write their browser applications, is available without the limitations of a browser window.

Node.js offers the same degree of comfort that JavaScript developers have when developing for Google Chrome, because the same JavaScript engine is underneath. But the JavaScript engine is just the core. Figure 1.5 shows which Node.js blocks are

The core functionality is provided by the Node.js developers. Those packages require operating system support for file access, network traffic, and memory management.

Programs are software written in JavaScript by you or the huge Node.js community.

Modules are programs that access core functionality and are run on the V8 runtime but packaged and written for reuse. All modules are stored in the NPM registry: http://npmjs.org.

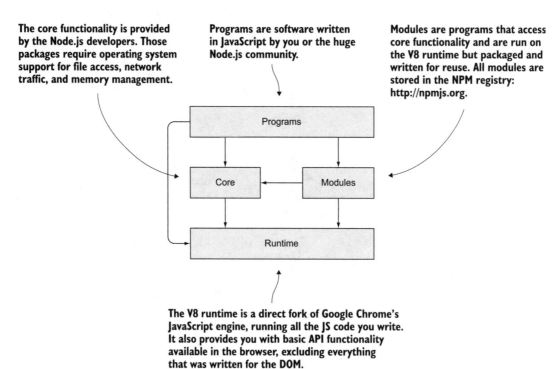

The V8 runtime is a direct fork of Google Chrome's JavaScript engine, running all the JS code you write. It also provides you with basic API functionality available in the browser, excluding everything that was written for the DOM.

Figure 1.5   The parts of the Node.js ecosystem

stacked above the JavaScript engine. At its base is the V8 runtime, a fork of Google Chrome's JavaScript engine. The Node.js developers provide you with core functionality, which is meant to access parts of the operating system. On top of those are programs and modules (programs bundled for reuse).

Let's look into them in detail:

- *The V8 runtime* is a fork of Google Chrome's JavaScript engine. It has been stripped of all browser APIs and provides a compilation and execution environment for JavaScript code.
- *The Node.js core* consists of an API close to the operating system. This includes file system access, networking protocols, and streaming—briefly speaking, everything that has to do with input and output and thus everything that requires functionality from the operating system.
- *Programs* are any JavaScript that can be written and run using Node.js.
- *Modules* are a concept of Node.js assuring the reusability of code. Every program that you write can be bundled into a module and packaged for distribution. Modules provide encapsulated functionality that you can use and reuse in your new programs.

For tooling, one of the most crucial points lies in the Node.js core layer. Node.js provides functionality that's close to the operating system. Most of this functionality works with the file system. With the ability to navigate the file system, read files, and operate on the data of those files, Node.js is a perfect environment for writing tools that transform source code into deployment-ready bundles.

Node.js has just one huge difference from other environments like Ruby or Java: developers don't have to make a mental switch when going from development for the browser to development for their tools. Because it's the same language, and much of the runtime environment is also the same, JavaScript developers can easily create their own tools: JavaScript tools to transform JavaScript code.

Even with interchangeable tools, we'll focus on three popular ones found in the JavaScript world: Yeoman, powered by Google, will be our scaffolding tool of choice. Bower by Twitter will take care of package management. And for the building processes, we'll take a good look at Gulp.

> **NOTE** All upcoming examples that feature calls on the command line are written compliant to Unix bash notations. This doesn't mean that they can be run only on Unix systems. The Unix/Linux bash, the Mac OS X terminal, and the Windows command prompt all run the same commands in the same way.

1.3 Scaffolding with Yeoman

Scaffolding gets your project up and running. It creates the necessary folders, copies initial files (like build scripts), applies boilerplate code, and triggers the installation of dependencies. Throughout development, scaffolding tools are used to create the base structure of new modules inside your project. But they do a little more than just copy files from one point (most of the time, a source repository) to another by listening for some parameters you can add. Parameters can be the name of the project or switches that allow for the inclusion or exclusion of different modules (for example, "include jQuery"). See figure 1.6 for details.

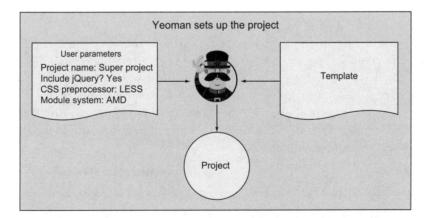

Figure 1.6   Yeoman takes predefined templates from a generator and integrates additional data based on user input. The adapted templates will be added to an existing project or— depending on the generator—will result in an entirely new project.

1.3.1   *The benefits of a Yeoman as a scaffolding tool*

Scaffolding can be done by machines and is usually one of those features covered by integrated development environments (IDE). In tools like Eclipse (with Aptana), Web-Storm, or IntelliJ, you have the option to create a new project or create a new module. Specifying an option usually pops up a wizard that provides you with a questionnaire prompting you for the parameters required by scaffolding.

Choosing an IDE for scaffolding conditions allows you to use this IDE throughout development, and indirectly you force the same IDE onto your coworkers. This is where independent scaffolding tools like Yeoman have their biggest advantage: their sole purpose is to roll out new projects and modules, independent from the rest of your development environment. Therefore, no matter how your environment or tool-chain may change over time, Yeoman can still be used to kick-start new projects. And should you decide to drop Yeoman at some point in your project's lifespan, you're still able to work on it without problems. Also, Yeoman works from the command line like many other Node.js tools do, so you remain in the same ecosystem as Bower or Gulp.

The biggest advantage, though, comes from its extensibility by using a plugin system called generators.

1.3.2   *The concept behind generators*

A *generator* is a simple JavaScript application that's run by the yo command-line tool, which does little more than create new folders or copy files. Of course, there's more to its complexity, like listening to parameters and altering the copied files accordingly, but, generally speaking, those are the tasks. So a generator comes with a folder full of templates that have to be transferred and altered by the generator script.

Yeoman's only task is to run one of those generators, which, in turn, knows which files to deploy where. It integrates a simple prompting API that allows different parameters to change the output generated by the generator. The Yeoman team brought some generators with them: their original web app generator and, among others, generators for the popular frameworks of Ember and Angular. There's a strong focus on the latter one since it's also from Google.

The usage is easy; once you've installed a certain generator, you can call it easily with the command yo in your command line. You can directly access a generator with the command yo generator-name. Take the Angular generator from Yeoman, for instance. Open the command line (or terminal) and move to the folder where you want to have your new project. With the command yo angular you tell Yeoman to boot up the Angular generator. You're then prompted by a short questionnaire where you can select various options:

```
$ yo angular                              ◁────── ❶ The command to start Yeoman

Out of the box I include Bootstrap and some AngularJS recommended modules.

? Would you like to use Sass (with Compass)? Yes
? Would you like to include Bootstrap? Yes
? Would you like to use the Sass version of Bootstrap? Yes
```

❷ Most questions require a yes/no answer.

```
? Which modules would you like to include? (Press <space> to select)    ◁——┐
?? angular-animate.js                                                        │
 ? angular-aria.js                                      There are more       │
 ? angular-cookies.js                             advanced questions.  ❸  ───┘
 ? angular-resource.js
 ? angular-messages.js
 ? angular-route.js
```

Execute the command to start Yeoman on your shell or command line ❶. The command is yo and the parameter it takes is the name of the generator. Questions set a flag as to whether to include certain code ❷. There is a multiple-choice prompt, with a few recommended modules preselected, which you can remove by pressing the spacebar ❸.

With Yeoman you can set up a new project in mere seconds. In the Angular example, you can benefit from a structure that's trusted by many developers and is standard among the community. This allows you to spend more time developing your project rather than wasting time with details on folder and file structures and names.

Next, let's look into dependency managers.

1.4   *Dependency management with Bower*

Dependencies are self-contained modules that your application uses as a foundation for new software parts or as an extension to existing software. These can be libraries like jQuery or Angular, UI widgets like in-page light boxes for images, or complete frameworks like Bootstrap. Another term for them is *packages*. The benefit of using such modules is that you don't spend time developing those parts but rather use them as they are.

The main purpose of dependency managers is to search in community and company repositories, fetch the needed packages from there, and add them to your project. Packages can also have dependencies. This is where a dependency manager differs from a simple command-line tool that just downloads files. If two or more of your packages require jQuery, for instance, but in different versions, it's the duty of your dependency manager to handle and resolve the conflict. The solution can be choosing one over the other, installing both, or marking it as a conflict and letting the users decide which version they should go for. Figure 1.7 illustrates this.

1.4.1   *The benefits of Bower*

Bower calls itself the "package manager for the web," and that's pretty much all it is. Created by Twitter, it was developed to install frameworks, libraries, and other modules from internet repositories, as long as they're hosted with Git and feature a bower.json file, telling Bower what to install.

Bower was developed for front-end developers. This doesn't necessarily mean that the packages have to include JavaScript, CSS, or some related language. But given its original purpose, it's not used by other developers, and you most likely won't find packages that don't have code to be included somewhere in your HTML file. Bower

**Bower downloads found dependencies
and their subdependencies to the project.**

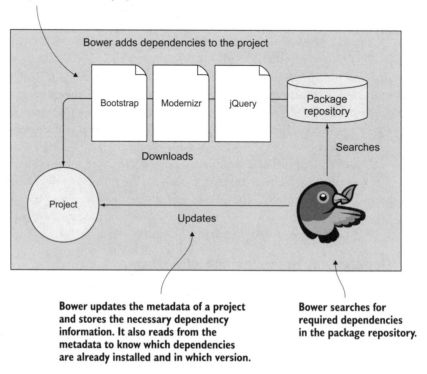

**Bower updates the metadata of a project
and stores the necessary dependency
information. It also reads from the
metadata to know which dependencies
are already installed and in which version.**

**Bower searches for
required dependencies
in the package repository.**

**Figure 1.7   Bower as a package manager calls the repository and checks for availability of this
package. It compares installed dependencies and will update them if needed or let the user know if
there's an issue. If everything is okay, those components will be downloaded and added to the project.**

provides commands for searching, installing, and updating packages. Once you're
ready to install a package, Bower will check if this package requires the installation of
more packages, like a common library (jQuery, for instance) that's used by others.
Also, it will see if there might be duplicates or version violations on installation. If it
doesn't cause conflicts, the new package will be added to your project.

From all the different package managers out there, we'll select Bower for the following reasons:

- *Bower was designed for front-end developers.* All major front-end libraries are tailored for use with this tool.
- *Package repositories tend to grow rapidly.* With Bower's focus on the front end, the
  number of packages is manageable and it's harder to lose one.
- *Bower's dependency tree is extremely flat.* Not only is this unique to Bower, but it's
  also necessary for web developers. As it turns out, this structure is the most
  native to web applications because you don't (or at least shouldn't) install two
  versions of the same package.

1.4.2 Bower's dependency tree

Dependency trees are used to show dependencies between components. Bootstrap, for instance, needs jQuery to run. In a dependency tree, jQuery would be a child node of Bootstrap. If you install another component that's dependent on jQuery, you'll have two options:

- Download jQuery again and set the child node of this component to the new package.
- Point the new downloaded package to the already installed version of jQuery.

Figure 1.8 shows those two options.

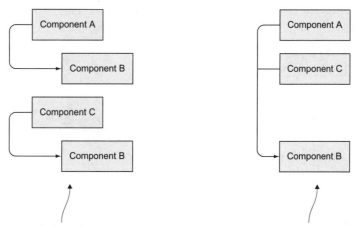

If one component is dependent on another component, the dependency manager will usually download this dependency separately, to ensure that there are no conflicts. But you might end up with several duplicates.

Bower, on the other hand, installs this dependency just once. Should conflicts arise (due to different versions), Bower will alert you with a call to action: overwrite, ignore, or cancel.

Figure 1.8 The two kinds of dependency trees: a deep dependency tree, which installs each dependency again, and a flat one, in which a dependency is installed just once

Both ways have their pros and cons. The deep dependency tree ensures that the version installed for this component fits perfectly and that the API is the one that the component expects. But installing the component every time results in duplicates. The other version, the flat dependency tree, makes sure that the component is installed just once and used throughout the project, but this might result in API conflicts with other dependencies.

Bower uses the latter version for one good reason: in web applications, you don't want to transfer the same package multiple times over the wire. If you install jQuery, use this version throughout the project. Also, browsers have a hard time handling the same software in two different places. The flat dependency tree is more suitable for front-end developers. Bower will alert the developer should version conflicts occur during installation. The developer then has the following choices:

- Cancel the installation of the component.
- Overwrite the old dependency with the new one.
- Choose the older dependency in favor of the newer one.

With Bower you now have a tool that takes care of all your third-party modules and components. Choosing the third option will make sure those dependencies and your own code are processed correctly.

1.5   *Gulp: the streaming build system*

The build system is the heart of your toolchain. It will process all your source files and create distributable, bundled versions of it. It will also check on code quality and do all repetitive tasks automatically for multiple files. Figure 1.9 shows how a build tool works.

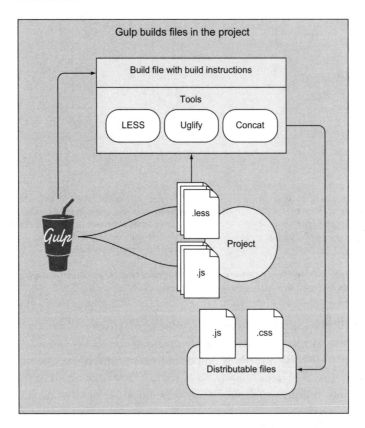

Figure 1.9   Gulp, as a build tool, triggers other tools that transform your source files into distributable files. The commands needed for those builds are stored in a build file. Gulp, in particular, takes input files, runs them through different commands (or tools), and saves the results in a new folder.

Build tools take a build configuration—or build file—and define three things: the source files, the process they should run through, and the destination path where the processed files should be saved. Source is run through this process and saved in the destination. For your toolchain, you use Gulp as the build tool.

1.5.1 *The benefits of Gulp*

Gulp wasn't the first JavaScript build tool on the block. Its direct predecessor, Grunt, is arguably a lot bigger and has been around for much longer than Gulp. But Gulp has a totally different approach to building, which is unique not only to the JavaScript world but also to build systems in general:

- Gulp's underlying technology works completely in memory and makes access to data incredibly fast. This allows for fast file transformations and for flexible building pipelines. Don't need a tool in your building pipeline? Just remove the line where you call it; the files can still be processed.
- Gulp can run tasks in parallel, and developers have the freedom to decide which tasks to run in sequence and which to run at the same time. This gives another performance boost over other tools.
- Gulpfiles are pure Node.js code, and developers are free to run any Node-compatible JavaScript code inside their Gulp tasks. This is even heavily promoted by Gulp's authors, who favor a generic Node.js module compatible with Gulp over a self-written Gulp plugin. In return, many Gulp developers try to make their functionality as generic as possible in order to return something to the Node.js community that can be used outside Gulp.
- Gulp allows you to create enormously advanced building pipelines that exceed the standard one-tier processes of other tools.

1.5.2 *Build pipelines*

Gulp's main goal is to define a file-processing pipeline that runs your source files through multiple stages. Each stage changes the contents and passes the results to the next stage. That's why Gulp calls itself "the streaming build system." A plugin is executed by calling a method. The rest is done by the code behind the interface provided by the plugin. Figure 1.10 illustrates this process.

The code closely mimics this process. Because Gulp is a wrapper for other tools, you first have to load the necessary Gulp plugins.

```
var gulp = require('gulp'),                ◁————① Load Gulp.
  uglify = require('gulp-uglify'),         ◁————② Load the Uglify plugin.
  concat = require('gulp-concat');         ◁————③ Load the Concat plugin.
```

You first need to load Gulp ①. The Uglify plugin includes the original Uglify software—a tool to optimize JavaScript code to reduce its file size—but also provides an easy-to-use API for Gulp ②. You can achieve the process of concatenating files by

The concatenation process then
takes all files from the input and
creates one file out of them.

Finally, the result
is stored in a file.

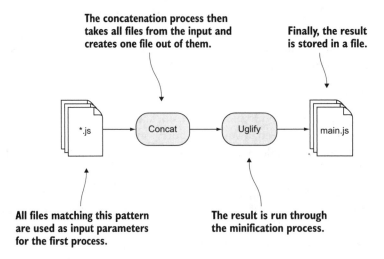

All files matching this pattern
are used as input parameters
for the first process.

The result is run through
the minification process.

Figure 1.10   A basic file process. All JavaScript files are first concatenated (bundled into one file) and then minified using the Uglify program. The result is stored in the main.js file.

loading the Concat plugin, which the original Gulp authors provided because the task is a common one for all developers ❸.

You then define the task you want to run, which is a straightforward implementation of figure 1.10:

```
gulp.task('scripts', function() {        ⊲—— Define your task and give it the name "scripts."
    return gulp.src('src/**/*.js')       ⊲—— Select all your JavaScript files in "src."
        .pipe(concat('bundle.js'))       ⊲—— Concatenate them into one file.
        .pipe(uglify())                  ⊲—— Run the minifying process.
        .pipe(gulp.dest('dest'))         ⊲—— Save your result.
})
```

The intermediate results are stored in memory, and costly disk-saving operations happen at the end. This makes the whole process really fast. Since its release in 2013, Gulp has become the mainstay for front-end developers who are desperate for automation and speed.

Gulp is also executed from the command line. Just call gulp scripts from your bash or shell, and Gulp will execute the scripts task defined. Gulp will then read the building instructions from the Gulpfile and pass it through the Node.js runtime environment.

With Gulp, you have the ability to integrate a multitude of file-processing tools into one tool. An easy-to-use interface allows you to execute these tools from the command line. Gulp as a build tool is the first of the three major tools we'll cover in this book. Because its file-processing nature provides the foundation of all the processes needed for a project, we're dealing with it first.

1.6 *Summary*

In this chapter you found out how automation and tooling help front-end developers to handle their huge task list, to become more efficient, and to provide better quality in their results:

- A front-end developer must perform a multitude of tasks, including heavy file transformation tasks such as minification and bundling, to create sophisticated web applications. All of those tasks are closely tied to tools that work on different levels.
- To reduce complexity you focus on three tools: a scaffolding tool that creates the code you want to adapt, a dependency manager that downloads and installs the code you want to use, and a build tool that processes the code you write into something edible for the browser.
- The three tools define a new workflow: create a new project with the scaffolding tool, download the dependencies you need, and develop your application using the authoring tools (among others) via your build tool.
- All three tools have Node.js-based variants. The first one, Yeoman, is a scaffolding tool provided by Google. The concept of plug-in generators allows you to scaffold various project templates in different flavors.
- Bower, as a dependency manager, checks for versions of various modules and components and integrates them into a project. It uses a flat dependency tree, meaning it avoids duplicates, which is preferred for web applications.
- The build tool Gulp has an easy-to-use command-line interface and various plugins that add file-processing tools into its roster of executables. With a few lines of code it's possible to chain file transformation tasks like concatenation and minification to each other.

With Gulp being the heart of your project and the main tool you need for your setup (after all, it will be scaffolded by Yeoman), you'll start with the build tool in chapter 2.

Getting started with Gulp

2

This chapter covers

- An introduction to Gulp
- The concepts of streams
- Creating simple tasks to automate tools
- Creating execution pipelines for multifunctional tasks

You start your new workflow by concentrating on the build system. Although this was the last step in the previous chapter, it serves as the necessary foundation for the upcoming elements of our new workflow. The build system deals with a number of tasks that occur in our day-to-day workflow, like concatenating, minifying, and testing our code. The build tool is initialized by the scaffolding tool and integrates the dependency manager's components into the project. Figure 2.1 shows the part of the build tool in our tooling workflow again.

Gulp is the foundation for your workflow automation. It's the first element that's being initialized by the scaffolding tool, and it integrates components into the project. Also, because it's creating an actively used development environment, it will become one of the most used and integral parts of your development cycles.

Gulp is a build tool written in JavaScript and running on Node.js. Because Gulp is a JavaScript program, and Gulp's build instructions are also written in JavaScript,

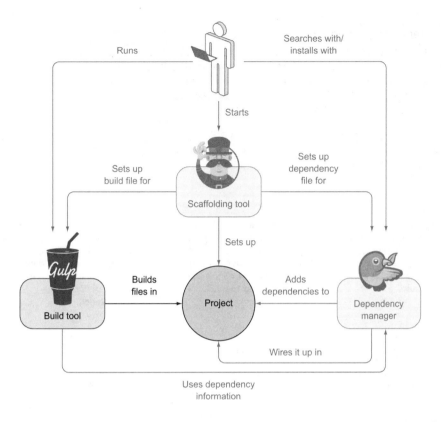

Figure 2.1   Your workflow setup from chapter 1

it's very close to the environment JavaScript developers use every day. This makes Gulp a perfect choice for automating the daily tasks of a front-end developer. In this chapter, I'll show you how to set up Gulp for your projects. You'll learn about the individual bits and pieces of a Gulp setup, and you'll develop your own building instructions for your JavaScript applications and CSS files.

2.1   Setting up Gulp

Gulp as a Node.js tool is a conglomeration of little pieces that make up a whole. In this section you'll learn about the different building blocks of Gulp and how to install both the command-line interface and the local Gulp installation.

2.1.1   The building blocks of Gulp

Build tools in general consist of at least two parts: the tool executing the build and a build file containing all the instructions for the build tool. Gulp is no exception: the tool executing the build is called Gulp. Gulp's build file is commonly referred to as a Gulpfile. Gulp can be broken down into several other parts. Figure 2.2 shows a quick overview of Gulp's parts and how they interact.

Sample project and Node.js

For all the upcoming samples in this book, I've prepared a sample project, which you can find under http://github.com/frontend-tooling/sample-project-gulp. If you're familiar with Git, you can use the `clone` command to get its contents. Otherwise, there's a Download Zip button on the website you can use to get the files onto your system.

To re-create the samples, you need to have Node.js installed and ready on your system. You'll find the necessary binaries and installation instructions on https://www.nodejs.org for your system (Windows, Linux, or Mac OSX).

1. The globally available Gulp CLI just checks if the local Gulp is available at the current project. If so, it boots up the local Gulp.

2. The local Gulp installation has two purposes: It provides you with the basic Gulp API, and it loads your building instructions and runs the tasks defined there.

3. The Gulpfile.js is a JavaScript file where all the tasks you want to run are defined. Those tasks use the Gulp API provided by local Gulp installation as well as the Gulp plugins that are also installed.

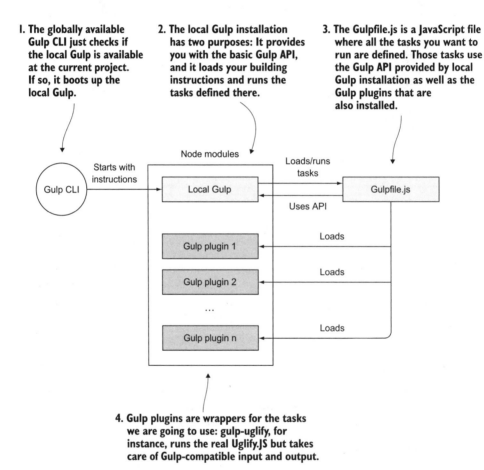

4. Gulp plugins are wrappers for the tasks we are going to use: gulp-uglify, for instance, runs the real Uglify.JS but takes care of Gulp-compatible input and output.

Figure 2.2   The Gulp CLI starts the local Gulp installation with the parameters provided on the command line. The local installation takes the local Gulpfile, which in turn loads Gulp plugins and defines tasks using the Gulp API. Gulp itself runs and loads these tasks.

A complete Gulp installation consists of the following parts:

- *The Gulp CLI*—A command-line interface to start the build tool
- *The local Gulp installation*—The actual software running your build
- *The Gulpfile*—The building instructions that tell you how to build your software
- *Gulp plugins*—Lots and lots of tiny executables that know how to combine, modify, and assemble parts of your software

That's quite a lot! But don't worry; in this chapter we'll deal with all of these. Let's start with the CLI.

2.1.2   The Gulp command-line interface

Node.js modules can be installed globally. That makes them usable as a command-line executable tool. Or you can install modules locally as a library for your own projects. Both ways are shown in figure 2.3.

The same goes for Gulp, with the exception that Gulp has two separate packages for the global tool part and the library. One is the Gulp command-line interface; it's installed globally and can be executed from your terminal/bash/command prompt. The other package is the local Gulp installation, which is the actual Gulp runtime, handling all the tasks and providing the entire API. Gulp's command-line interface provides a *global* entry point for the *local* Gulp installation, forwarding all the parameters entered to the local installation and kicking off the version of the runtime you've installed for your project. From there on, the local installation takes the lead and executes your build.

Gulp's CLI is rather dumb, meaning that its only functionality is to check for a local installation that it can execute. The reason for this is to allow for a version-independent execution. Imagine you have a project running the legacy version of Gulp 3.8. The CLI will be able to execute this project because the interface to the local Gulp installation

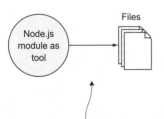

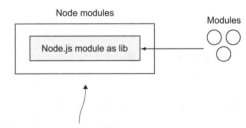

Global installations of Node.js modules provide the tool component. Run from the command line, you can apply this tool to files located anywhere in your file system.

A local installation of Node.js modules allows other programs to use them as libraries in their own code.

Figure 2.3   The two ways a Node.js module can be installed. If you install a module globally, it provides its functionality as an executable from the command line, working with the files you want to change. It becomes a tool. Installed locally, you can use the same functionality but in your own programs.

is the same. A newer project running on Gulp 4 can be executed with the same CLI. In the end, you'll most likely never update your command-line interface but will be able to run all the Gulp projects you'll ever create, no matter which local installation they require.

To install it, boot up your bash, terminal, or Windows command prompt (it works on all of them) and check to see if Node.js is installed:

```
$ node --version
```

If you have Node.js installed, this command should output the current version of your installation. Next, you need to check for Node's package manager, NPM. It comes with Node.js; check for it with this command:

```
$ npm --version
```

Again, you should get a correct version output. Should one of those programs not be available, please check appendix B for installation instructions or visit the Node.js website at https://nodejs.org. With Node.js and NPM installed and your command line booted up, install the Gulp CLI with

```
$ npm install -g gulp-cli
```

Note the -g parameter after `install`. It tells your Node package manager to make this installation globally available. Once NPM has finished, you have a new command available on your system. Type the following on your command line to make sure the installation worked:

```
$ gulp --version
```

It should output something like this:

```
[12:04:15] CLI version 0.2.0
```

The first step is done. You have the Gulp CLI installed on your system! Let's continue with the local installation.

2.1.3   *The local Gulp installation*

The local Gulp installation has two main purposes: loading and executing the building instructions written in the Gulpfile and exposing an API that can be used by the Gulpfile. The local Gulp installation is the actual software executing your builds. The global installation kicks off the local software installed separately for each project. Figure 2.4 illustrates this.

To install Gulp locally, open your command line and move to the directory where you unzipped (or cloned) our sample project—not in the app folder directly, but one

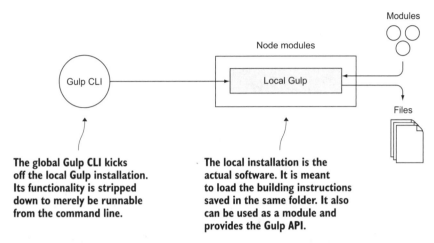

The global Gulp CLI kicks off the local Gulp installation. Its functionality is stripped down to merely be runnable from the command line.

The local installation is the actual software. It is meant to load the building instructions saved in the same folder. It also can be used as a module and provides the Gulp API.

Figure 2.4   The global installation of Gulp is the Gulp CLI. Its purpose is to check the availability of a local installation, which it starts on call. The local Gulp is located in the local node_modules folder of a JavaScript project. It contains all the necessary runtime functions and provides an API for build files (Gulpfiles).

level up where the README.md file is located. There, promote the whole folder to a Node module by typing

```
$ npm init
```

What follows is a short questionnaire asking you several pieces of information about your project, but because you probably don't want to publish your new module to the NPM registry (at least not now), you can leave everything at its default value. Once you've finished, you'll see that a new file called package.json is available in your folder. This file will store all the information on which Node modules are necessary for your application—the so-called dependencies—and which version they have to be. This file is the core of every Node project, and some plugins access it directly to get information on installed modules.

The package.json file stores the information of the Node modules that your project depends on. It divides this information into runtime dependencies (modules the project needs to work properly) and development dependencies (modules you need to develop your project). Because your build tool falls into the latter category, you install the local Gulp installation with the following command:

```
$ npm install --save-dev gulp
```

Gulp is downloaded, and the save-dev parameter stores the correct version in your package.json file:

```
{
  "name": "sample-project-gulp",
  "version": "1.0.0",
```

```
    "description": "The sample project we will use throughout the Gulp
        chapters",
    ...
    "devDependencies": {
        "gulp": "^4.0.0"
    }
}
```

Doing a version check again (with `gulp --version`), you can see that the output has changed. The Gulp CLI recognizes your local installation:

```
[20:40:12] CLI version 0.2.0
[20:40:12] Local version 4.0.0
```

> ### Gulp 4
> This chapter and some parts of the book were written with the newest version of Gulp, version 4, in mind. But at the time this book went into production, Gulp 4 was still in a pre-release state. So we don't know if at the time of this book's release Gulp 4 will have been released to the public. If `gulp --version` gives you a 3.x version number, then Gulp 4 is still in the pre-release state. To install Gulp 4, use this command instead:
>
> ```
> $ npm install --save-dev gulpjs/gulp.git#4.0
> ```
>
> This will download and install the pre-release branch.

You now have both the CLI and the local Gulp installed. The next step is working on your Gulpfile.

2.2   Creating Gulpfiles

In the previous section you set up the basic software that runs Gulp. You installed the global CLI and made sure that the local Gulp installation is available. The chain up until now is to start the local Gulp installation with the globally available CLI (figure 2.4). Now you're ready for the next step in the chain: the Gulpfile.

2.2.1   A Gulp "Hello World" task

The Gulpfile is a JavaScript file containing all your building instructions. Building instructions contain a series of commands that can be bundled into tasks. In Gulp, a *task* is a plain JavaScript function containing all the commands you want to execute. Any function will do, as long as it's defined using the first method of Gulp's API: the `gulp.task` method. Figure 2.5 shows the method's signature.

The `gulp.task` method serves one purpose: it gives the task function—which is plain JavaScript—a unique name. This name pushes the function into Gulp's execution space. In doing so, Gulp "knows" of this function's existence and can use this reference to execute it. This means that `gulp.task` provides a direct interface from the command line to that function.

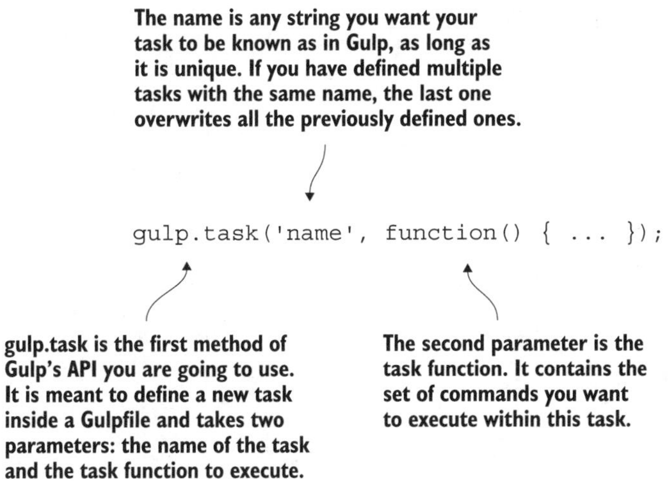

The name is any string you want your
task to be known as in Gulp, as long as
it is unique. If you have defined multiple
tasks with the same name, the last one
overwrites all the previously defined ones.

```
gulp.task('name', function() { ... });
```

gulp.task is the first method of
Gulp's API you are going to use.
It is meant to define a new task
inside a Gulpfile and takes two
parameters: the name of the task
and the task function to execute.

The second parameter is the
task function. It contains the
set of commands you want
to execute within this task.

Figure 2.5   The signature
of the gulp.task method

Let's write your first task. In true programming tradition, you'll go for the output of
"Hello World!" on the command line. Create a new, empty text file called Gulpfile.js
in the same folder where your package.json and node_modules folders are located.
The following listing shows the contents to add.

Listing 2.1   Hello World in Gulp–Gulpfile.js

```
var gulp = require('gulp');          ◁────❶ Require the local Gulp installation in your Gulpfile.

gulp.task('test', function () {      ◁────❷ Define a new task named test.
  console.log('Hello World!');       ◁──┐
});                                      │ Print "Hello World!"
                                         │ on the command line.
```

In requiring the local Gulp installation in your Gulpfile, you have Gulp's API available ❶.
Gulp and the Gulpfile are here inherently connected: Gulp loads the Gulpfile to know
which tasks are available, and the Gulpfile loads Gulp to use its API ❷. In defining the
test task, the task is available within Gulp. The second parameter is the function you
want to execute.

Gulp and the Gulpfile share a unique connection: whereas Gulp needs the Gulpfile to know which tasks are available and can be executed, the Gulpfile needs Gulp to
have access to the API. See figure 2.6 for details.

With gulp.task, the first method provided by Gulp's API, you can promote task
functions to Gulp tasks. In listing 2.1 you created the "Hello World" task that now runs
by the name test. This name is available in Gulp's execution space, and you can refer
to it directly when calling Gulp from the command line. With the command

```
$ gulp test
```

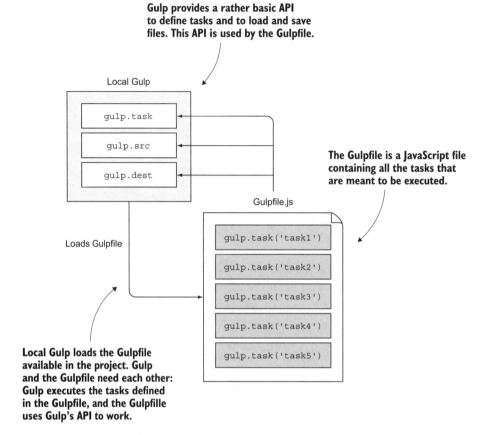

Figure 2.6   The local Gulp installation interplays with the Gulpfile. It loads the Gulpfile available in the project and executes the available tasks, as instructed by the command-line interface. It also provides the Gulpfile with a basic API, which is needed to create and define tasks.

you are able to execute this particular task. The various parts of executing tasks kick in (as shown in figure 2.7) as follows:

1 The global Gulp CLI loads the local Gulp installation.
2 The local Gulp installation loads the Gulpfile.
3 The Gulpfile loads the local Gulp installation and defines a new task called `test`.
4 The local Gulp installation is passed a command-line parameter. This is the name of the task to execute.
5 Because the task of the same name is available, the local Gulp executes the function attached to it.

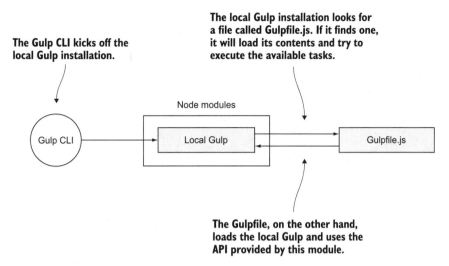

The Gulp CLI kicks off the local Gulp installation.

The local Gulp installation looks for a file called Gulpfile.js. If it finds one, it will load its contents and try to execute the available tasks.

Node modules

Gulp CLI

Local Gulp

Gulpfile.js

The Gulpfile, on the other hand, loads the local Gulp and uses the API provided by this module.

Figure 2.7   The global CLI kicks off the local Gulp. The local Gulp looks for a Gulpfile and loads its contents.

The output looks like this:

```
[15:01:06] Using gulpfile ~/Project/playground/test/gulpfile.js
[15:01:06] Starting 'test'...
Hello World
[15:01:06] Finished 'test' after 95 µs
```

You can now execute functions defined in your Gulpfile via the command line. Of course, a "Hello World!" isn't something you need a build tool for. Let's do something useful with it.

2.2.2   *Dealing with streams*

With Gulp, you want to read input files and transform them into the desired output, loading lots of JavaScript files and combining them into one. The Gulp API provides some methods for reading, transforming, and writing files, all using streams under the hood.

Streams are a fairly old concept in computing, originating from the early Unix days in the 1960s. A *stream* is a sequence of data coming over time from a source and running to a destination. The source can be of multiple types: files, the computer's memory, or input devices like a keyboard or a mouse. Once a stream is opened, data flows in chunks from its origin to the process consuming it. Coming from a file, every character or byte would be read one at a time; coming from the keyboard, every keystroke would transmit data over the stream. The biggest advantage compared to loading all the data at once is that, in theory, the input can be endless and without limits. Coming from a keyboard, that makes total sense—why should anybody close the input stream you're using to control your computer? Input streams are also called readable

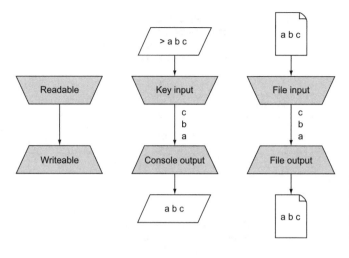

Figure 2.8   Streams can be of two types: readable streams, which access data, and writeable streams, which write data.

streams, indicating that they're meant to read data from a source. On the other hand, there are outbound streams or destinations; they can also be files or some place in memory, but also output devices like the command line, a printer, or your screen. They're also called writeable streams, meaning that they're meant to store the data that comes over the stream. Figure 2.8 illustrates how streams work.

The data is a sequence of elements made available over time (like characters or bytes). Readable streams can originate from different sources, such as input devices (keyboards), files, or data stored in memory. Writeable streams can also end in different places, such as files and memory, as well as the command line. Readable and writeable streams can be interchanged: keyboard input can end up in a file, and file input can end up on the command line.

Not only is it possible to have an endless amount of input, but you also can combine different readable and writeable streams. Key input can be directly stored into a file, or you can print file input out to the command line or even a connected printer. The interface stays the same no matter what the sources or destinations are.

2.2.3   *Readable and writeable streams with Gulp*

In Gulp, you can use the `gulp.src` method to create readable file streams. It allows you to select which files you want to process in your task. Because you're going to deal with many different files and most likely won't know how your files are called directly, you can define some selection patterns using *globs*. The counterpart for `gulp.src` and your writeable stream is `gulp.dest`. Here you define where you want to put your files. The parameter that `gulp.dest` takes is a simple string pointing to the directory, relative to the directory where the Gulpfile is located. Should this directory not be available, Gulp will create it accordingly. Figure 2.9 shows this process.

Globs

Globs are a well-known concept in computer science and programming, and if you've ever deleted all files of a certain type on your command line, then you're familiar with how they work. The asterisk in `*.js` stands for "everything" and is a wildcard. With that, every JavaScript file in the app/scripts folder gets selected. Node globs are more advanced, though, and allow for more sophisticated patterns. One such pattern is the double asterisk right before the `*.js` part. This pattern, called *globstar*, is also a wildcard that tells your selection engine to select practically everything, but in this case you want to match for zero or more directories in that particular subdirectory. For example, the glob `app/scripts/*.js` with a single wildcard before the filename allows you to select any JavaScript file inside the scripts directory but not its subfolders. Using the globstar pattern `app/scripts/**/*.js`, you include JavaScript files in subdirectories.

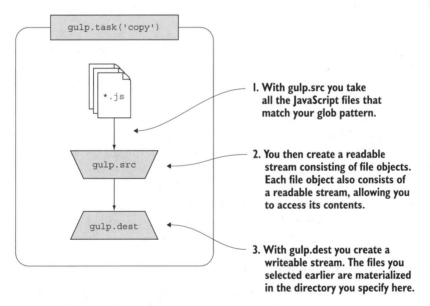

1. With gulp.src you take all the JavaScript files that match your glob pattern.

2. You then create a readable stream consisting of file objects. Each file object also consists of a readable stream, allowing you to access its contents.

3. With gulp.dest you create a writeable stream. The files you selected earlier are materialized in the directory you specify here.

Figure 2.9 A basic Gulp task working with `gulp.src` and `gulp.dest`. You read files from one place and pipe their contents to a destination.

So far you know that `gulp.src` reads files according to a pattern and `gulp.dest` stores files in a certain directory. With this knowledge, you can create your first Gulp task that makes use of this part of Gulp's API. `gulp.src` reads files and `gulp.dest` writes files, so a combination of both copies files from one point to the other. See the next listing for a sample implementation.

Listing 2.2   Copy files from one directory to the other—Gulpfile.js

```
var gulp = require('gulp');                    ➊ Create a new task called copy.

gulp.task('copy', function() {
  return gulp.src('app/scripts/**/*.js')          Create a new readable
    .pipe(gulp.dest('dist'));                   ➋ stream of file objects.
});                                                Streams provide
                                                ➌ a pipe function.
```

In creating the `copy` task, the following function is available in Gulp's task execution space ➊. The glob pattern provided selects all files ending with "js" in all subdirectories of app/scripts (including files inside app/scripts) ➋. You can pipe the contents of a stream through to other functions ➌. In this case, you pipe them through Gulp's `gulp.dest` function. This function materializes all files inside your stream in the specified directory. In this case, you save them in the dist folder. If the folder isn't available, it will be created.

> **NOTE**   Running `gulp copy` from the command line kicks off your execution chain again, this time running the `copy` task.

`gulp.src` opens a readable stream of files. The chunks of data processed are all the files selected by the glob specified in the first parameter. Once this stream is opened, you can steer your stream toward a certain process using a pipe. Pipes are not a Gulp specialty per se, but rather a concept used by Node streams in general. In listing 2.2 you piped the contents to the `gulp.dest` function. The `gulp.dest` function opens a writeable stream. Writeable streams are meant as a sink for data, the end point for the data to stay. This can be output on the screen or in a file. In this case, it's output on the file system. The writeable stream created from `gulp.dest` accepts the same type of data that the readable stream from `gulp.src` creates.

So you read files from the file system and stored them back into the file system, creating a copy functionality. You'd agree that copying is essential but also boring. Let's spice it up with transformable streams in the next section.

2.3   *Handling tasks with Gulp plugins*

So far you've used Gulp as a layer for running functions from the command line and reading files from one place on the file system and writing them back to another place. But Gulp's true power comes when you start to use Gulp plugins. Gulp plugins are little pieces of software that allow you to transform the files in a stream. This section shows you the possibilities and technologies used by Gulp.

2.3.1   *Transforming data*

Streams aren't just good for transferring data between different input sources and output destinations. With the data exposed once a stream is opened, developers can transform the data that comes from the stream before it reaches its destination, such as by transforming all lowercase characters in a file to uppercase characters.

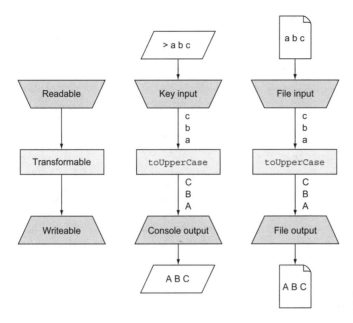

Figure 2.10 Streams are good not only for transferring data but also for modifying it.

This is one of the greatest powers of streams. Once a stream is opened and you can read the data piece by piece, you can slot different programs in between. Figure 2.10 illustrates this process.

To modify data you add transformation blocks between the input and the output. In this example, you get your input data from different sources and channel it through a toUpperCase transformation. This changes lowercase characters to their uppercase equivalent. Those blocks can be defined once and reused for different input origins and outputs.

In Gulp, transformation is done via plugins. The Gulp ecosystem contains more than 1500 plugins that allow you to transform data in various ways. Let's see how you can transform your JavaScript files using a common transformation in the JavaScript world: Uglify.

Uglify is a minification library written in JavaScript. It removes all unnecessary white spaces, reduces variables and function names to a possible minimum while keeping global APIs intact, and takes on every JavaScript code optimization in the book (like writing true as !0, for example, because it saves two bytes!). Your code gets reduced to an absolute minimum, which allows for faster parsing and transfer over the network. For example, the popular jQuery library gets pared down from roughly 250 KB to 90 KB, which is a little more than a third of its original size. Once the process runs, the code becomes unreadable by human eyes, hence the name Uglify. Uglify has Gulp bindings you can install with

```
$ npm install --save-dev gulp-uglify
```

This installs the Gulp plugin for Uglify to your Node modules and saves an entry in the package.json file. You're now able to use this plugin within your Gulpfile, as shown in the following listing.

> **Listing 2.3   Uglifying JavaScript—Gulpfile.js**

```
var gulp = require('gulp');
var uglify = require('gulp-uglify');

gulp.task('scripts', function() {
  return gulp.src('app/scripts/**/*.js')
    .pipe(uglify())
    .pipe(gulp.dest('dist'));
});
```

Next to Gulp, you require the previously installed gulp-uglify module. This allows you to transform contents from Gulp's readable streams with the Uglify process.

You use this plugin directly after creating the readable stream and before saving it with a writeable stream. It's as easy as calling a function.

Each file gets piped through the Uglify process, transforming its contents accordingly. If you run the task with `gulp scripts` and take a good look into the dest directory, you'll see that all the perfectly clear JavaScript from earlier is now an unreadable mess. Mission accomplished!

2.3.2   *Changing the file structure*

When you want to load JavaScript applications over the wire, you want to make as few requests as possible (see chapter 1 for the reasons for this). That's why you want to combine all JavaScript files into one file. This can be done using concatenation. Concatenation combines the contents of many files into one. This new file contains all the contents from the concatenated files and needs a new name that you can define. The same goes for Gulp and the virtual file system.

In standard streams, it's usual to see the file just as a possible input source for the real data, which has to be processed. All information on the origin, like the path or filename, is lost once the stream has opened up. But because you're not just working with the contents of one or a few files, but most likely with a huge amount of files, Gulp needs this information. Think of having 20 JavaScript files and wanting to minify them. You'd have to remember each filename separately and keep track of which data belongs to which file to restore a connection once the output (the minified files of the same name) must be saved.

Luckily, Gulp takes care of that for you by creating both a new input source and a data type that can be used for your streams: virtual file objects. You use a special symbol for those objects, which is shown in figure 2.11.

Once a Gulp stream is opened, all the original, physical files are wrapped in such a virtual file object and handled in the virtual file system, or *Vinyl*, as the corresponding software is called in Gulp.

Vinyl objects, the file objects of your virtual file system, contain two types of information: the path where the file originated, which becomes the file's name, as well as a stream exposing the file's contents. Those virtual files are stored in your computer's memory, known for being the fastest way to process data. There all the modifications

A virtual file object contains the filename of the original file, including its path. This distinguishes it from standard streams, which forget all about file origin once they're opened.

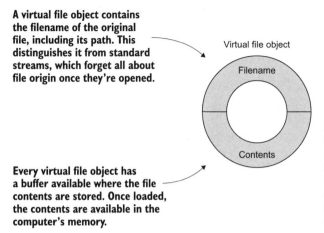

Virtual file object

Figure 2.11 The symbol of a virtual file object. A virtual file consists mainly of two parts: data about the file's path and name, as well as a buffer containing the original contents. Both types of information are available in the computer's memory.

Every virtual file object has a buffer available where the file contents are stored. Once loaded, the contents are available in the computer's memory.

are done that would usually be made on your hard disk. By keeping everything in memory and not having to perform expensive read and write operations in between processes, Gulp can make changes extraordinarily quickly.

You can use this virtual file system to modify the structure of your files during the Gulp task. During concatenation, you specify a new virtual file that contains all the contents from the previous stream. You just have to give it a name. See the next listing for more information.

Listing 2.4 Concatenating files—Gulpfile.js

```
var gulp = require('gulp');
var concat = require('gulp-concat');

gulp.task('scripts', function() {
  return gulp.src('app/scripts/**/*.js')
  .pipe(concat('bundle.js'))
    .pipe(gulp.dest('dist'));
});
```

❶ Require a module called gulp-concat that handles concatenation.

❷ Use this module again after the readable stream is created and before the writeable stream is created.

This module can be installed as before with npm install --save-dev gulp-concat ❶. You pipe your contents (all JavaScript files) through the concat process ❷. The Concat plugin needs one parameter: the name of the new file. Internally, the Concat plugin creates a new virtual file object with the name provided by the parameter. The contents of this virtual file object are all contents from the stream files.

2.3.3 Chaining plugins

In the previous examples, you used different programs to transform the contents of a certain input set before storing the result to the hard disk. The possibilities don't end here. You can slot in any number of programs before you get to the destination, piping your data stream through multiple transformation processes.

Transformation processes are meant to do just one thing and do that one thing well. By compositing more of those processes by connecting them, you can create more advanced and sophisticated programs. To quote Doug McIlroy, who created the concept of streams back in 1964 for the Unix operating system:

> *We should have some ways of connecting programs like garden hose—screw in another segment when it becomes necessary to massage data in another way.*

Opening your data and piping it through a series of processes or subtasks is the very essence of how Gulp works. See figure 2.12, where you use both uglify and concat from the previous example in one process chain.

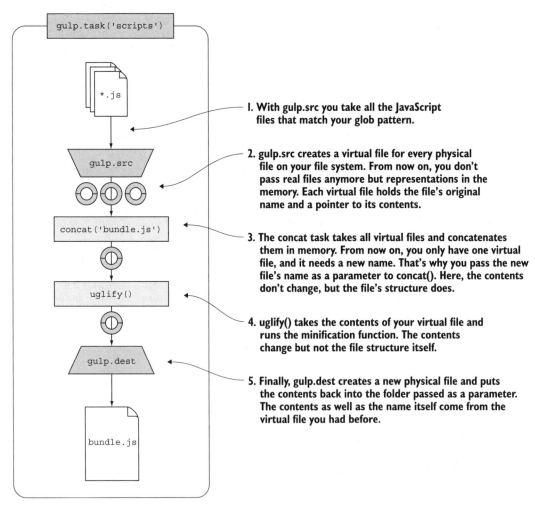

1. With gulp.src you take all the JavaScript files that match your glob pattern.

2. gulp.src creates a virtual file for every physical file on your file system. From now on, you don't pass real files anymore but representations in the memory. Each virtual file holds the file's original name and a pointer to its contents.

3. The concat task takes all virtual files and concatenates them in memory. From now on, you only have one virtual file, and it needs a new name. That's why you pass the new file's name as a parameter to concat(). Here, the contents don't change, but the file's structure does.

4. uglify() takes the contents of your virtual file and runs the minification function. The contents change but not the file structure itself.

5. Finally, gulp.dest creates a new physical file and puts the contents back into the folder passed as a parameter. The contents as well as the name itself come from the virtual file you had before.

Figure 2.12   Streams applied to the virtual file system and Gulp. With gulp.src, you select a sequence of files, promote them to the virtual file system as file objects, and access their contents for a series of transformation processes provided by the Gulp plugins.

So you're concatenating all files and then uglifying them. All of this is happening in the computer's memory, without costly read and write operations from the hard disk in between. This makes Gulp extremely fast and also exceptionally flexible. You can now create advanced programs that take care of multiple things, just by chaining the right plugins in order:

1 Create a `scripts` task that concatenates all files and then uglifies them.
2 Create a `styles` task that compiles the "less" files, minifies them, and then runs Autoprefixer on it to automatically add vendor prefixes.
3 Create a `test` task that does some quality checks on your JavaScript files, making sure you have a good coding style.

> **Vendor prefixes**
>
> Vendor prefixes are used by browser vendors to denote experimental features, where syntax or functionality is subject to change. Browser vendors use a specific abbreviation that's put before JavaScript methods and CSS properties to differentiate between other browser vendors' implementations, their own, and the final specification. For instance, `-webkit-animation` is the vendor-prefixed version of the CSS `animation` property found in browsers using the WebKit rendering engine.

The following Gulpfile takes care of your scripts and stylesheets and also does some extra testing. Install all necessary plugins as you did earlier with `npm install --save-dev <plugin-name>`.

Listing 2.5   A complete Gulpfile.js

```
var gulp        = require('gulp');
var jshint      = require('gulp-jshint');
var uglify      = require('gulp-uglify');
var concat      = require('gulp-concat');
var less        = require('gulp-less');
var minifyCSS   = require('gulp-cssnano');
var prefix      = require('gulp-autoprefixer');

gulp.task('scripts', function() {
  return gulp.src('app/scripts/**/*.js')
    .pipe(concat('main.min.js'))
    .pipe(uglify())
    .pipe(gulp.dest('dist/scripts'));
});

gulp.task('styles', function() {
  return gulp.src('app/styles/main.less')
    .pipe(less())
    .pipe(minifyCSS())
    .pipe(prefix())
    .pipe(gulp.dest('dist/styles'));
});
```

❶ Require all the modules necessary for this Gulpfile.

❷ The script task

❸ The styles task

```
gulp.task('test', function() {                    ◄──4 The test task
  return gulp.src(['app/scripts/**/*.js',
➡ '!app/scripts/vendor/**/*.js'])#D
    .pipe(jshint())
    .pipe(jshint.reporter('default'))             ◄──┐  JSHint works a little differently
    .pipe(jshint.reporter('fail'));                5  than the previous tasks.
});
```

Install each module with npm install --save-dev <plugin-name> ❶. The script task ❷ loads all JavaScript files in the app's scripts directory and combines them into one uglified JavaScript file. The styles task ❸ loads one LESS main file and pipes it through three processes: LESS, CSS Minification with CSS Nano, and automatic vendor prefix inclusion with Autoprefixer. Like the script task, the test task ❹ loads all scripts, but there's a second glob excluding all the files in the vendor directory. This is because you don't want to have code style checks on third-party libraries in the vendor directory, because those files most likely have a different coding style. JSHint's output is not transformed files but a report telling you whether all style checks have been passed ❺. You can pass this report to the reporter plugins of JSHint.

That's quite a lot that you can achieve with just a few lines of code. Running gulp scripts, gulp styles, or gulp test from the command line activates those specific tasks. You now have a fully functioning build file that takes care of all your assets.

2.4   Summary

In this chapter, we introduced you to our building system, Gulp:

- Gulp's runtime environment, Node.js, comes with a package manager called NPM. NPM can install Node.js modules globally to be used as a tool and locally to be used as a library. Gulp has both a command-line interface that's to be installed globally and a library that's installed locally for every project.
- Gulpfiles are build instructions written in JavaScript. They use the local Gulp installation to access an API. You can now require Node modules from within JavaScript files and use them in your code.
- Gulp's gulp.task API makes functions available and runnable from the command line. A call with gulp <taskname> executes the defined task in your file.
- gulp.src and gulp.dest create readable and writeable streams, allowing you to copy files from one place in the file system to another.
- Plugins like Concat and Uglify allow you to transform your JavaScript contents.
- Plugin chaining allows more advanced software, such as a script task that does both uglification and concatenation, or a styles task that takes care of running a preprocessor using CSS minification and automatic prefixing of properties.
- Code style checks with JSHint make sure your software is well written.

With this simple Gulpfile, you can process your source files as needed. In the next chapter, we'll expand this file to provide a full-fledged development environment for you.

A Gulp setup
for local development

This chapter covers

- Dependency chains
- Sequential and parallel execution chains
- Watch processes
- On-demand development servers with live reload capabilities

In the previous chapter you learned how to use Gulp to create build pipelines to allow for a chain of different file transformations. You selected files according to different patterns, created a stream of data out of them, and transformed their contents by using several Gulp plugins, each designed to fulfill a special task.

Even though you created different processes and were able to run a multitude of transformations by the simple click of a button, you're still a few steps away from the bigger and more comprehensive concept of automation. As the term *automation* might suggest, you're aiming for a collection of processes bound together in a system that does a set of tasks automatically and without your explicit intervention.

In other words, you start your finely tuned task collection and let your automation tool do the rest for you during the entire development lifecycle.

Gulp provides the functionality to create automation. In this chapter, you'll get to know the rest of Gulp's API, which allows you to order the execution of your previously defined set of tasks. Furthermore, you'll create so-called *watch processes*, which keep an eye on your source files and trigger transformation tasks automatically should one of those files change. You'll even automate the reloading of your browser window, using an on-demand development server, bringing your Gulp setup to a totally automated and full-fledged development environment. To re-create the samples shown in this chapter, you can either continue from the previous chapter or check out branch chapter-3 from the GitHub repository at https://github.com/frontend-tooling /sample-project-gulp.

> **GULP   4** Most of the contents in this chapter require the functionality of version 4 of Gulp. Chaining tasks in series and parallel especially requires an API that's not available in older versions. We strongly suggest you use Gulp 4 to continue.

3.1   The local development environment

Your main goal for this chapter is to create a local development environment that allows for rapid development cycles. Instead of executing the various tasks manually, you'll define processes that automatically trigger the right tasks at the right time and in the right order.

Imagine how you'd usually operate when working on a project, given your Gulpfile from the previous chapter, as shown in figure 3.1. You'd follow this process:

1   Delete your build folder (named dist in previous examples) to make sure you start with a clean slate and without artifacts from your previous work.
2   Run the tasks you created earlier: `tests`, then `scripts`, and then `styles`.
3   For many JavaScript features, your app needs to run with the file transferred over HTTP or HTTPS. Therefore, you boot up a development server.
4   Start iterating over your source files. You add new functionality or new styles and run your previously defined tasks again. This last phase continues as long as you're actively developing.

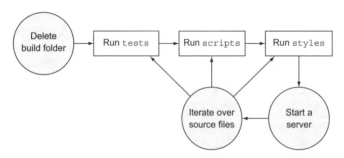

Figure 3.1   **The phases of your local development environment. You clean your build folder and then make calls to the three build tasks you defined earlier. Then you start a server. Once this basic setup is complete, you iterate over your source files and call** `tests`, `scripts`, **and** `styles` **again.**

The first two steps—deleting and running the original tasks in a defined order—require considerable attention from you as a developer. You might forget to perform one of those tasks, such as deleting your build folder, or you might mix up the execution order of other tasks, such as compiling your scripts before running tests on them. Defining the order of execution and thus automating it helps you reduce errors. The third step—booting up a development server—is required, and there are different ways to achieve this. It would be good if you could define the server's setup once and execute it whenever you like. Installing and configuring a server takes time and effort, but most of the steps are the same, so it's another step you can automate. The last point—iterating over the source files—again requires some attention from the developer, plus it gets boring the more often you have to do it and the smaller your coding iteration steps are.

A local development environment takes care of all of those tasks. It knows which tasks should be executed in which order, and it knows which files have to be served from your development server.

3.1.1 Grouping the tasks

If you take a closer look at figure 3.1, you'll see that you can categorize all your tasks into three different groups, as depicted in figure 3.2:

1. *Reset*—Getting rid of the results of your previous build
2. *Initial build*—Re-creating the compiled files from your source files
3. *Iteration*—Making small adaptions over the time and showing the results in your browser

Let's take a closer look at each of those steps.

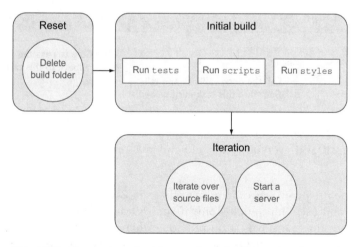

Figure 3.2 The previous steps for your local development environment combined into three different groups: a reset to create a clean state to begin with, an initial build to create a first result, and build iterations to update your build with incremental changes from your source files

3.1.2   *The reset step: a clean task*

The reset step for your local development environment is straightforward: get rid of any results from your previous build. You need this clean slate to make sure you don't have any leftovers from the previous build that might interfere with your current development status. You need to create a new task that takes care of this. When you created all your building tasks in chapter 2, you stored the results in a folder called dist. You now have to tell Gulp to get rid of everything inside it.

The Node.js ecosystem has a package for this functionality called del, which you can incorporate in your Gulpfile written in the previous chapter. Install the package with npm install --save-dev del via the command line, and add the following code into your Gulpfile.

Listing 3.1   Gulpfile.js—clean task

```
var del = require('del');       ◁—— Require the del package in your Gulpfile.

gulp.task('clean', function() {
    return del(['dist']);       ◁—— Call the del method you required earlier.
});
```

Place this particular line with your other require statements. The first parameter is a list of patterns you want to delete (in this case, the dist folder). The del package isn't a Gulp plugin per se, but it has an interface that's compatible with Gulp.

As shown in the previous listing, you don't need a Gulp plugin or file streams to work with. Rather, you take a Node.js module and incorporate it into your Gulp setup. Another way of closing tasks without streams is by passing a done callback to the function, as shown in the next listing.

Listing 3.2   Demo code

```
gulp.task('report', function(done) {      ◁——┐ Allow Gulp to pass the
    console.log('We are done!');              │ done callback to this task.
    done();       ◁——┐ Call the done callback and tell
});                  │ Gulp that this task has finished.
```

The done callback function notifies Gulp when this task has finished (instead of returning streams), and everything inside your task relies purely on other Node functionality.

> **NOTE**   This is the preferred way of handling things in Gulp: use Node.js modules if possible and use Gulp plugins only if you're transforming files and if you have to store the transformed output somewhere on your file system. Gulp streams have a defined beginning and end, which connect to physical files on your file system. Although you're transforming files when deleting them (the transformation being removing them), you don't have an output in your file system in which to store the result.

With this `clean` task, the reset step is complete. Next, we take a look at the initial build and iteration steps.

3.1.3 Build and iteration

The initial build and iteration phases seem very similar at first: they're both meant to run the previously implemented tasks you defined earlier in chapter 2. But there's a subtle but important difference.

The initial build is meant to run through all compilation tasks you have (`styles`, `tests`, `scripts`) in a defined order that not only makes sense for the developers but also ensures that build results don't interfere with each other. With your current setup, you don't have possible interferences inside your build phase but rather at the beginning of the phase and the end. Your build folder, dist, has to be cleared *before* compilation starts; otherwise, you could possibly delete the newly compiled files. Also, the server from the next phase has to start *after* the compilation; otherwise, your compiled files won't be ready. The build phase takes care of this.

The iteration phase, on the other hand, just picks a subset of all those tasks from the build phase based on the incremental changes of your source code. When you change a JavaScript file, you don't want to run the `styles` task, because the two don't have anything to do with each other. And vice versa is also true—a LESS file that's being changed doesn't need to trigger the `scripts` task.

Those two phases require a little more attention than the reset phase. They also need some major updates in the Gulpfile you carried over from chapter 2. We'll look at both of those phases in the next two sections.

3.2 The initial build step

The initial build step takes care of compiling all your files, bringing the whole app into a deployment-ready state. From there on, you want to either deploy your application or iterate over the build files in the next step of your development process.

As a quick recap of which tasks to execute for your build step, take a look at figure 3.3.

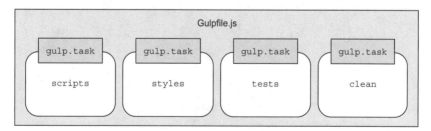

Figure 3.3 The four tasks you want to bring in order: your `scripts` compilation task, the `styles` compilation task, and the JavaScript `tests` task from the previous chapter, along with your new `clean` task, which removes the build directory to start a new build entirely

Follow these steps:

1 Delete your build folder from a possible previous build step and start with a clean slate; call `clean`.
2 Run `tests` for your JavaScript files.
3 Run `styles` and `scripts` to make sure your assets are compiled and put into the right folder.
4 To achieve such an order of execution, you define different dependency and execution chains and wire them up using the Gulp functions `gulp.series`—which allows for sequential execution of tasks—and `gulp.parallel`—which is used to run tasks alongside each other.

3.2.1 *Dependency and execution chains*

When you take a closer look at the purpose of each task and how they relate to each other, you'll find a small but significant difference, as illustrated in figure 3.4. `tests` has to run every time before `scripts`, which means that `scripts` *depends* on `tests` passing successfully. `styles` doesn't have such a dependency, but you want to clean your build directory before starting both `scripts` and `styles`. You have to define an execution order: first `clean` and then `styles` and `scripts` in parallel, with the latter executing after `tests` has finished running.

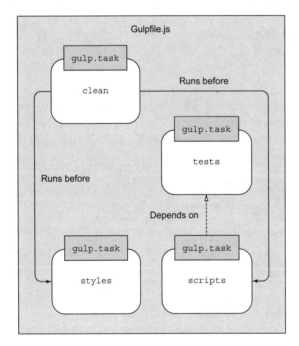

Figure 3.4 How your tasks relate to each other

DEPENDENCY CHAIN

The first concept introduced here is dependency chains, as shown by the dotted line with the empty arrow in figure 3.4. In this example, `scripts` is tightly coupled to `tests`. You don't want to run the `scripts` compilation task without first testing your sources. Every time you want to run `scripts`, you have to run `tests` first. We call this relationship a *dependency*.

Dependencies are defined at the task itself. In our example, `scripts` is defined to call `tests` first. The caller of `scripts` doesn't need to know that this will happen. Dependencies can also have other dependencies. The path from the outmost dependency to the very root task is called a *dependency chain*.

EXECUTION CHAIN

The second concept is execution chains, as shown in figure 3.4 by the straight lines and full arrows. There are tasks that should be run in a certain order, such as `styles` and `scripts` needing to call `clean` first, but that aren't as tightly coupled as dependencies. It's fine to call `styles` and `scripts` separately on their own, without deleting the whole build folder first. It's just on special occasions—like your initial build—that you need to call them. To achieve this, you define an *execution chain*: a set of tasks that are called in order, either sequentially or in parallel.

Gulp offers two chaining functions used for both dependency and execution chaining.

3.2.2 *Serial and parallel task execution*

To create execution chains you can use two task-execution functions from Gulp's API: `gulp.series` and `gulp.parallel`. As their names suggest, they're used to run tasks in either sequential or parallel order:

- `gulp.series`—This function call allows you to run a sequential order of Gulp tasks. It takes an infinite amount of parameters of either string (pointing to a defined Gulp task) or functions.
- `gulp.parallel`—This function takes the same parameters as `gulp.series` but executes those tasks in parallel. To do so, it spawns a series of processes that are executed at the same time.

Figure 3.5 shows how to create a sequential execution chain with `gulp.series`.

You can see that you create a new task (called `default`), which doesn't have a function per se but rather a `gulp.series` call pointing to the three tasks you want to run. In the order in which you added them to the function, you first run `clean`, then `styles`, and then `scripts`. Note that you're skipping the `tests` call for the moment. `gulp.series` makes sure that none of those tasks gets executed before the other has finished.

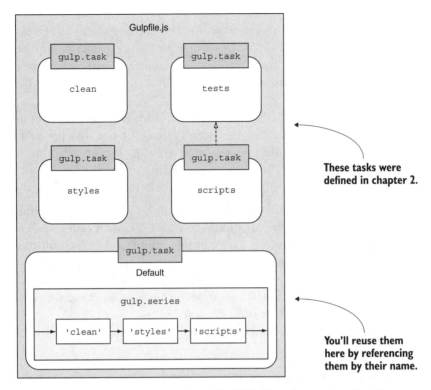

Figure 3.5   A sequential task execution order. With the `gulp.series` function, you can define to run `clean`, `styles`, and `scripts` in that order. The API takes the names of your previously defined tasks.

With `styles` and `scripts` not having any common dependency in terms of tasks or files, you can run them in parallel. With the `gulp.parallel` function you can combine those two tasks to still run in parallel but behave as one building block inside the sequential order you defined previously. See figure 3.6 for details.

Running these tasks in parallel allows for a much faster execution because Gulp spawns two separate processes executing both tasks asynchronously. `gulp.series` and `gulp.parallel` can be combined freely and almost endlessly, so both methods can contain multiple variations of task names and series/parallel calls, allowing for complex and rich execution chains.

The new `default` task will be your main execution chain for this example. Here all necessary calls are being made to build and kick off your project.

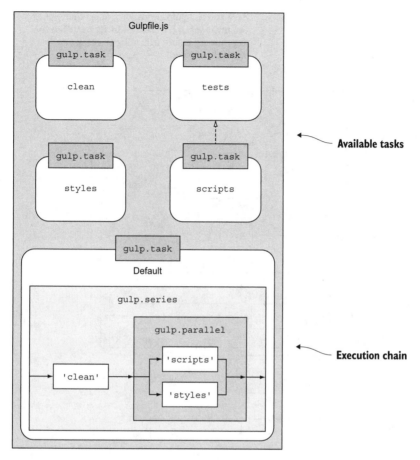

Figure 3.6 Because `scripts` and `styles` don't depend on each other, you can run `scripts` and `styles` in parallel. The `gulp.series` API allows you not only to define task names but also to add other functions, like a call to `gulp.parallel`, which in turn provides the same API where you call your `scripts` and `styles` tasks. The running order is now first `clean` and then `scripts` and `styles` at the same time.

3.2.3 *Task execution functions for dependency chains*

You can use the same API calls to `series` and `parallel` to create dependency chains. The difference is where you put them—remember that you ignored the call to `tests` earlier. This is because you wanted to tightly couple it to your `scripts` task, making sure that every time you call `scripts`, `tests` is executed beforehand. Figure 3.7 shows the adaptations you need to make to your `scripts` task.

Here you use gulp.series for a dependency chain:
You make a call (referenced by its name) to the
dependency before executing the task you
originally defined.

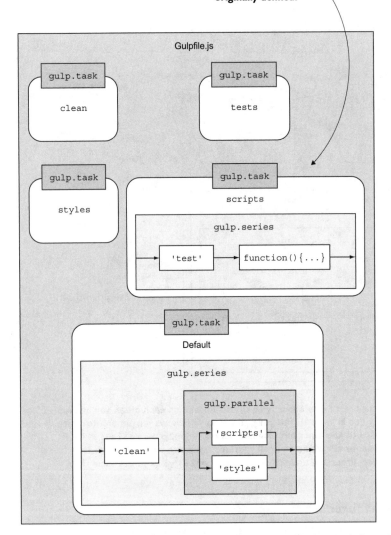

Figure 3.7   You can use this execution chain to also describe your task dependencies.
tests must run before scripts no matter what. To achieve this, you use a gulp.series
function that executes tests and directly after that the original function you defined earlier.
Coupling this with scripts and not in the default execution order allows you to freely
work with the scripts task without having tests always on your mind.

You create another sequential execution chain, with the first being a call to `tests` and the second being the original task function you created earlier. In this case you don't want to call those tasks in parallel, because both `tests` and your task function access the same files.

With this dependency added to your `scripts` task, the execution of `default` becomes a little more complex. The original `scripts` call is replaced with the `gulp.series` chain in this task, nesting this sequential execution inside your parallel one. Let's put those changes into the Gulpfile.

3.2.4 *Updates to your Gulpfile*

First, you create the dependency call in your `scripts` function, as shown in the following listing.

> **Listing 3.3   Gulpfile.js excerpt—revised scripts task**

The first parameter of this function stays the same.

The second parameter is now a call to the gulp.series function.

```
gulp.task('scripts',
  gulp.series('tests', function() {
    return gulp.src(['app/scripts/vendor/**/*.js', 'app/scripts/**/*.js'])
      .pipe(concat('main.min.js'))
      .pipe(gulp.dest('dist'));
  })
);
```

You still call your task `scripts`. You pass `tests` as the first parameter and your original function is the second parameter. This method takes as many parameters as you pass to it but at least one of these:

- A string pointing to a task
- A function containing JavaScript code to execute
- Another call to `gulp.series` or `gulp.parallel`, where those rules apply again

Now when you run `gulp scripts` from the command line, you see that the execution stack is a little more advanced:

scripts is called.

```
$ gulp scripts
[18:09:26] Using gulpfile ~/Projects/book/sample-project-gulp/gulpfile.js
[18:09:26] Starting 'scripts'...
[18:09:26] Starting 'tests'...
[18:09:26] Finished 'tests' after 30 ms
[18:09:26] Starting '<anonymous>'...
[18:09:26] Finished '<anonymous>' after 15 ms
[18:09:26] Finished 'scripts' after 48 ms
```

Before the main goal of your function is executed, Gulp sees the dependency to tests and runs that function in advance.

The anonymous function holds your original task and is executed after tests.

The whole scripts task is finished; the time given is the execution duration of the whole scripts task, which includes the durations of tests and your anonymous function.

The output of a call to anonymous happens because your passed function doesn't have a name. It isn't scripts anymore, because scripts is now a sequential execution of two functions. You can change this by naming it in the truest JavaScript sense, as shown next.

Listing 3.4 Gulpfile.js excerpt—naming anonymous functions

```
gulp.task('scripts',
    gulp.series('test', function scriptsInternal() {        ◁——┐  You can name
        … // same as before                                     │  this function
    })                                                          │  as you like.
);
```

This function won't be available in your global function scope, just printed by Gulp. A good naming convention is to have the original task name postfixed by "Internal" in camel case.

After making your changes in the scripts task, you have to make some adaptations in your default task as well. The following listing is a direct transition from figure 3.6.

Listing 3.5 Gulpfile.js excerpt—using series and parallel

```
gulp.task('default',                    ◁—— Create a new task.
    gulp.series('clean',                                    ◁——┐
        gulp.parallel('styles', 'scripts')      ◁——┤  The first parameter is
    )                                                          │  a call to gulp.series.
);                          The second parameter is
                            a call to gulp.parallel.
```

You create a new task and name it default. It takes a pointer to your clean task as the first parameter and then points to both styles and scripts.

As you can see, even if the basic structures of default and scripts are roughly the same, both having a task name as well as a call to gulp.series as their first parameter, everything beyond that is different. This showcases the flexibility of chaining functions. You can call now your new default task by running gulp on your command line. If no task is specified as a parameter when calling Gulp, it will automatically search for a default task and execute it. Here's the output:

```
$ gulp
[18:26:51] Using gulpfile ~/Projects/book/sample-project-gulp/gulpfile.js
[18:26:51] Starting 'default'...
[18:26:51] Starting 'clean'...
[18:26:51] Finished 'clean' after 12 ms
[18:26:51] Starting 'parallel'...
```

Run your parallel execution of scripts and styles.

clean is the first task executed via default, as described in your Gulpfile. It also ends before any other task starts due to its sequential order.

scripts and styles start at the same
time. No other task starts and/or
finishes before them.

With the call of scripts, the same execution
order as in the previous sample begins.

```
[18:26:51] Starting 'styles'...
[18:26:51] Starting 'scripts'...
[18:26:51] Starting 'test'...
[18:26:51] Finished 'test' after 164 ms
[18:26:51] Starting 'scriptsInternal'...
[18:26:51] Finished 'styles' after 185 ms
[18:26:51] Finished 'scriptsInternal' after 14 ms
[18:26:51] Finished 'scripts' after 189 ms
[18:26:51] Finished 'parallel' after 190 ms
[18:26:51] Finished 'default' after 206 ms
```

The notable exception is that
styles finishes long before the
scripts task. Gulp now waits
for both tasks to end...

...so it can finish both the parallel
execution and the default task in general.

With that code you've finished your initial build step. Let's move on to the iterations.

3.3 The iteration step

After your initial build you iterate over your source files during development. From now on, you don't want to build the whole batch but rather increments representing the changes. For example, if you're going to change one of your style files, you don't have to rebuild all your JavaScript files, because there are no changes to be tracked.

You use Gulp to keep an eye on your source files and trigger processes once a change occurs. For this you create *watch processes*. To see your changes directly in the browser, you need to boot up a development server and inject those changes into your open browser window.

3.3.1 Watch processes

File watch processes constantly poll the file system to see if something on the hard disk has changed. Because Gulp is all about transforming files from one state into another, it just makes sense to include this feature in Gulp's API.

With the `gulp.watch` function call, Gulp provides an interface to start a watch process, listen for file changes to a specific pattern, and trigger task execution accordingly. The `watch` function spawns a watch process that listens for change events on a certain set of files you define. Should a change occur, it triggers a callback function, which most of the time is a set of Gulp tasks but can also be any other function. Figure 3.8 illustrates how you can add file watchers to your existing `default` task in your Gulpfile.

You add a new function to your sequential execution chain you defined before. You put it after the compilation of both scripts and styles to make sure the trigger tasks from your watch processes aren't executed at the same time. Because `gulp.series` takes not only task names but also functions as parameters, you can add one function as the last parameter in `gulp.series`. The contents of this function are two watchers—or two `gulp.watch` calls—that you set off, one looking for changes in styles and

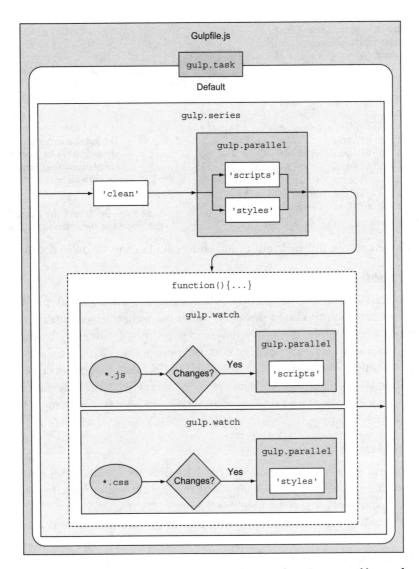

Figure 3.8   After the execution of `clean`, `scripts`, and `styles`, you add a new function to your sequential (or serial) execution chain. In this function you define two watch tasks, one watching the JavaScript files and one watching the CSS files. Depending on which file changes during the run, `gulp.watch` will execute the tasks you add there. Once a `gulp.watch` function is called, Gulp blocks the Gulp process from terminating, still keeping an eye on the files you want to watch. You can close Gulp via Ctrl-C.

one for changes in scripts. Once the watchers have been added, Gulp looks for three different types of changes and triggers the task that's referenced in `gulp.watch`:

- *Changes in existing files*—The task is triggered once the file's contents have been saved to the file system and the timestamp changes.
- *Additions to the file system that follow the given pattern*—The task is triggered once this file has been added.
- *Deletions from the file systems that follow the given pattern*—The task is triggered once the file has been removed.

Gulp watchers are set to match a specific glob pattern, much like the one you provide when selecting files with `gulp.src` (for example, `scripts/**/*.js` selects all JavaScript files in the scripts folder as well as in subfolders). Once a change occurs on the file system, your watcher is notified and checks to see if the change matches the provided pattern. If so, your watcher calls the function passed as the second parameter. Again, this can be any function: a self-defined one as well as calls to `gulp.series` or `gulp.parallel`.

With your watch processes in place, you can now trigger incremental builds with each iteration of your original source files.

3.3.2 *Using Browsersync for an on-demand server with live reload*

For iteration purposes, running a local development server gives you access to one thing that's wonderful to have during the coding phase: you can inject changes directly and on the fly to the rendering of your application inside the browser window, making the browser reload the current page and assets, doing one more step for you automatically.

Usually, one PC runs one web server at a time, with the developer adding more subdomains or folders as they add more projects. This is also time-consuming and can easily be automated. With Browsersync, you can achieve both. First, you boot up a new, clean development server on the go, serving your project and nothing else, and it can be torn down just as easily. Second, you inject the changes made into your styles and script files at the same moment that the source files are saved, creating an immediate update in your browser window.

BROWSERSYNC

Browsersync is one tool that does exactly that. Among many other features, it can easily be booted up with one call in your JavaScript and pointed to a set of directories to serve. It also has methods to reload the browser window on call. Figure 3.9 shows how to add Browsersync to your execution chain.

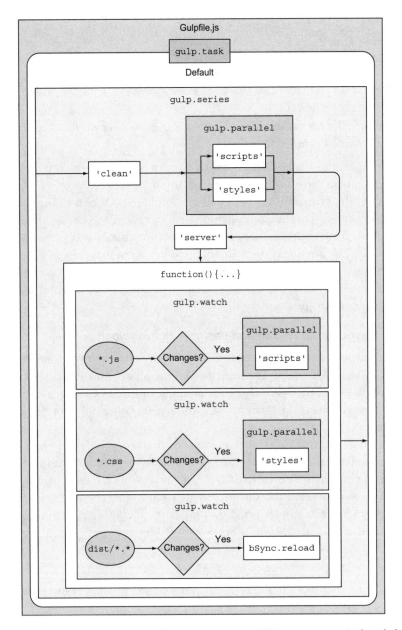

Figure 3.9   To start your development server, you add a new `server` task and place its execution well in your previously established execution chain. Because you want to run the server before your watchers start up but after your assets (`scripts` and `styles`) go off, you add it in your series execution chain after the parallel run tasks. You also add a new watcher to your function. This time you listen to all changes in your distribution folder, the folder that contains your build results. You don't call a Gulp function then but call the `reload` method of Browsersync.

With the execution of both server and file watcher established (see the concrete implementation in the upcoming subsection), you create a connection between your client (the browser) and server, as shown in figure 3.10.

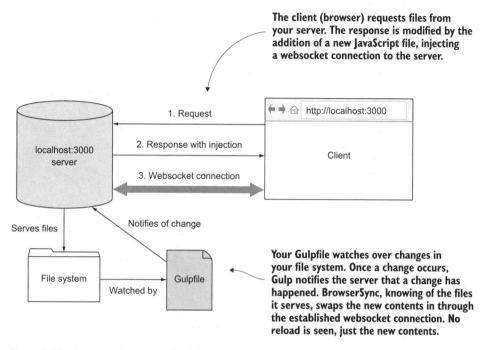

The client (browser) requests files from your server. The response is modified by the addition of a new JavaScript file, injecting a websocket connection to the server.

Your Gulpfile watches over changes in your file system. Once a change occurs, Gulp notifies the server that a change has happened. BrowserSync, knowing of the files it serves, swaps the new contents in through the established websocket connection. No reload is seen, just the new contents.

Figure 3.10   A request from your client triggers a response from the Browsersync server. The server modifies the response by injecting a JavaScript file, which in turn opens up a direct websocket connection to the server. Now when a change in your file system occurs, Gulp notifies the server that this change has happened, which in turn swaps the new contents of this file into the representation in your browser.

With every request to an HTML file on your web server, Browsersync manipulates the returned response by injecting a JavaScript snippet at the end. This JavaScript snippet opens up a websocket connection to the server. Websockets are a way to directly communicate between client and server without the need for any user interaction or HTTP request. This allows for real-time calls to the web application on your client. Websockets are commonly used for small data updates, and in this case those updates are the new contents of your JavaScript and CSS files. Browsersync uses this direct connection for many more possible updates. It transfers not only changes in content but also scroll positions and clicks to other clients. You can open more browsers to look at the same site, and Browsersync makes sure you have the same view on every client, hence the name *Browsersync*.

3.3.3 Updates to your Gulpfile

In this section you learn the following concepts, which give you more automation possibilities:

- Watch processes listen to file changes and trigger one or more tasks.
- A socket connection between client and server allows you to inject resources like styles and scripts programmatically.

Those two ideas have been integrated to our build pipeline in figure 3.9, and you'll adapt your Gulpfile accordingly. You start with the new server task, because it can be used as a standalone component that you'll integrate later into your build execution chain.

First, you need to install a new package with npm install --save-dev browser-sync. The changes to your Gulpfile are shown in the following listing.

Listing 3.6 Gulpfile.js excerpt—adding Browsersync

```
var bSync  = require('browser-sync');
...
gulp.task('server', function(done) {
    bSync({
        server: {
            baseDir: ['dist', 'app']
        }
    });
    done();
});
```

Require Browsersync as you did with other packages and store it ❶ in the variable bSync.

Create a new task named server. ❷

❸ Pass a configuration object.

Give this configuration ❹ object two folders.

❺ Call the respective callback.

Place this statement ❶ with the other require statements in your Gulpfile. The function you pass has the done callback as a parameter to be called afterward ❷. Starting the Browsersync server is a simple function call ❸. This configuration object ❹ defines the base directories of your server. Give it two folders, dist and app. If a request occurs, Browsersync will first look into dist to find this file; if not, it searches for it in an app. If it can't be found in either of those directories, Browsersync will emit a 404 error. Once you've finished opening your server, call the respective callback ❺.

Browsersync doesn't take many arguments and has a set of good defaults to get your server going. If your system is configured correctly, Browsersync will even open the browser for you and open a new tab with the correct URL. If you're not comfortable with so many options preselected for you, go to http://browsersync.io and see which options you can change.

It's important to call the done callback afterward. Browsersync starts a new process, and without the callback, Gulp would be stuck there, unable to call the functions afterward. The done callback function makes sure you return to the next step in your previous execution chain, which you adapt in the next listing

---

Listing 3.7   Gulpfile.js excerpt—watcher function

```
gulp.task('default',
  gulp.series('clean',
    gulp.parallel('styles', 'scripts'),
    'server',
    function watcher(done) {
      gulp.watch(
        ['app/scripts/**/*.js', '!app/scripts/vendor/**/*.js'],
        gulp.parallel('scripts')
      );
      gulp.watch(
        'app/styles/**/*.less',
        gulp.parallel('styles')
      );
      gulp.watch(
        'dist/**/*',
        bSync.reload
      );
      done();
    }
  )
);
```

Adapt your series execution chain by first putting a call to the server task.

1 Add your watcher function.

The first watcher is called with the gulp.watch function.

Pass an array of globs as the first parameter. **2**

You don't need to put in arrays; **3** you also can use just strings.

Call the last watcher. **4**

Add the reload function of **5** browserSync as the second parameter.

For completeness, tell Gulp you're finished with your watcher function.

You name your watcher function so you see the call to this function on the command line **1**. These **2** are the same globs as in the scripts example in chapter 2. You want to rebuild just your own files, not your vendor files that have been changed. You then make a parallel call to `scripts`. This glob **3** points to your LESS files. The last watcher you call is to your created files in the dist folder **4**. You look out for every file in there. Instead of a call to a Gulp function, you just add the `reload` function of Browsersync as the second parameter **5**. This gets executed every time a change occurs in your dist folder.

If you execute Gulp now (by typing `gulp` into the command line), you'll see the whole execution chain fire off. First is `clean`, followed by `scripts` and `styles` run in parallel (with `tests` running before the `scriptsInternal` method). Once those are done, you boot up your server and run the file watchers. Note that Gulp won't stop afterward because you have a multitude of processes running that shouldn't stop on their own. Hit Ctrl-C at your command line to stop Gulp. All child processes will also be terminated.

With those changes applied, you've implemented all your processes. Your local development environment is ready.

3.4   Summary

In this chapter you created a local development environment, running a defined process of reset, initial build, and build iterations. Each of those steps leads to automation of the tasks you defined in chapter 2 and gets executed by calling one command at the beginning:

- For the reset, you created a `clean` task using the `del` Node.js module. This provides a clean state with no artifacts of previous builds remaining.
- The initial build task was done by an execution chain, implemented with the `gulp.series` and `gulp.parallel` functions from Gulp's API, allowing for sequential and parallel execution of tasks.
- You learned the concept of dependency chains, which are also implemented using `gulp.series`. Dependency chains tightly couple the execution of dependencies and tasks. Thus, you can make sure that you run your JavaScript tests before JavaScript compilation takes place.
- For the build iterations and incremental builds, you used Gulp's file watchers. They keep an eye on changes on the file system and trigger functions if such a change should occur.
- You also booted up a local development server with Browsersync, which allows you to see those iterative changes. File watchers again notify your server to inject changes into the visual representation in your browser.

With your local development environment in place, you'll leave the world of Gulp for now and move on to the next tool in your toolchain. You've seen that with your vendor scripts still in the same place as your self-written files, you need to make exceptions to your building instructions. You want to get rid of those exceptions by promoting vendor scripts to their own space in your project and dealing with them exclusively.

Dependency management with Bower

This chapter covers

- An introduction to dependency management
- Bower as a front-end dependency manager
- Flat versus nested dependency trees
- Gulp plugins for Bower integration

After creating a solid build definition file for Gulp, you're ready to move on to the next step in your new front-end development workflow: dependency management.

Dependencies are self-contained and reusable code packages. You don't want to change the code but simply want to use it. The packages include frameworks like Bootstrap or jQuery but also smaller components like carousels or various widgets you want to include in your application. The latter ones also might have dependencies of their own. And those might be dependent on one of the frameworks you're already using.

The more code you use, the harder it gets to keep track of. Imagine having 10 jQuery plugins on your website and trying to update the main framework to a newer version. It's hard to ensure that all of the plugins still work with the new jQuery release.

61

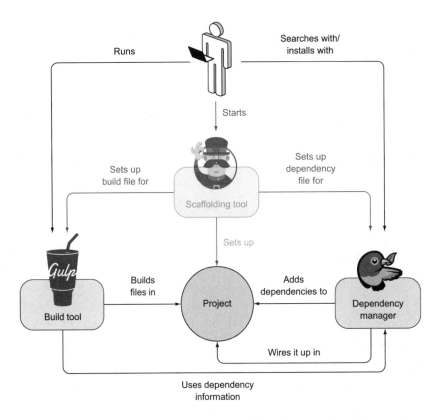

Figure 4.1 **The next tool in your development workflow: Bower, a dependency manager for front-end development. You'll learn how to search for and install new dependencies and how to add them to your project files.**

This is where dependency managers come in. Tools like Bower help you to install, search for, and update dependencies, as shown in figure 4.1. They also keep an eye on cross-references and possible version conflicts with other frameworks and components you've installed.

In this chapter, you'll learn how dependency managers work and how you can use them for your own projects. Among all the dependency management tools out there, we'll focus on Bower, which was specifically designed for front-end developers. Its unique architecture of allowing you to have just one version of a certain library at a time ensures the browser doesn't end up with multiple versions of the same dependency. Also, it provides a more flexible way of dealing with versions than other package managers, which is more aligned to the backward-compatible nature of the web.

To start, let's see what we're dealing with when talking about *components* and *dependencies*.

> ## NPM for client-side dependencies
>
> In recent times, NPM and the related Yarn tool have also become choices for front-end developers to handle their dependencies. To work with NPM on the client side, however, requires an entirely different workflow, which isn't as flexible as the one used with Bower. But this chapter was written with other dependency managers in mind. You should be able to transfer the information easily to any other tool that deals with JavaScript components.

4.1 Dependency management basics

Before we go into the depths of our selected tool, it's necessary to examine the basics of dependency management. To do so, we'll define the term *dependency* and take a more detailed look at dependency trees. The latter provide the basis for a dependency manager to actually fulfill its purpose.

4.1.1 Components and dependencies

In this chapter and throughout the book we'll use two terms to describe our reusable code packages: *component* and *dependency*. Although they're the same content-wise, there's a subtle difference in how they're handled.

COMPONENT

A component is a bundle of reusable, self-contained code. The idea is that this piece of software encapsulates a set of functionality that works on its own. This component provides an API to access the functionality intended to be used. Throughout this chapter we'll use the symbol shown in figure 4.2 to depict a component.

Figure 4.2 We'll use this image to depict a component.

Components can range from general-purpose frameworks like jQuery (which provides an API to access cross-browser functionality in a comfortable and error-free way) to more specific sets of code like UI widgets. The most important factor is the self-containment rule: a component developer ensures that with the installation of such a component, every requirement to work properly is given. This leads us directly to the next term.

DEPENDENCY

Because the term *component* encompasses a broad variety of software, we immediately run into a problem: what if the functionality a component provides requires some other functionality to work? Think of a carousel component, which is a rather specific set of functionality that uses jQuery as the preferred way of selecting HTML elements. Without jQuery, the most important rule for a component wouldn't be met. Of course, you could include the entire jQuery library inside the component to make up for this. But given that jQuery itself can be seen as a component that's likely to be

Figure 4.3   This image shows two components connected to each other. The arrow connecting them has an unfilled triangle at the end, indicating a dependency. The image reads "Component B depends on component A" or "Component A is a dependency of component B."

reused within various other components, you could make it a dependency. Figure 4.3 shows how we depict dependencies in this book.

A dependency is a component that's necessary for another component to fulfill the self-containment rule. It provides functionality that the component relies on. Without this functionality, the component wouldn't work and thus would break the rule of providing software that works on its own. In figure 4.3, component A provides its functionality independently of any other components. Component B, on the other hand, can only work with component A available. The link between those components is mandatory for B, and it's the task of a dependency manager to ensure that this requirement is met.

COMPONENT REPOSITORIES

Another term that has to be defined is *component repositories* or *component registries*. Component repositories are servers where all the necessary metadata from all the registered components is stored. Usually, a dependency manager communicates with such a repository to retrieve meta information on a component's version, its dependencies, and an endpoint from which to download the component. In most cases, the component itself is also stored in the component repository.

In Bower's case, however, the repository (or registry) just stores meta information. The files themselves can be stored on any available Git endpoint. Usually they're hosted on GitHub. This is another advantage of Bower. With components being stored somewhere other than the component's meta-information registry, you can easily swap one of those. Instead of using GitHub, you might use an internal Git repository. Instead of having to communicate with the official registry, you can create a private registry that stores information just for your components.

Now that you know what components a dependency manager needs to work, let's look at how it handles the organization.

4.1.2   *Dependency trees*

Figure 4.3 shows a simple link between two components, making just one component a dependency of the other. But every component can have as many dependencies as needed, and those dependencies can also have other dependencies. These chains of dependencies can be as deeply nested as necessary. Furthermore, multiple dependencies might require the same component but in different versions. To make this mass of interconnected components manageable, dependency managers organize them in *dependency trees*. There are three types: a nested dependency tree, a flat dependency tree, and some sort of hybrid of these two. To create such dependency trees, each component must meet the following requirements:

> A component that should work as a dependency must have a name that makes it uniquely identifiable. For instance, a component with the name jQuery can appear only once in the component registry. The component must provide metadata in the form of a version number to ensure identifiability of the API it provides. Versioning patterns of different kinds (like the one shown in appendix A) can be used to give a hint of API compatibility. Again, with jQuery, several versions are registered in the Bower component registry, from version 1.0.1 up to the latest (for example, 3.0.0). Each of those versions provides an API that follows certain rules, and it might or might not be compatible with your code. With the version number attached, you know which API you're dealing with.

With these requirements given, let's take a closer look at the different types of dependency trees.

NESTED DEPENDENCY TREES

The nested dependency tree is the most straightforward type. Figure 4.4 shows an example organization.

The idea is that every component comes with its dependencies right away, not relating to any duplicates that might be around in the same space. This ensures that a component uses the dependency version that fulfills its requirements to work properly. Should two or more of versions of component A in figure 4.4 be required by the definitions in the components' metadata, no conflict would arise.

On the other hand, you also end up with lots of duplicates. Having those duplicates can result in redundancy. Should two or more copies of a specific component differ in terms of version, it's possible that the API has huge differences and that certain components behave differently. This can cause confusion.

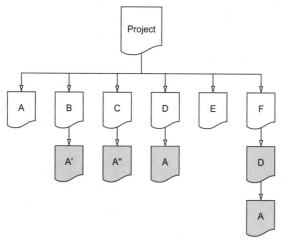

Figure 4.4   A nested dependency tree. Components B, C, and D are dependent on A and each of those components come with its own copy of A. This ensures that the version of this package is compatible with the necessary dependency (for instance, B and C need a different version, but D would need the same one as in the project). Component E is standalone, whereas component F is dependent on D, which in turn is dependent on A. Both D and A are being downloaded again. Duplicates are shown shaded.

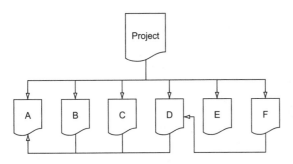

Figure 4.5 A flat dependency tree. Flat dependency trees make sure that just one version of a component is available. If some component requires another one (like B, C, and D, which are dependent on A), they all have to work with the same version of this component.

FLAT DEPENDENCY TREES

The flat dependency tree is the direct opposite. Figure 4.5 shows a sample organization of the same structure described previously.

Instead of allowing multiple copies of a single component, each of them can exist only once in your project space. This ensures that you don't have the same code or the same API provided redundantly. But this approach is prone to conflicts. Two components requiring the same dependency but with incompatible APIs will cause an error that can't be solved without a user's interaction. Usually, the user has to decide which of those components to use and will be informed of possible inconsistencies. Because flat dependency trees are Bower's way of handling components, we'll take a closer look at this topic in the next section.

SEMI-NESTED/SEMI-FLAT DEPENDENCY TREES

A compromise between those two approaches is the semi-nested or semi-flat dependency tree, shown in figure 4.6.

This approach aims for the most efficient way of handling API-compatible versions of the same package where necessary, just like a flat dependency tree. Once a conflict occurs, the semi-flat dependency tree will make an exception to this rule and allow a variation of the same component. Although the latter approach seems like the most reasonable one, there's a reason why Bower uses the fully flat dependency tree approach, as you'll see in the next section.

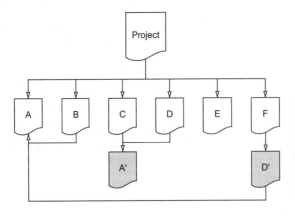

Figure 4.6 A semi-nested or semi-flat dependency tree. If a component's dependency is compatible with an already installed version of the same, it doesn't get installed again but instead is referred to. If the dependency isn't compatible, another copy with the correct version is installed.

4.2   *Flat dependency tree management with Bower*

Bower, as a dependency manager made exclusively for front-end developers, was designed to work with fully flat dependency trees. This is because all those components have to work in a browser in the end. The browser as the execution environment operates quite differently than other platforms:

- A browser usually has one big, global scope where all the components are thrown in. Although there are several ways to create scopes, the most common way for many websites and applications is to reserve variables in the global namespace. Having two versions of the same component running there will cause conflicts.
- The more versions of a component you have, the more bytes of data you have to transfer over the wire. Because network connection speed (and stability) is a variable over which developers have no control, every byte counts. Front-end developers can't afford redundancies in their code.

With those factors in mind, the decision was made for Bower to use flat dependency trees. And that's also why we chose Bower as the dependency manager for our projects.

But as you know, this approach is prone to conflicts and requires that you pay strict attention to version components and their dependencies. Let's take a look at Bower's way of handling things during different installation processes.

4.2.1   *Installation and update of a component*

Because you've worked with NPM in the previous chapters, initializing, installing, and updating components with Bower should be familiar to you. The command palette for the command-line tool is exactly the same as with Node's package manager. If you haven't yet installed Bower on your system, boot up your favorite command line and install it via NPM:

```
$ npm install -g bower
```

This makes the command-line tool available for you. To try the examples shown here, navigate to an empty folder that you can use as a playground. To initialize your folder to be manageable with Bower, you have to provide a file with metadata. This promotes your project folder to a component on its own and also stores all the necessary information on your dependencies:

```
$ bower init
```

After answering the short questionnaire that pops up, you're ready to install your first component. Figure 4.7 shows what happens when you type `bower install --save jquery` into your command line.

The `save` parameter makes sure that you save that entry in your metadata file bower.json. The `install` command downloads a bunch of files for the jQuery framework

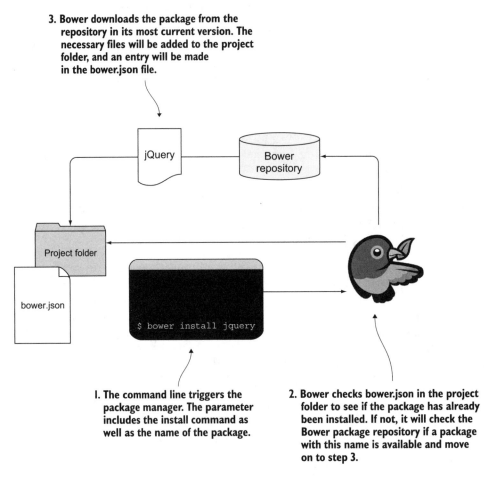

3. Bower downloads the package from the repository in its most current version. The necessary files will be added to the project folder, and an entry will be made in the bower.json file.

jQuery

Bower repository

Project folder

bower.json

```
$ bower install jquery
```

I. The command line triggers the package manager. The parameter includes the install command as well as the name of the package.

2. Bower checks bower.json in the project folder to see if the package has already been installed. If not, it will check the Bower package repository if a package with this name is available and move on to step 3.

Figure 4.7   The installation process of a single component. With the command given to install jQuery, Bower will check for the most current version and add it to the project. An entry with both the component name and the version number will be made in the metadata file. The same process takes place with an update, with the original files being replaced with the new ones.

to a folder on your file system called bower_components. This is where all your components and dependencies are stored. When you enter this command, Bower will fetch meta information on the component from the Bower repository and compare the component's metadata with the data stored in your bower.json file. If the component isn't already installed, the most recent version will be downloaded by default. Otherwise, Bower will successfully terminate the process, notifying you that the component has already been installed.

If you want a specific version, you can add the version number after the component's name. For instance,

```
$ bower install --save jquery#1.8.0
```

will download the 1.8.0 version to your project. We're intentionally choosing this version for this example. If you want to update the jQuery component to the newest version, simply type

```
$ bower install --save jquery
```

into your command line. This will re-trigger the installation process, forcing Bower to download the most recent release.

4.2.2 *Installation of components with dependencies*

The previous step was straightforward: you installed a component and made it a dependency of your own project. The `save` parameter stored the necessary metadata in your bower.json file, recording jQuery as a component you rely on. Now let's see what happens if you install a component that has other dependencies. For this sample, you use the Ember.js framework, because its dependency on jQuery makes it a good use case. You're not required to know what's going on *inside* the framework, though. First, install a specific version of jQuery:

```
$ bower install --save jquery#1.8.0
```

To install Ember, you type in the same command as previously but with `ember` as the desired component.

```
$ bower install --save ember
```

If you're in a project that doesn't have any components already installed, Bower will fetch the most recent version of Ember and the most recent yet compatible version of its dependency, jQuery. It will add both to your project folder and add the necessary version information to your metadata in the bower.json file. In our sample project we already have jQuery in version 1.8 installed. Here a special case occurs, which is shown in figure 4.8.

Ember stores a specific version range in its metadata file. It says that its one dependency, jQuery, has to be at least version 1.7 and not higher than version 2.2. Bower fetches this information and compares this data with the information stored in our bower.json file. Because the installed version of jQuery 1.8 satisfies this criterion, the new component will be downloaded without any error.

Here, the creators of the Ember.js component specifically state that this range of versions is compatible with the version of Ember they provide. The only criterion on the version of the installed dependency is that it fit into this range. This requirement is unique to Bower and separates the dependency manager from similar tools like NPM (see appendix A on how versions have to be defined in NPM to ensure compatibility). But this requires attention to detail and a good knowledge of their dependencies on the part of the authors and maintainers of the component.

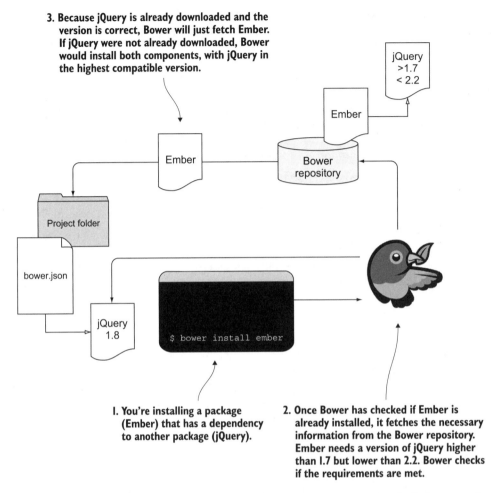

3. Because jQuery is already downloaded and the version is correct, Bower will just fetch Ember. If jQuery were not already downloaded, Bower would install both components, with jQuery in the highest compatible version.

I. You're installing a package (Ember) that has a dependency to another package (jQuery).

2. Once Bower has checked if Ember is already installed, it fetches the necessary information from the Bower repository. Ember needs a version of jQuery higher than I.7 but lower than 2.2. Bower checks if the requirements are met.

Figure 4.8 The installation of a component that has a dependency. The metadata for Ember suggests that the jQuery version it depends on has to be at least version 1.7 and is not allowed to be higher than version 2.2. This information is compared with the information stored in the bower.json file in our project. If the requirements are met, the package will be downloaded.

4.2.3 *Resolving dependency conflicts*

So far, the setup we've chosen holds up: the versions of the components we're going to install for our sample project are compatible with the dependencies we already have in our project. Things get interesting, though, once a version mismatch occurs. We're now going to install Bootstrap, a popular UI framework that's also based on jQuery. Figure 4.9 shows the installation process.

Install Bootstrap with the following command:

```
$ bower install bootstrap
```

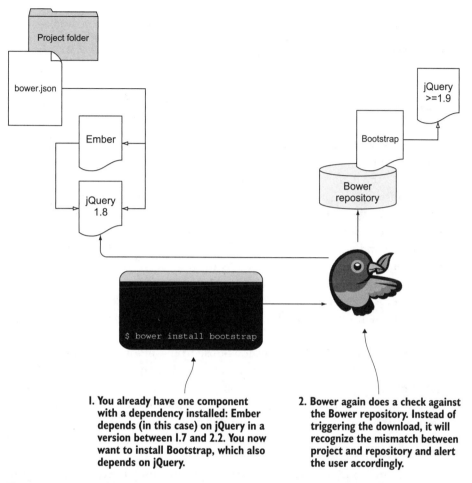

1. **You already have one component with a dependency installed: Ember depends (in this case) on jQuery in a version between 1.7 and 2.2. You now want to install Bootstrap, which also depends on jQuery.**

2. **Bower again does a check against the Bower repository. Instead of triggering the download, it will recognize the mismatch between project and repository and alert the user accordingly.**

Figure 4.9   With the installation of Bootstrap, the same process is triggered as in the previous example. But Bootstrap requires a different and incompatible version of jQuery to work. Bower compares the versions from our project with the versions listed for the new dependency in the component repository, finds a mismatch, and throws an error.

In this case, the installed version of jQuery 1.8 is not compatible with the required version of at least 1.9. Instead of taking the matter into its own hands, Bower will throw an error and require user action to resolve this dependency conflict. See the following command-line output for more information:

Bower validates dependencies. ❶

```
$ bower install bootstrap
bower cached        git://github.com/twbs/bootstrap.git#3.3.5
bower validate      3.3.5 against git://github.com/twbs/bootstrap.git#*
bower cached        git://github.com/jquery/jquery.git#2.1.4
bower validate      2.1.4 against git://github.com/jquery/jquery.git#>= 1.9.1
bower cached        git://github.com/jquery/jquery.git#2.1.4
bower validate      2.1.4 against git://github.com/jquery/jquery.git#>= 1.7.0 < 2.2.0
```

Suggests possible version options ②

```
Unable to find a suitable version for jquery, please choose one:
    1) jquery#1.8.0 which resolved to 1.8.0 and is required by bowerplayground
    2) jquery#>= 1.9.1 which resolved to 2.1.4 and is required by bootstrap#3.3.5
    3) jquery#>= 1.7.0 < 2.2.0 which resolved to 2.1.4 and is required by
       ember#1.13.5
Prefix the choice with ! to persist it to bower.json
? Answer:
```

Version required by Bootstrap ③

Versions compatible with Ember ④

These two points ❶ show the validation of the dependencies that are installed or should be installed. The first line is the jQuery version required by Bootstrap; the second one is the jQuery version required by Ember.js.

Because Bower can't find a suitable version, it prompts the developer with the possible options ❷. The first one is to keep the version that's already installed; bower-playground is the name of our project.

The second option is to go with the version required by Bootstrap ❸. You see both the requirement (>= 1.9.1) as well as the version it would resolve to. Here Bower again aims for the most recent, compatible version.

Ember.js is also fine with the most recent version, because it fits the rule given by the component's metadata ❹. But Ember has a different range of compatible versions than Bootstrap.

Bower prompts the developer to choose from one of these options and optionally to persist that choice into their own metadata file. Should such a situation occur, it's generally recommended to update all your dependencies first to determine if you have any outdated components. Then go with the version number most options resolve to and give it a good and thorough test.

4.3   *Integration with Gulp*

With the necessary concepts in place, you'll now update your previous project with Bower as a dependency manager. To do so, first remove the vendor folder from the scripts folder. This includes a (most likely) outdated version of jQuery you now want to handle with your dependency manager. Second, promote the project folder to a Bower component by executing bower init. Install jQuery with bower install --save jquery.

This is all it takes to handle your one dependency. But it doesn't take care of the integration to your existing project. Because everything is pretty well automated, you'll aim for an automatic integration with your existing files rather than manual insertion.

For this, you have two possibilities concerning the JavaScript libraries:

- *Adding referrers to the Bower components in your HTML files*—This is the place where jQuery was originally to be referenced and would be a direct replacement of the existing code.
- *Adding the JavaScript library code to your scripts build pipeline*—This would mark a huge change because vendor scripts would be integrated into the deployment of your main.js file.

Which one you choose depends on whether you like your vendor scripts separated from your own code. For fast delivery, merging both dependencies and your own files into one would be the preferred choice. This might cause larger build times due to an increase in file size, though. We'll tackle those issues in the advanced Gulp chapters. Until then, the first option will help you make quicker iterations. We'll look at both possibilities in turn.

4.3.1 *Wiring up dependencies to your application files with Gulp*

For both solutions, you require a certain entry from the bower.json metadata, which well-maintained components have recorded to aid your development workflow: the main-array. This entry includes an array of filenames that are considered the main files of this project. Because many components come with more files than you probably need (including documentation and possible theming features), a few files stand out as being the ones you really have to include in your project. Thankfully, you can access this data through various plugins.

First, we look at how to change your HTML to include the Bower components instead of the hard-wired reference to a vendor script. As a preparation, remove one line from the index.html file:

```
<script src="scripts/vendor/jquery.js"></script>
```

This is the old reference to the jQuery module that you don't want to use anymore. To insert the dependencies to your HTML files, you use a special plugin called wiredep. This is short for "wiring up dependencies," which is exactly what you're looking for. How wiredep works is shown in figure 4.10.

With wiredep, you add specific markers to your HTML files and tell the plugin where to put all the main files. Wiredep will then run through all the listed components in your bower.json, will find the related main files, and will create a series of references to be put at the exact spot.

The implementation starts at the index.html file. At the point where you removed the previous call to jQuery, add the following marker in the form of HTML comments:

```
    ...
    <!-- bower:js -->        ⟵────❶ Beginning of comment
    <!-- endbower -->                           ⟵
    <script src="scripts/main.min.js"></script>  ❷ End of comment
</body>
</html>
```

The wiredep marker listens to a comment that starts with bower ❶. The part after the colon shows which file type should be included here. In this case, it's JavaScript files. Place the endbower comment to show wiredep where to stop ❷. Note that everything in between will be removed by the tool.

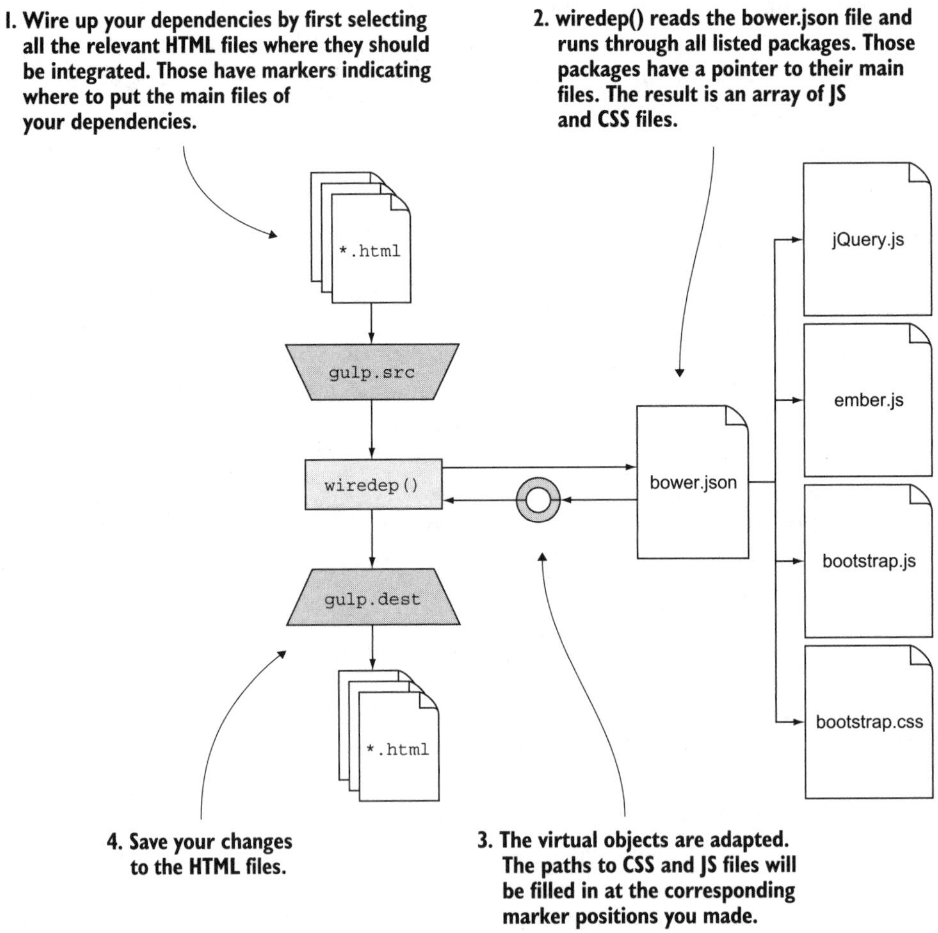
1. Wire up your dependencies by first selecting all the relevant HTML files where they should be integrated. Those have markers indicating where to put the main files of your dependencies.
2. wiredep() reads the bower.json file and runs through all listed packages. Those packages have a pointer to their main files. The result is an array of JS and CSS files.
*.html
gulp.src
wiredep()
gulp.dest
*.html
bower.json
jQuery.js
ember.js
bootstrap.js
bootstrap.css
4. Save your changes to the HTML files.
3. The virtual objects are adapted. The paths to CSS and JS files will be filled in at the corresponding marker positions you made.

Figure 4.10 A build pipeline to include references to the main Bower files in HTML files. The wiredep plugin reads the contents of the bower.json file and retrieves the necessary path information for the main files of the package. Those are included by type at the markers added by the developer.

The HTML file is now ready, so it's time to make the necessary changes in your Gulpfile. First, install wiredep as a development dependency:

```
$ npm install --save-dev wiredep
```

Note that the plugin is missing the "gulp" prefix. This is because wiredep is not only a Gulp plugin but a Node.js tool that's also suitable for Gulp. The following code shows your new deps task, which will integrate the main Bower files to your HTML:

```
var wiredep  = require('wiredep').stream;          ❶ Require the wiredep package.

gulp.task('deps', function() {
    return gulp.src('app/**/*.html')          ❷ Select all HTML files in your app folder.
```

Call wiredep. ❸──▷ `.pipe(wiredep())`
                `.pipe(gulp.dest('dist'));`   ◁─── ❹ **Store it in the dist folder.**
       `});`

With wiredep not being a Gulp plugin but a Gulp-compatible plugin, you have to use it a tad differently ❶. Instead of just requiring the package, you require it and load the `stream` component. In your `deps` task, select all HTML files in your app folder ❷. This currently includes just the index.html file that you've adapted. Because you didn't change any paths or other options, you can use wiredep as is without passing options ❸.

Because the HTML files are now processed, you store wiredep in the dist folder, which holds all your compiled files ❹. You can now call this task with `gulp deps` on the command line. To integrate it into your development lifecycle, you have to adapt the original `default` task:

```
gulp.task('default',
    gulp.series('clean',
        gulp.parallel('styles', 'scripts', 'deps'),       ◁──┐  Put the dependency
        'server',                                              wiring in the parallel
        function watcher(done) {                               task where you prepare
            …                                                  all your assets.
        }
    )
);
```

You've now successfully replaced the old way of handling vendor scripts with an integration of your dependency files. Updates to your jQuery dependency will be smoothly included in your application by entering a single command (`bower update jquery`) on the command line. New dependencies will also find their way to your application without you having to do anything in particular.

4.3.2 *Including dependencies in our build chain with Gulp*

There's a second way to integrate the new JavaScript dependencies, instead of wiring them all up in your HTML. Until now you've avoided processing vendor files. This is perfectly okay for testing and linting because you don't want to lint other people's code. But for creating a deployable bundle, you might want to consider putting vendor files in your build pipeline. This ensures that you deliver just one JavaScript file instead of multiple files to save requests.

Usually, you'd be fine with the task you created in section 4.3.1. For later chapters, however, this example will serve as a base for further optimizations.

In the previous section you saw that you can easily access the main Bower files through an API, provided by the wiredep plugin. A similar plugin, main-bower-files, does the same process of browsing through files. Instead of modifying HTML files, though, it just returns an array of file paths. You can use this plugin to create an even more sophisticated globbing array for your scripts task in the original Gulpfile. Figure 4.11 shows the concept.

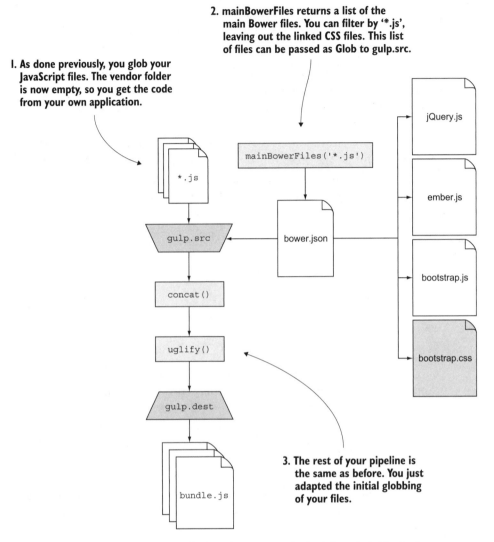

2. mainBowerFiles returns a list of the main Bower files. You can filter by '*.js', leaving out the linked CSS files. This list of files can be passed as Glob to gulp.src.

1. As done previously, you glob your JavaScript files. The vendor folder is now empty, so you get the code from your own application.

3. The rest of your pipeline is the same as before. You just adapted the initial globbing of your files.

Figure 4.11 The main-bower-files plugin does the same as wiredep internally but just returns an array of file paths. You can filter this array by type. You use these strings to adapt your source globbing for the scripts pipeline.

The implementation also requires you to remove the reference to jQuery in the HTML files. The rest is done in the Gulpfile. To add the new package to your project setup, type the following in the root folder of your project:

```
$ npm install --save-dev main-bower-files
```

This will add the necessary package. You now can adapt your Gulpfile.

```
var mainBowerFiles = require('main-bower-files');

gulp.task('scripts',
    gulp.series('test', function scriptsInternal() {
        var glob = mainBowerFiles('*.js');
        glob.push('app/scripts/**/*.js');
        return gulp.src(glob)
            .pipe(concat('main.min.js'))
            .pipe(uglify())
            .pipe(gulp.dest('dist/scripts'));
    })
);
```

❶ Require the module to your Gulpfile.

❷ Prepare a variable called glob.

❸ Add your own scripts glob to the globbing array.

Pass that array to gulp.src.

Note that this also is not a Gulp plugin but a module that can be used in any other Node.js project ❶. You also assign the array that's the return value of the mainBower-Files call ❷. The one parameter it takes is a glob filter. You set it to filter JavaScript files. The order is now all main Bower files and then your own files ❸. The rest of your pipeline is already in place, so you don't need to make any further changes. A call to the scripts task will now include all JavaScript components you've installed.

4.4   Summary

In this chapter, you learned how dependency management works for front-end developers and how to make use of it in your development lifecycle:

- You learned the basics of dependency management and the definitions of *component*, *dependency*, *dependency tree*, and *component repository*.
- You learned the different types of dependency trees—flat dependency trees, nested dependency trees, and a mixture of both—as well as their pros and cons. With a focus on front-end development, you found out why flat dependency trees are the one to go for: strictly no duplicates.
- Bower is a dependency management tool designed exclusively for front-end developers and implementing a flat dependency tree. You learned how Bower communicates with the component repository to decide if it's okay to download a dependency or if a developer's action is required.
- Finally, you removed all your vendor scripts from the demo project and created a setup not only to replace them with their Bower counterparts but also to include them automatically with Gulp.
- In the next chapter, you'll take your current project setup of Bower and Gulp and make it reusable for a multitude of new projects.

Scaffolding with Yeoman 5

This chapter covers

- Scaffolding as way to reproduce a solid project foundation
- Yeoman's generator concept for scaffolding at scale
- A generator's assembly line
- Template engines as a way to handle options

The last three chapters have shown you the first essential steps in creating a new front-end development workflow. You created a local development environment with Gulp, building all your assets automatically and booting up a local web server for you to instantly check iterations. You instructed Bower to keep track of your dependencies and integrated the third-party libraries in your main application, also automatically. This sounds—and definitely feels—like a lot of effort has been put into the setup of how to handle projects. Let's not waste this effort on a single instance; let's make it available for all your future projects!

If you have many different projects going on, it's likely that the structure and setup of those often resemble one you created previously. That's quite common; nobody wants to reinvent the wheel. So you know where to put your files, which folders to create, and which components you need from the get-go. You discover patterns, maybe with some variations for each project. The creation of files and folders is repetitive; you want to focus on only the variations of your new project. This is a perfect opportunity to automate! It's a crucial step. Imagine that not only do you have to work on lots and lots of projects, but also your team of front-end developers has to touch certain parts of your code from time to time—and vice versa. Sharing the same setup with everybody and keeping the variations to a minimum help you find your way through other people's code and reduce settling-in periods. Sticking to conventions in your team helps you and your coworkers keep focused on critical tasks, creating fewer errors and differences with the basic chores.

To tackle all those issues, you can use Yeoman. As you saw in chapter 1, Yeoman creates the necessary folders, copies initial files (like build scripts), applies boilerplate code, and triggers the installation of dependencies. It distributes the setup you created earlier, which helps you and your team stick to code conventions. It leaves the creation of the groundwork to a specified, automated generator, making sure there are no unforeseen variations in your code's and project's structure. In this chapter, you'll learn how to create a generator for Yeoman. This is the final step in creating your new front-end development workflow (figure 5.1).

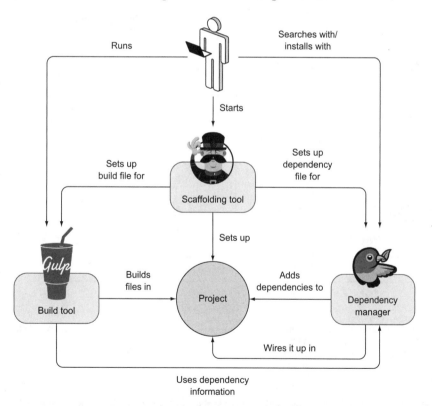

Figure 5.1   The complete development lifecycle. With Yeoman you will create new projects with files reused from other projects. These include a basic project structure, as well as the Gulp setup from chapters 2 and 3 and the bower.json file from chapter 4.

5.1   *Yeoman generators*

When starting new projects you usually have a good idea how to construct them. Software projects grow naturally over time, with lots of new files and modules added to the codebase. But if you compare the initial state of two projects that have been started with a short amount of time in between, you'll recognize some similar patterns. Take figure 5.2, for example.

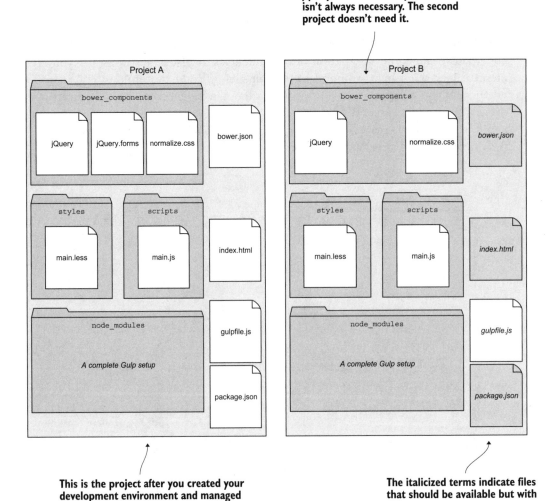

jquery.forms is a handy tool but isn't always necessary. The second project doesn't need it.

This is the project after you created your development environment and managed your dependencies with Bower. You want to reuse this structure and environment for more projects.

The italicized terms indicate files that should be available but with different contents.

Figure 5.2   The original project A and its copycat. Project B should be an almost identical copy of project A, so developers can easily start coding. But some parts should be optional or different. The name of the project has to be included in package.json, bower.json, and index.html files. And the jquery.forms component should be included only on occasion and not by default.

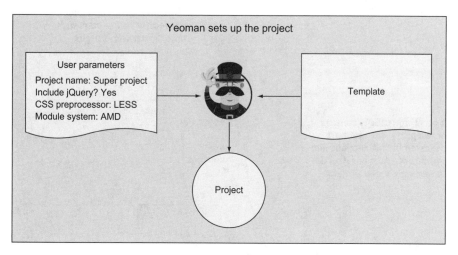

Figure 5.3 **Yeoman's purpose is to fill the necessary gaps of a project structure with user input and to transfer the newly generated contents to the project folder.**

Projects A and B have the same folder structure, and some parts are even completely identical. In other parts they differ only in nuances, most of which are located inside a file. Those nuances are hard to maintain, and you might easily overlook one spot where they need to be changed, especially when you roll out the same structure over and over again for future projects. That's why you need to automate this process. With Yeoman, this automation is done using generators.

A Yeoman *generator* is a tool that sets up new projects and provides the necessary files. Let's say you want to create a new AngularJS project. You call the corresponding Yeoman generator, which engages you in some sort of dialog. You can pick a few options, like selecting some libraries to include. Yeoman than takes a predefined template, and based on your options, it modifies the outcome for you. In the end, you'll end up with a new project tailored for your needs. Figure 5.3 shows the process.

5.1.1 *Parts of a generator*

Like many front-end development tools, Yeoman was designed to provide a small core with a few API functions. The real heavy lifting is done by generators, and there are many of them. At the time of this writing, the Yeoman website features over 2,000 generators. Developers can choose the generators that fit their needs. There are some official generators, either by framework vendors or the Yeoman team, that are not only excellent in quality but also continuously updated.

Installing a generator happens with NPM. Instead of installing generators locally, you install them globally to make them available anywhere on your command line. As a quick rehash of chapter 1, this is how you install a generator for scaffolding of an AngularJS project:

```
$ npm install -g generator-angular
```

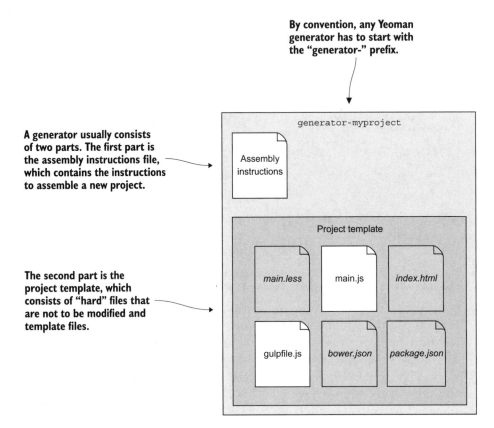

By convention, any Yeoman generator has to start with the "generator-" prefix.

A generator usually consists of two parts. The first part is the assembly instructions file, which contains the instructions to assemble a new project.

The second part is the project template, which consists of "hard" files that are not to be modified and template files.

Figure 5.4   The typical parts of a Yeoman generator. It includes a project template as well as the assembly instructions.

The AngularJS generator will provide you with assets, dependencies, and a recommended project structure to start a new AngularJS project. So a generator provides Yeoman with the building blocks of a new project as well as instructions on how to install them. Figure 5.4 gives an overview. Next, we'll look at some considerations.

THE NAME

A Yeoman generator has to start with the "generator-" prefix by convention. Because those generators are plain Node.js modules installed globally (see appendix A), Yeoman relies heavily on the file system to find them. It queries all modules starting with "generator-" to filter at a great scale. The remaining packages are filtered by looking at their metadata in the generator's package.json file. We'll look at those in section 5.4.

THE PROJECT TEMPLATE

The project template includes all files that are necessary to construct a new project along with its structure. It includes "hard" files that are just to be copied, as well as files that you want to modify before copying them to the destination. Creating a new project template is a delicate process. You have to ask yourself which files you want to copy, which files you want to modify, and which files you want to include at all. We'll look at project template generation in section 5.2.

ASSEMBLY INSTRUCTIONS

One file inside your Yeoman generator is dedicated to telling Yeoman how to scaffold your new project. It knows which options are available and also prompts for user input to select the values for those options. It also knows which files are put where and how files have to be modified. These assembly instructions are discussed in section 5.3.

5.1.2 *Calling generators*

Executing generators for scaffolding happens with the yo command-line tool. yo is provided by Yeoman and works as the bridge between the installed generators and your project folder. Think of it as the executer of generators. yo knows where to find them and in which phase to execute when. Because it's based on Node.js and should be called from the directory where you want to start your scaffolding, yo has to be globally available. That's why you install the tool with the -g flag:

```
$ npm install -g yo
```

yo is able to do some tasks, like browsing the NPM repository for new generators or updating existing ones, but its primary task is to execute a generator. It takes one parameter, the name of the generator. First, you create a new and empty project folder in your file system and enter it. On Mac and Linux/Unix systems, this is done like this:

```
$ mkdir projectfolder
$ cd projectfolder
```

Inside, you call the Angular generator by its name:

```
$ yo angular
```

generator-angular is the name of the generator, and yo angular is the call to the generator. This is Yeoman's only convention to follow. Figure 5.5 shows the installation process.

The yo command-line tool checks to see if a generator is available, and if so, it calls the necessary assembly instructions. The generator takes over from there and copies as well as modifies the necessary files.

yo's primary function is to find the generator you want to call and plug in the interface to the generator. After that, yo hands over the execution to the assembly instructions. The assembly instructions prompt the user for some information, take those options to modify certain elements, and then copy all the files from the project template to the destination folder on the file system.

If you want to create a generator on your own, you have to create two parts for Yeoman to work: the assembly instructions and the project template. Let's look at both of those.

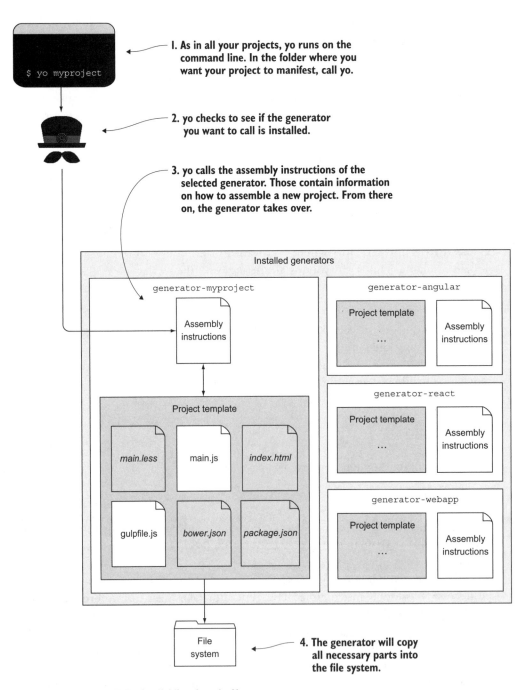

1. As in all your projects, yo runs on the command line. In the folder where you want your project to manifest, call yo.

2. yo checks to see if the generator you want to call is installed.

3. yo calls the assembly instructions of the selected generator. Those contain information on how to assemble a new project. From there on, the generator takes over.

4. The generator will copy all necessary parts into the file system.

Figure 5.5   Scaffolding done by Yeoman

5.2 *Project templates*

A term often used with this type of automation is *scaffolding*. Coming directly from the construction business, its metaphor is clear: it provides you with the necessary elements to create new things. But you might wonder what your scaffolding consists of.

To determine the necessary scaffolding parts, you should look at your projects and find the common elements that form a project template. Each file you want to include in your template has a different purpose. Some you want to have in your project every time and to be completely identical. Some of them should be without content, so that you can add them afterward. And some should be flexible enough that you can modify part of the content with every rollout.

It helps to put them into different categories so you know how to treat them once you have to create a new project out of them. The two projects from figure 5.2 are stripped down to their bare essentials in a template in figure 5.6.

The figure shows fixed parts (bold), flexible parts (italic), and optional parts (normal). All elements located in shaded areas are not part of your project template because they're restorable parts. All the required information to restore those files is saved in other files (package.json, bower.json). You re-create them on demand to keep your project template's data footprint as small as possible.

Looking at each element in the previous project, you can identify four types of project parts: fixed parts, flexible parts, optional parts, and restorable parts. The first three parts will be included in your project template; the latter ones will be—as the name might suggest—restored from your scaffolding.

5.2.1 *Fixed parts*

Fixed parts are elements that are identical in every project you want to initialize. Not only are they identical, but they are also a must for every project. Without these, you can't consider your project initialization complete:

- *Your build system with Gulp, along with all the Gulp plugins you need for that*—You designed your local development environment to be as flexible within your project structure as possible. So you can reuse these files without any alteration between projects.
- *Essential libraries and dependencies*—In your sample project, jQuery is a must if you want to create any application. With other projects, those libraries might include AngularJS, Ember.js, or any other components that are required for a project to work.
- *Project files that are meant to be filled with new content but in their initial state are identical*—Compared to flexible parts, they don't contain any variable elements during scaffolding. The main.js file, for instance, is empty at the beginning, featuring just a few lines for encapsulation of modules. You'll implement your own application inside, but the blank, initial state is the same with every new project you start.

Your project template includes those files untouched.

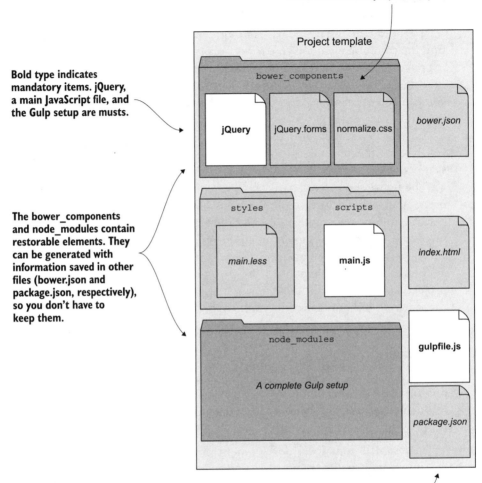

Plain type font here indicates optional items. It's up to the developer to include them in the initial project setup.

Bold type indicates mandatory items. jQuery, a main JavaScript file, and the Gulp setup are musts.

The bower_components and node_modules contain restorable elements. They can be generated with information saved in other files (bower.json and package.json, respectively), so you don't have to keep them.

Project template

bower_components

jQuery   jQuery.forms   normalize.css

bower.json

styles   scripts

main.less   main.js

index.html

node_modules

A complete Gulp setup

gulpfile.js

package.json

Italics indicates files that are mandatory, but require some modification due to their optional counterparts. Both package.json and bower.json require a project name, bower.json includes optional component names, and the main.less file will optionally include normalize.css.

Figure 5.6   A project template

5.2.2 *Flexible parts*

Flexible parts are similar to fixed parts because they're also mandatory for a project to be complete. But their contents are subject to change with every new project. Those changes can range from huge to subtle. Let's look at some examples:

- For each project you want to define a different project name. This name is required by both bower.json and package.json to work properly. Also, you want to include the name of the project in the title attribute of your index.html. The name is a variable that changes every time you scaffold your template. So index.html, package.json, and bower.json become flexible project parts. This is a subtle change.

- You have some optional parts (see the next section) that have a direct influence on some other parts. For instance, the inclusion of normalize.css (which is a rather conservative CSS reset, bringing all browsers to a common denominator) has a direct effect on main.less, because you want to a place a reference to this file. Depending on the number of files you want to consider, this type of change can be relatively large.

Flexible parts are also the first elements in your project template that are influenced by the user, because the user gets the opportunity to decide on the changes during the scaffolding process.

5.2.3 *Optional parts*

Optional parts, as mentioned before, are elements that aren't necessary for your scaffolding to be considered complete but provide a nice addition and a good default in some cases. Here are some examples:

- The aforementioned normalize.css is a good default to start any project with because it brings all browsers to a common display of standard HTML elements. In most cases you want to include this file with your project setup. But if you should decide to use a CSS framework like Bootstrap, normalize.css becomes redundant because it's already included in Bootstrap. This is why you want to make that optional.

- This also goes for other components, like jquery.form in the example shown in figure 5.3. It might be a good idea to have it if you're dealing with forms, but you might run into instances where this just adds bloat to your application. Dead code has no place in your project.

Depending on your way of handling projects, this list of optional parts might be huge. On the other hand, if you know you can manage with a smaller component footprint, or you know your must-have components really well, this list can be empty.

5.2.4 *Restorable parts*

This is one of the most important things for a project template: you don't have to include every file. You can use several parts in your project as a sort of black box. You take their API but don't care about the implementation or fiddle with their internals. The packages for your local development environment with Gulp are a good example: you install gulp-less, but you don't look at the elements of this package. All you care about is putting the package in its original spot so all functionality of your application stays intact. Why not tell your generator to do exactly that? Fetch the necessary components and put them in the spot where you needed them originally. Package and dependency managers have one crucial feature that you use in this case: they can restore all necessary files, as long as the meta information is intact and available. Because package.json and bower.json store all the necessary data you need for your dependencies, you don't have to include the dependencies themselves—just the files that know everything there is to know. Calling npm install in a directory that just features a package.json will download all packages that are mentioned there. The same goes for a bower install where a bower.json is available. So there's no need to include them.

Those different categories help you create a project template you can use with a Yeoman generator. It's good to know that you don't have to include restorable parts in your project template, because they'll be taken care of afterward. Fixed parts can be copied with no thought spent on how to modify them. Flexible and optional parts require extra care. The part of a Yeoman generator that knows how to take care of them is the assembly instructions. We'll look at those instructions in the next section and will create both a project template and an assembly file in section 5.4.

5.3 *Yeoman's assembly line*

With your project template in place, you can focus now on the assembly instructions: detailed orders for Yeoman to create the necessary files for your project. To bring some order to those instructions, Yeoman works along a predefined assembly line. It consists of three phases that are executed consecutively, providing the necessary flow for your contents. Those three phases are filled with your assembly instructions. Figure 5.7 gives an overview.

The three phases are

- *Prompting*—Asking the developer a list of questions to determine the amount of customization.
- *Writing*—Copying files from the project template to the desired directory. This is essentially the part where you put up your scaffolding.
- *Installing*—After copying all necessary files, you install your Bower dependencies and the node modules necessary for your local development environment.

Let's look at those phases in detail.

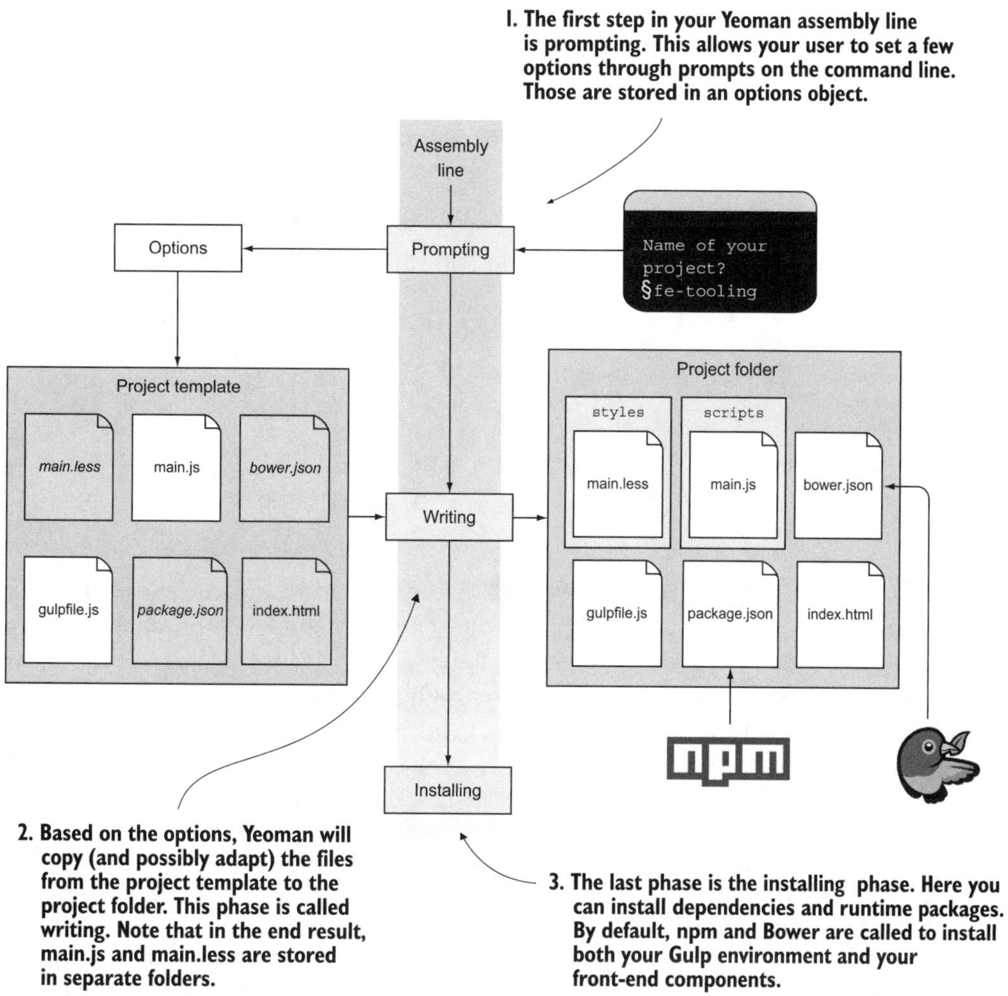

1. The first step in your Yeoman assembly line is prompting. This allows your user to set a few options through prompts on the command line. Those are stored in an options object.

2. Based on the options, Yeoman will copy (and possibly adapt) the files from the project template to the project folder. This phase is called writing. Note that in the end result, main.js and main.less are stored in separate folders.

3. The last phase is the installing phase. Here you can install dependencies and runtime packages. By default, npm and Bower are called to install both your Gulp environment and your front-end components.

Figure 5.7 The typical Yeoman assembly line is split into three major steps. The first one is prompting, where the user can choose among some options or fill out the necessary blanks to complete your template files. The second is writing. Based on the options chosen by the user, project files are copied to the desired destination. The third is installing. All your third-party libraries saved in bower.json and package.json are downloaded and installed, so your development environment is complete and functional.

5.3.1   Prompting

Prompting is the first step in Yeoman's assembly line and the last one where the user has to interact with your generator before the rest gets automated. The prompting phase determines which options your generator has to consider by directly asking your developer for them on the command line.

Yeoman executes the prompting phase as its first step in the assembly line, and you have the option here to provide your own questionnaire. For that, you'd use a package called `inquirer` to deal with the prompting. This package allows you to choose among a multitude of options. See the following code:

```
var prompts = [{
  type: 'confirm',                              ◁————————❶ The confirm prompt
  name: 'someOption',
  message: 'Would you like to enable this option?',
  default: true                                 ◁————————❷ Optional default value
}, {
  type: 'list',                                 ◁————————❸ The list type
  choices: ['Bootstrap', 'Foundation', 'None'],  ◁————❹ The list of options
  name: 'someList',
  message: 'Do you want to select an UI framework',
  default: 'None'
}, {
  name: 'textinput',                            ◁————————  The default prompt
  message: 'Enter something'                    ❺ is simple text input.
}];
```

The first option is the `confirm` prompt ❶. A `confirm` needs a name and a message. This will result in a yes/no question. You can optionally add a default value ❷. `true` maps to `Yes`; `false` maps to `No`. This allows faster input. The list type results in a single-choice select input ❸. The user can choose from the options in the next line. The list needs choices, which are provided through an array. You also need the default properties of `name`, `message`, and an optional `default`. Just leave out `type` and you can enter any text you like ❺. A possible output is shown in figure 5.8.

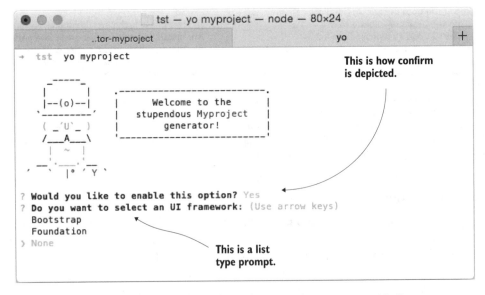

Figure 5.8   Example output from both a `confirm` (Y/N) and `list` type prompt in Yeoman

The only fields required for each prompt are `name` and `message`. The `name` is the property field from the object in which the result gets stored, so be sure to name this property as you would any JavaScript variable. The other field is to show the message when prompting.

> **NOTE** For the full list of prompt types, check out the `inquirer` package at https://www.npmjs.com/package/inquirer.

Once you've defined your prompts, you can call inquirer with them. A callback function allows you to access the results:

```
this.prompt(prompts, function (props) {          ① Calling the prompt function
    console.log(props.someOption);
    console.log(props.someList);
    console.log(props.textInput);
  this.props = props;
    done();                          ③ Finish the prompting stage.
  }.bind(this));                     ④ Bind results to the generator
```

Accessing the results ②

The `inquirer` package is connected to the Yeoman generator ①. That's why you can call the prompt method via `this.prompt`. The prompts from the earlier example are the only parameter it takes. The callback function gets you the results stored in `props`. You can access each result by the name you specified earlier ②. The first one gives you `true` or `false`; the second produces either `None`, `Bootstrap`, or `Foundation` in a string; the third prints out the string you entered. The `done` callback is called to denote that you're finished with the phase ③. You bind `this` to your callback function ④. This allows you to access all generator properties inside the callback (`this.props`).

Once you've finished (and called the `done` callback), you can access the second phase: writing.

5.3.2 *Writing*

The writing phase deploys your project template to the desired directory. For that, Yeoman gives you access to a file system package, which in turn exposes two functions for you:

- `fs.copy`—Allows you to create an identical copy of the original file in your desired output folder
- `fs.copyTpl`— Does the same but runs the file through a template engine first

`fs.copy` is the simpler one. Figure 5.9 shows how it works.

This is the Yeoman way of copying files as you would on the command line or in your file manager. A typical call to that would look like this:

Calls the fs object you decide to copy

```
this.fs.copy(
    this.templatePath('_package.json'),        Allows you to access files
    this.destinationPath('package.json')       inside the project template
);
                                               Defines the point to put it, usually
                                               where you called your generator
```

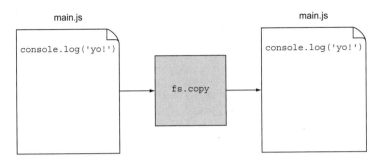

Figure 5.9   One way to bring files from point A to point B is via `fs.copy`. This creates a full and identical copy in the desired output folder.

The second function, `fs.copyTpl`, is a bit more advanced. See how it works in figure 5.10.

Here you can use the options you defined earlier in the prompting phase. The template engine will interpret certain calls inside the file and swap out different parts. For instance, if you only want to include some parts in your file if a certain confirm option is set (`someOption`), you can prepare your bower.json like this:

```
"dependencies": {
  "jquery": "~2.1.4"    <% if(someOption) { %>,      ❶  Is the someOption
  "bootstrap": "~3.3.5" <% } %>                           parameter set?
}                                                    ❷  If so, echo the comma in the previous
                                                         line and add the bootstrap line.
```

The template engine's markers are denoted with `<%` for start and `%>` for end ❶. Here you execute basic JavaScript and ask if the `someOption` parameter has been set. If so,

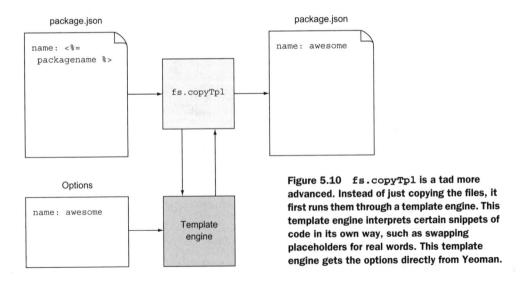

Figure 5.10   `fs.copyTpl` is a tad more advanced. Instead of just copying the files, it first runs them through a template engine. This template engine interprets certain snippets of code in its own way, such as swapping placeholders for real words. This template engine gets the options directly from Yeoman.

the comma in the previous line and the bootstrap line are echoed ❷. Because this is JavaScript, you have to close the angle brackets to avoid causing a syntax error.

The option you want to call is stored in your `props` property. You can pass this to the `fs.copyTpl` function:

```
this.fs.copyTpl(                              ◁──┐  The call to the fs object in Yeoman;
   this.templatePath('bower.json'),              │  the first three lines are identical.
   this.destinationPath('bower.json'),
   this.props                    ◁──┐
);                                   │  The object where you originally
                                     │  stored your properties
```

> **NOTE** The template language used by Yeoman is EJS. Read more on http://www.embeddedjs.com/.

The writing phase takes care of optional and flexible parts with `fs.copyTpl`. Fixed parts are taken care of with `fs.copy`. The last things to take care of are the restorable parts.

5.3.3 Installing

The last phase in your Yeoman assembly line is the installing phase. You have everything in place at your destination directory; now you only need to call both npm and bower to download and install your dependencies and node modules for the Gulp setup. For this phase, Yeoman also provides you with a method to call:

```
this.installDependencies();
```

That's it. This will call both Bower and NPM (if available) and install every package noted in package.json and every component depicted in bower.json. Yeoman also provides separate functions for Bower and NPM, should you decide to make one of those optional to install:

```
this.npmInstall();
this.bowerInstall();
```

You can also call your own installation commands via the `this.spawnCommand` function. For example, if you want to wire up all your Bower dependencies with Gulp once you install them, you can use this method:

```
this.installDependencies(function() {   ◁──❶  installDependencies takes a callback.
   this.spawnCommand('gulp', ['deps']);   ◁──❷  Call gulp via spawnCommand.
}.bind(this));                             ◁──❸  Bind your generator to this callback.
```

This code allows you to execute other calls after the installation processes from NPM and Bower have finished ❶. The parameter is deps, calling the task from chapter 4 ❷. Binding your generator to the callback allows you to execute all the functions inside ❸. All of these commands are executed in the destination directory.

With all your phases in place, it's time to create your very first generator.

5.4 *Creating a generator*

Yeoman comes with numerous community generators. But if you aren't in a certain project dedicated to a specific technology, you most likely have your own ideas of how a generator should be structured. That's why for this case you'll create your own Yeoman generator. With the concepts you've learned so far, you can do this in three steps. For the first time, you're leaving your project directory and moving to a separate folder on your file system. Create one with a name to your liking, where you can start creating the project template.

5.4.1 *Preparing the project template*

For the template, you want to pick some files you had in your sample-project and make them flexible enough to continue. Create those parts in a folder anywhere on your file system. Later you'll move them to a specific destination. Figure 5.11 shows the elements in your project template.

Inside the project template are all the files you have to copy from the original project. Your template should consist of the following:

- *Fixed part: main.js*—An empty JavaScript file ready for your application. You create this one new.
- *Fixed part: package.json*—Copy the same Gulp setup you created up to chapter 3.
- *Fixed part: gulpfile.js*—You're also happy with this one.

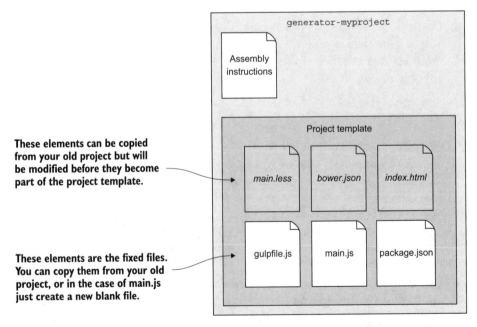

Figure 5.11 A symbolic representation of your generator, including the assembly instructions and the project template

- *Flexible part: main.less*—If you have normalize.css installed, import it into your main.less file. Otherwise, it will be empty.
- *Flexible part: bower.json*—If you have normalize.css installed, add it into your bower.json file.
- *Flexible part: index.html*—This will contain a project name.

Create a new folder and copy all the files described here. For main.js and main.less, create two new empty files. There's no need for subfolders; you'll create them with the generator.

> **NOTE** If you feel lazy, you can always get the sample template at https://github.com/frontend-tooling/sample-template.

Open bower.json and add the following line to your dependencies:

```
{
  "name": "sample-project-gulp",
  "version": "0.0.0",
  "license": "MIT",
  "ignore": [
    "**/.*",
    "node_modules",
    "bower_components",
    "test",
    "tests"
  ],
  "dependencies": {
    "jquery": "~2.1.4" <% if(includeNormalize) { %>,
    "normalize.css": "~3.0.3" <% } %>
  }
}
```

Always include jQuery; if the Normalize flag is set, include Normalize as well.

This line provides normalize.css.

In the main.less file, add the following:

```
<% if (includeNormalize) { %>
@import (css)
    '../bower_components/normalize.css/normalize.css';
<% } %>
```

The import directive from LESS

This import directive from LESS allows you to include any CSS file. This is the path relative to a styles directory.

Finally, you need to make a change in index.html. Open the file, and change it to the following:

```
<!DOCTYPE html>
<html lang="en">
<head>
    <meta charset="UTF-8">
    <title><%= projectTitle %></title>
```

This line echoes the projectTitle, when set.

```
            <link rel="stylesheet" href="styles/main.css">
        </head>
        <body>
            <!-- bower:js -->
            <!-- endbower -->
            <script src="scripts/main.min.js"></script>
        </body>
        </html>
```

Note that the template call is <%= instead of <% …, which tells the template engine to directly echo the property.

With those three files changed, your flexible parts are also ready. The bower.json and package.json files include all the restorable parts, and normalize.css is optional for this example.

5.4.2 *Providing the assembly instructions*

If you had to generate your Yeoman generator from scratch, it would take quite some time. Fortunately, the Yeoman crew sticks to the concept of scaffolding and provides a generator for generating generators. Besides being a tongue twister, it's really handy. Install the generator, and call it in your desired directory:

```
$ npm install -g generator-generator
$ yo generator
```

Answer the questionnaire accordingly. Yeoman will prompt you to make it publishable and available for the community, but you don't want to do that yet, so ignore those parts. Once you've finished, you have a complete setup. Copy your templates into the generators/app/templates folder, and start editing the index.js file. This file contains your assembly instructions. As you can see, it already includes preparations for the three phases. It's time to make adaptations.

THE PROMPTING PHASE

You can find the prompting call pretty easily. It already includes a simple questionnaire, which allows you to make just a few adaptations. The bold parts in the following listing are the ones to change:

```
prompting: function () {
  var done = this.async();

  // Have Yeoman greet the user.
  this.log(yosay(
    'Welcome to the stupendous ' + chalk.red('Myproject') + ' generator!'
  ));

  var prompts = [{                        The flag for including Normalize;
    type: 'confirm',                      this will be a yes/no question.
    name: 'includeNormalize',        ⟵
    message: 'Would you like to include normalize.css?',
    default: true
  },{
```

```
    name: 'projectName',
    message: 'Enter the name of your project'
  }];
```
◁ **A string containing the project's title; you'll add this in index.html.**

```
  this.prompt(prompts, function (props) {
    this.props = props;
    done();
  }.bind(this));
},
```
◁ **Copy all your props to your generator object.**

With those changes you have a new object—the props object—in your generator object. Let's move on to the writing phase.

THE WRITING AND INSTALLING PHASES

The writing phase is also already in your generator. It's time to adapt it. Again, you'll change the bold parts:

```
writing: {
  fixed: function () {
    this.fs.copy(
      this.templatePath('package.json'),
      this.destinationPath('package.json')
    );
    // Same for gulpfile.js
    this.fs.copy(
      this.templatePath('main.js'),
      this.destinationPath('scripts/main.js')
    );
  },

  flexible: function () {
    this.fs.copyTpl(
      this.templatePath('index.html'),
      this.destinationPath('index.html'),
      this.props
    );
    // Same for bower.json, main.less
  }
},
```

❶ ◁ **You can fill the writing object with functions.**

❷ ◁ **You can specify subfolders.**

◁ **The flexible function executes all your fs.copyTpl calls.**

These functions ❶ can include and execute anything you like. To make the separation a bit clearer, you distinguish between flexible and fixed. In fixed, you do all your copy calls. In this case ❷, a scripts directory will be created in the destination folder.

With the writing phase finished, the only thing you have to do is install your dependencies. This code is already in place. If you want to adapt it, you can include the call to Gulp, as shown in section 5.3.3.

5.4.3 Bundling and testing

Now that both the template and assembly instructions are ready, you can try your generator. To check if your NPM package works, type

```
$ npm link
```

in the directory where you scaffolded it. This allows you to globally access the generator without having to install it globally or publish it anywhere. If you want to make your generator available for your coworkers, you have two options:

- *Publish it to NPM.* This requires you to register at npmjs.com. Once you have credentials, type `npm publish` in the directory of your generator. This will make it available on yeoman.io and npmjs.com.
- *Push it up to a Git endpoint.* If you want to keep your generator private—perhaps because your company's policy requires that—you can store the files somewhere on a Git repository. Your coworkers can install it then from the Git URL: `npm install -g git://path/to/your/repository.git`.

Whatever you decide, you and your coworkers are now ready to scaffold your projects.

5.5 Summary

In this chapter, you learned what scaffolding is and how Yeoman works underneath its hood:

- You looked at the different elements of a Yeoman generator: the project template and the assembly line. You also saw how Yeoman's command line tool `yo` decides which generator to use.
- You learned what project templates are and what parts they consist of: fixed parts, which should be used as-is; flexible parts, which have to be adapted; optional parts, which can be there if you choose; and restorable parts, which can be re-created through other files. With this knowledge, you can more easily decide which files to take from a real-world project into a project template.
- Speaking of the assembly line, Yeoman generators usually consist of three phases: prompting, writing, and installing. Each of those is connected to an API from Yeoman, which you learned to use. You also learned what template engines are and how they operate with Yeoman.
- Finally, you created your first Yeoman generator by adapting the project from the previous example and creating an assembly instructions file with Yeoman's generator-generator.
- This chapter concludes part 1. The new development workflow is now in place and working. But we've merely touched on the basics of each technology. In part 2, we'll revisit each of our main technologies to create more advanced build files, generators, and your own Bower components.

Part 2

Integrating and extending the platform

With workflow and tooling in place, it's time to dig deeper into the internal technologies of the three selected tools. In part 2, you'll learn how to extend each technology with additional software to get more benefits from it.

In chapter 6, you'll improve your local development environment by introducing incremental builds and sourcemaps to your Gulp setup. You'll also learn how to create different output for different deployment environments.

Chapter 7 digs deep into the underlying technology of Gulp: file streams. By using streams, you'll be able to avoid redundancy and create reusable build pipelines.

Chapter 8 shows how to extend Gulp with tools outside the Gulp plugin scope. You'll learn about Promises and Gulp's virtual file system.

Chapter 9 returns to Bower and the concept of components. It shows how components can be split up into modules and how modules can help integrate components into project code more effectively. You'll also learn how to create and distribute self-made Bower components.

Finally, in chapter 10, you'll learn what Yeoman sub-generators are, and how you can use them to automate module generation.

Gulp for different environments

6

This chapter covers

- Incremental builds and build caches
- Debugging original files through sourcemaps
- Environment specific switches and noop blocks

In part 1 of this book you learned how to create a good, solid build setup we referred to as the local development environment. This setup allowed the automation of repetitive but common tasks, as well as a development server along with the ability for automated iterative builds.

If you take a good look at the artifacts of your build, you'll see that the result is production-ready code. JavaScript and CSS are optimized and minified, and all your dependencies are wired up, ready to be published on a production web server. One huge advantage in having such a result is that you can be sure that the code you deploy is the same code you built and tested earlier when developing locally. There are some shortcomings, though. Imagine that you find a bug in your application; JavaScript no longer executes and the developer tools of your browser spit out an error message. With optimized, production-ready code, you'll most likely find something like what's shown in figure 6.1.

The minified output might be good
for running in production mode, but
to develop locally, you can't debug and
step through a source code's execution.

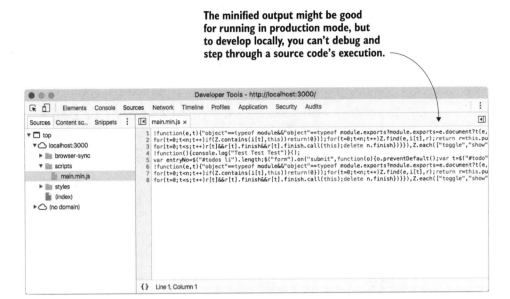

Figure 6.1   The minified and concatenated output of your main.js file inside Chrome's developer tools. The code is obfuscated and nowhere near the original source you used when developing.

The outcome of your build pipeline is obfuscated beyond recognition. It's very hard, even for experts, to make out where the error actually occurred. So you start guessing, searching for the culprit line of code that breaks your deployment. You try to map the outcome to the original source files and do quick checks in the build where you suspect the error happened. This leads to the second problem: each shot triggers another iteration of your complete build. Every file gets read, linted, and minified again. And depending on the size of your application, this build could last for several seconds, slowing you down tremendously in your hunt for the problem.

Wouldn't it be better if you could see the error happening in the original source file, with a clear pointer to the line that breaks the execution? And wouldn't you like to tell your build pipeline to recompile just this fix instead of the whole application, making the build a lot faster and the results appear much more quickly in your browser? Wouldn't it be nice if all this could happen while retaining your build pipeline that produces optimized and production-ready code? Wouldn't you like a few extras that would help you in your development environment, without forgetting to produce for the production environment?

As it turns out, with Gulp you have some good options to achieve exactly that:

- You can use incremental builds and save intermediate results in build caches to speed up build times for each iteration.
- The browser-wide standard for sourcemaps brings back the original source in a browser's developer tools, while still executing the compiled and optimized

bundle. This helps you identify the error with ease, running the same code as you would in production.

- Switches deal with the optional addition of sourcemaps and incremental builds depending on which environment (production or development environment) you're building for.

In this chapter, you'll learn how those techniques will help you make your development environment even more efficient, while retaining an elegant and performant building pipeline.

6.1 *Incremental builds and build caches*

Your original Gulpfile was designed to execute related tasks every time a certain file changes on the file system. Each time you saved a JavaScript file, you called the `scripts` task, which in turn called the `tests` task you defined. Figure 6.2 recalls this process from chapter 3.

Although this is a good approach to begin with, you select all the JavaScript files with every iteration, read their contents, and pipe them through your various processes. But is it necessary to do a JSHint code convention check each time you save a file? Or should you just check the files that have changed? The latter is surely the way to go, because the other files have already been thoroughly checked and don't require a recheck. This is where you should go from iterative builds to incremental builds, meaning that with each iteration, you build just the new and changed files, incrementing the original result set. Let's explore how you can do this.

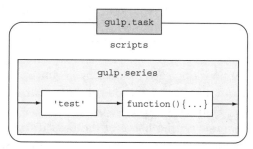

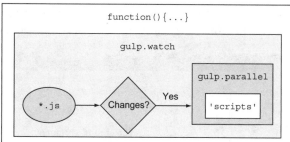

Figure 6.2 A recall from chapter 3: at the top is the `scripts` task, which executes `test` first, before running your JavaScript compilation. Below that is the watcher, looking out for changes in JavaScript files.

6.1.1   *Gulp's built-in functionality*

The desire for incremental builds has been around since Gulp first appeared. People started to realize that the true power of Gulp was in controlling and manipulating file streams. Thankfully, with the release of Gulp 4, a handy shortcut and feature has been introduced to Gulp's API: the ability to select files based on a timestamp. Let's see how those work on our original `test` task. Figure 6.3 shows the task that was introduced in chapter 2.

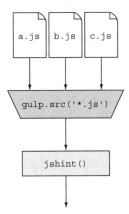

Figure 6.3   This is the pipeline for the original `test` task. Every time it's called, it selects all JavaScript files and passes them through JSHint.

With every call of your `test` task, you selected all files that end with js and ran your JSHint checks on them. Now you want to make your file selection a little more intelligent. Gulp provides a flag that you can pass to the options of your `gulp.src` method. It's called `since` and it accepts a timestamp, against which it will validate all files in the glob. If the files are older than the provided timestamp, they won't be included in your selection.

> **JSHint settings**
>
> Your application is now a lot more complex than it was in the beginning. Therefore, you need some settings to tell JSHint what to check and what to leave out. We've provided a .jshintrc settings file in the GitHub repository. Check out branch ch7 from the sample-chapter-gulp repo to see the changes.

Additionally, Gulp keeps track of how long each task has been run, as long as Gulp is running. With this information and the `since` flag, you can limit your selection to the newer files since the last iteration. Figure 6.4 illustrates this.

`gulp.lastRun` accepts one parameter: the name of the task. If that parameter is empty, Gulp will return the timestamp of the last execution of any task. Note that Gulp tracks execution times just during one run. If Gulp terminates, the reference to the previous iterations is lost. See the following listing for a demo implementation.

Listing 6.1   Gulpfile.js excerpt: Incremental run

```
gulp.task('test', function() {
  return gulp.src(['app/scripts/**/*.js',
    '!app/scripts/vendor/**/*.js'],
    { since: gulp.lastRun('test') })        ◁─── The second argument
    .pipe(jshint())                              of gulp.src is a
    .pipe(jshint.reporter('default'))            JavaScript object.
    .pipe(jshint.reporter('fail'));
});
```

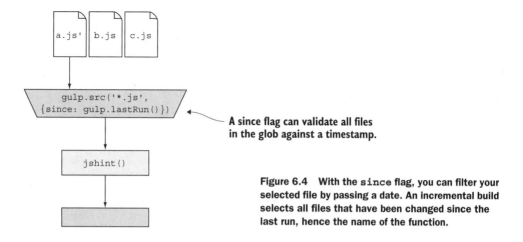

A since flag can validate all files
in the glob against a timestamp.

Figure 6.4 With the `since` flag, you can filter your selected file by passing a date. An incremental build selects all files that have been changed since the last run, hence the name of the function.

This JavaScript object passes additional information to the file-selection process. In this case, you activate the `since` flag. The value of this field is set to the timestamp from the last run of the `test` task.

Reduced reading operations and reduced calls to the JSHint plugin with every iteration speed up the linting task significantly. And if you want to create a production deployment (where you don't have build iteration cycles) or run the `test` task on its own, you can still select all the necessary files.

This works perfectly for any task that has the same number of files sent out to the destination directory as there are in the source directory, but with more file-transforming tasks, like the `scripts` task, there are some limitations. Let's see how to tackle those.

6.1.2 *Installing a build cache*

Although the built-in incremental runs work perfectly fine with single-file operations, you can't use them with the `scripts` task without some additional changes. Incremental builds are necessary for `scripts` because the Uglify process is performance-heavy. Just minifying the files that are new or those that feature different contents would reduce your execution time tremendously. But your output in the end is just one file, main.min.js, a compilation of all the JavaScript files you have in your application. So although you certainly need this filter operation for the Uglify process, you need all the other files unfiltered when concatenating them. With the `since` filter active during file selection, you'll lose all this information.

A helpful technique here is the introduction of a build cache: an in-memory store of all the files that you've ever selected. Remember, the first time you run your task, every file is new. You just have to keep them somewhere. The Gulp community provides this functionality with the gulp-cached plugin, which follows the simple algorithm shown in figure 6.5.

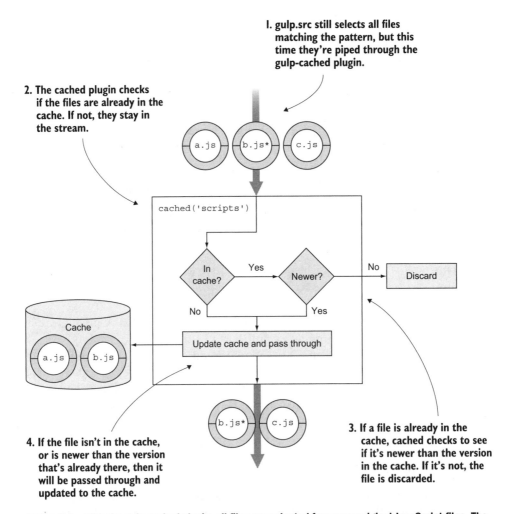

1. gulp.src still selects all files matching the pattern, but this time they're piped through the gulp-cached plugin.

2. The cached plugin checks if the files are already in the cache. If not, they stay in the stream.

3. If a file is already in the cache, cached checks to see if it's newer than the version in the cache. If it's not, the file is discarded.

4. If the file isn't in the cache, or is newer than the version that's already there, then it will be passed through and updated to the cache.

Figure 6.5 With the gulp-cached plugin, all files are selected from your original JavaScript files. The cache then checks to see if the files are already in the cache. If not, they'll be passed through to the stream and also added to your designated cache. If they're already in the cache, cached checks to see if the files from your selection are newer than the ones in the cache. If so, they will be passed through and updated to your cache. If not, they will be discarded from the stream.

The process seems like a more advanced version of the since flag introduced earlier. Files that you've already processed and that haven't changed are filtered, reducing the elements in your stream. But there are important differences: the since flag doesn't take the contents into account. If a file just happens to be newer in terms of the time-stamp, it will be added to the stream. Also, if you just use the gulp-cached plugin, you'll still read all the files using gulp.src, so you won't save any reading operations.

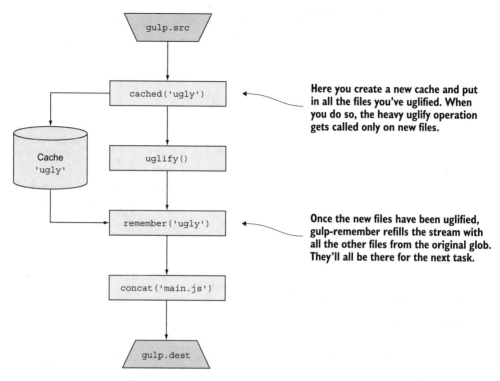

Figure 6.6   gulp-remember allows you to "unfilter" streams. The stream that has been filtered through the gulp-cached plugin is refilled with all the files from the original selection. In doing so, you can reduce execution time with performance-heavy tasks like Uglify.

A combination of both is the way to go. The biggest advantage of having a build cache is that you can recall all the processed files whenever you need them. With the accompanying gulp-remember plugin, you reintroduce your incremental builds from a previous iteration into the stream. Figure 6.6 illustrates this process.

With the plugins gulp-cached and gulp-remember you have the following optimizations:

- You can read files that you haven't read before.
- You can run a check on content differences.
- You can process files that haven't been processed before.
- You can reintroduce cached files for tasks where you need them.

The following listing shows how the implementation looks for your Gulpfile. Install gulp-remember and gulp-cached via NPM as you would have done before.

Listing 6.2   Gulpfile.js excerpt: Gulp caches

```
...
var cached        = require('gulp-cached');
var remember      = require('gulp-remember');
...

gulp.task('scripts',
  gulp.series('test', function scriptsInternal() {
    var glob = mainBowerFiles('**/*.js');
    glob.push('app/scripts/**/*.js');
    return gulp.src(glob, { since: gulp.lastRun('scripts') })
      .pipe(cached('ugly'))
      .pipe(uglify())
      .pipe(remember('ugly'))
      .pipe(concat('main.min.js'))
      .pipe(gulp.dest('dist/scripts'));
  })
);
```

> Keep using the since flag with gulp.lastRun of the scripts task to ensure you read only new files.

> Piping them through the cache ensures you have the same contents and fills your cache with new files or updates older files.

> At the concatenation step, you again have all the files at your disposal.

> After the uglify task, you remember all the processed files; the stream gets bigger with the files from the previous iteration.

This optimization speeds up the whole process from an initial six to seven seconds (depending on the machine) to mere milliseconds. New changes are introduced in a blink of an eye. There's only change left.

6.1.3   *Handling file deletions*

With your optimized scripts pipeline in place, you can now make fast iterations using incremental builds. With these changes, you rely heavily on the virtual file system and the ability to store files in memory. With every cached call, you update your memory, and with every remember call, you put the files back into a stream that will end up on the real file system. But there's one issue with that: the virtual file system has no clue as to what's happening with your files on the hard disk.

Every time you call remember and return files into the stream, you're putting all the files back, no matter whether they still exist on the file system. If file a.js is being deleted from the hard disk, but it's still inside your in-memory build cache, it will reappear when remember is called. Therefore, you must take care of your cache here on your own.

You can do this by using event handling on file watchers. In chapter 3, you learned how file watchers work and how they're able to call tasks when files have changed. You can hijack the events that happen on the file system and execute your own functions there. Figure 6.7 illustrates what to do.

Adapt your watcher to determine if the
change to the file was a deletion, and if
so, to remove the file from the cache.

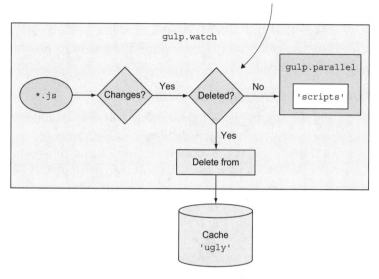

**Figure 6.7   If a file is deleted, it will still be part of your cache. This also
means that it will be reintroduced to your stream with gulp-remember, even
though it's no longer here. For this reason, you must remove deleted files from
your cache by adding an event handler to your Gulp watcher.**

`gulp.watch` returns an object, and you can add event listeners to it. The following
code shows how this works.

Listing 6.3   Gulpfile.js / function watcher()

```
var slash = require('slash');
var path  = require('path');
var watcher =
  gulp.watch(['app/scripts/**/*.js'], gulp.parallel('scripts'));

watcher.on('unlink', function (filepath) {
  delete cached.caches['ugly'][slash(path.join(__dirname,filepath))];
  remember.forget('ugly', slash(path.join(__dirname,filepath)));
});
```

**The slash package takes care of
❶ system independent file paths.**

**❷ The gulp.watch function
returns a watcher object.**

**Remove this element from
your gulp-remember cache. ❹**

**Watcher objects can
emit different events. ❸**

You use the slash package to make sure your software works for *NIX, OSX, and Windows systems ❶. You'll store the watcher object in the `watcher` variable ❷. One of
these events is the `unlink` event; developers can listen for those and add their own

callback functions ❸. The unlink event is fired once a file is deleted from the file system. Also delete it from the other gulp-cached plugin cache ❹.

With this last addition, your incremental builds for JavaScript are complete. Performance-heavy operations are done only on elements that need to be processed. The original time of more than five seconds is reduced to just milliseconds with each new iteration. You also keep track of changes on the file system to maintain a tidy cache. Let's move on to the next task.

6.2 *Debugging original files through sourcemaps*

Even though your build iterations are now lightning fast, you still see gibberish compilation results when you open your browser's developer tools. This is good for a production environment because it's highly optimized. But during development, you want to see what's going on. Think back to the introductory example: try debugging production-ready code with your browser's developer tools. It's downright impossible! You rely on those developer tools to see how your code behaves. You want to see how values change with each instruction and which errors are raised. Especially when working with JavaScript, browser developer tools provide you with highly sophisticated debugging environments, which are on par with debugger tools of high-level languages like Java or C#. There's just one major difference: the JavaScript debugger is not located in the development environment (like Visual Studio for C# or Eclipse for Java) but in the execution environment of your code: the browser. The browser runs the compiled and production-ready package that's comparable to the binary output of other programming languages. And nobody wants to debug binary output. Figure 6.8 shows an example.

To overcome this issue—having a development-like debugging experience in the execution environment—browser vendors Google and Mozilla combined their efforts to create sourcemaps, which are a way of tracking the output back to its original source files. In this section, you'll see how to generate sourcemaps with Gulp.

6.2.1 *What are sourcemaps?*

Sourcemaps are a way of letting the browser know where to find the original source of a certain file that has been loaded. There are two ways of letting the browser know of the existence of a sourcemap: either adding a reference URL in a comment of the output file or including the encoded sourcemap as a whole.

The contents of the sourcemap are created by splitting the compiled output file into several pieces. Each of those pieces gets a reference in the sourcemap, pointing to the following properties:

- The file from which the snippet originates
- The section inside the file where the snippet originates
- If you're using certain variables that are known in other sections, a reference to the original names of those variables

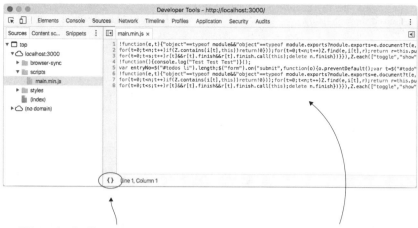

This option in Chrome's developer tools activates the formatted view below, which attempts to add sensible spacing to the minified code.

This is the output produced with your script's build pipeline.

Although the formatted view shows the fewest lines of code (and thus uses sensible breakpoints), the original variable and function names are still lost.

Figure 6.8   The browser's developer tools in action. On the first screen you can't make out anything. Some browsers, such as Chrome, allow you to format certain source code to get at least a little structure from the minified output. But you still don't know which variable names or function names you're debugging. It's becoming a guessing game.

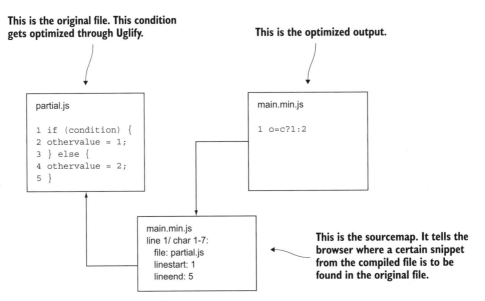

This is the original file. This condition gets optimized through Uglify.

This is the optimized output.

```
partial.js

1 if (condition) {
2 othervalue = 1;
3 } else {
4 othervalue = 2;
5 }
```

```
main.min.js

1 o=c?1:2
```

```
main.min.js
line 1/ char 1-7:
    file: partial.js
    linestart: 1
    lineend: 5
```

This is the sourcemap. It tells the browser where a certain snippet from the compiled file is to be found in the original file.

Figure 6.9 A sourcemap keeps a record of a code snippet's position in the original file. To do so, it stores both the original file's name and the start and end of this snippet.

Figure 6.9 shows what a basic mapping property might look like.

Also, the original source code is included in the sourcemap, ensuring that it can be loaded from any device, without having the original source available.

Should a browser like Chrome or Firefox see a reference to one of those sourcemaps, it will load the map and display the original contents in the debug window. Sourcemaps are generated during the modification of the files' contents. Uglify, for instance, keeps track of every transformation it makes and stores relevant information in a sourcemap if needed. Sourcemap-generating functionality is available in many tools and also in the wrapping Gulp plugins, which allows developers to readily use sourcemaps.

> **NOTE** Sourcemaps are very common nowadays and many tools and plugins feature a way to generate them. But if a plugin doesn't support sourcemaps, the Gulp output will also ignore it. If you experience such behavior, the plugin might be broken. Search for an alternative or try updating it. Most of the file-transforming core plugins feature sourcemap support. Alternatives that don't support sourcemaps are blacklisted by the Gulp community.

This feature has become significant because developers often rely on code transpilers like CoffeeScript, TypeScript, or Babel.js. Those tools allow you to write JavaScript code in a more modern or sophisticated language, which gets compiled into browser-readable JavaScript. Because the output isn't even in the same language anymore, sourcemaps have become the way to go for debugging. The same goes for CSS preprocessors like LESS or Sass, which can also output sourcemaps.

6.2.2 Built-in sourcemaps in Gulp

Sourcemap support is natively available in Gulp but with an additional feature: because files are usually piped through several transformation steps, Gulp has the ability to combine sourcemap output from each step into one. Figure 6.10 shows an example.

Several files are run through Uglify to generate a minified version. A sourcemap for each of those files is also generated. The next step is the concatenation of those files. The gulp-concat plugin also generates a sourcemap, referencing the contents from the previous step. To track the contents you started with, the Gulp plugin can

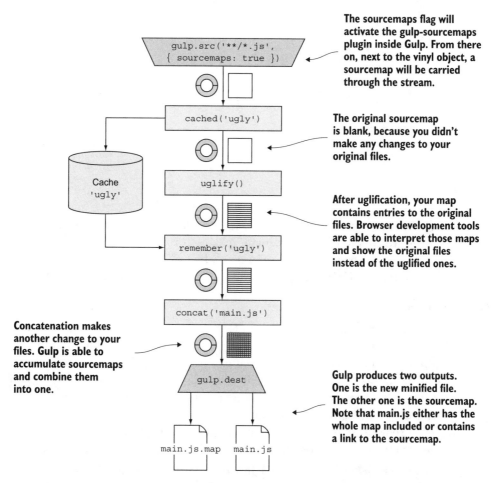

Figure 6.10 Built-in sourcemaps create a new property for your virtual file objects called `sourcemap`**. These properties will be filled with information about the transformations you make: which line and which character have been changed, what the original was, and what the new output is. Those sourcemaps can be interpreted by browsers, reimagining the original file, even though they don't have to be physically available anymore. Gulp sourcemaps are combinable, which means that every new task will modify the sourcemap with new data, so that the end sourcemap still has the references to the original files.**

combine the previous sourcemap with the new one. This means that the new snippet information (start and end data) gets mapped to the original mapping information.

> **NOTE** The NPM package plugin developers use to combine sourcemaps is called vinyl-sourcemaps-apply.

This technique can be used with both stylesheets and JavaScript files. The following sample implementation shows how it's done for your `scripts` task.

Listing 6.4 Gulpfile.js

```
gulp.task('scripts',
  gulp.series('test', function scriptsInternal() {
    var glob = mainBowerFiles('**/*.js');
    glob.push('app/scripts/**/*.js');
    return gulp.src(glob, {
        sourcemaps: true,
        since: gulp.lastRun('scripts')
    }).pipe(cached('ugly'))
      .pipe(uglify())
      .pipe(remember('ugly'))
      .pipe(concat('main.min.js'))
      .pipe(gulp.dest('dist/scripts'));
  })
);
```

The addition of the sourcemaps: true flag activates the internal sourcemaps plugin.

Once saved, the sourcemap output is stored within the original file. Also, the original sources are added to the sourcemap, making it relatively huge. This is done to make sure developers have the right reference when opening the files in a browser. This is not acceptable for production output, so you definitely want to change this behavior.

6.2.3 *The sourcemaps plugin*

Sourcemaps can be stored either inside the original file or in an extra map file, which is then referenced by the compiled output via a comment. The built-in function of Gulp to generate sourcemaps is specific in its handling. You can configure a lot more by using the sourcemap functionality via the gulp-sourcemaps plugin. This plugin is also used internally by the virtual file system itself, so the generation won't differ. Only the usage changes, as shown in figure 6.11.

You're now using gulp-sourcemaps as part of your process chain. Compared to the built-in version, this allows for more options when writing the sourcemap:

- You can specify a directory in which to store the file. If the directory name is blank, it gets added to the original file.
- You can opt out of including the entire source code in the sourcemap.
- You can define the source root. This is a virtual directory that's shown when opening the browser dev tools. By default, it's called source. This also means that if it generates sourcemaps for both JavaScript and CSS, all those files are shown in this directory. You can use a different name for this directory, like js-source for JavaScript or css-source for stylesheets, to help clarify.

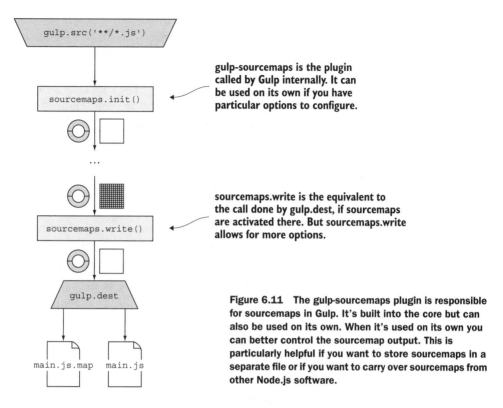

gulp-sourcemaps is the plugin called by Gulp internally. It can be used on its own if you have particular options to configure.

sourcemaps.write is the equivalent to the call done by gulp.dest, if sourcemaps are activated there. But sourcemaps.write allows for more options.

Figure 6.11   The gulp-sourcemaps plugin is responsible for sourcemaps in Gulp. It's built into the core but can also be used on its own. When it's used on its own you can better control the sourcemap output. This is particularly helpful if you want to store sourcemaps in a separate file or if you want to carry over sourcemaps from other Node.js software.

There are some other options, but these are the ones that you'll need most of the time. Refer to the documentation for more. Put in code, the alternative now looks like the following listing.

Listing 6.5   Gulpfile.js

```
var sourcemaps = require('gulp-sourcemaps');

gulp.task('scripts',
  gulp.series('test', function scriptsInternal() {
    var glob = mainBowerFiles('**/*.js');
    glob.push('app/scripts/**/*.js');
    return gulp.src(glob)
      .pipe(sourcemaps.init())
      .pipe(cached('ugly'))
      .pipe(uglify())
      .pipe(remember('ugly'))
      .pipe(concat('main.min.js'))
      .pipe(sourcemaps.write('.', {
        sourceRoot: 'js-source'
      }))
      .pipe(gulp.dest('dist/scripts'));
  })
);
```

Activate sourcemaps by calling the plugin in your build pipeline.

❶ After performing your transformations, call the sourcemap plugin again, but this time the writing functionality.

❷ The second parameter is a configuration object.

Here you pass two parameters, the first one being the directory where you want to save the sourcemaps ❶. The dot indicates that you want to save it in the same location as the file it describes. Rename the source root folder from source to js-source so you can easily spot it in your browser's developer tools ❷.

This completes the second point in our introductory checklist: you now have a good reference to the original source files, allowing for more complete debugging options. Still, you're generating production-ready code for a development environment. But what about the production environment? You'll find out in the next section.

6.3   *Environment-specific switches*

You've now optimized your local development environment to make it more comfortable to use, but you're still neglecting the production environment you're producing code for. Although the output is already highly optimized and production-ready, your workflow has some issues when it comes to creating a deployable bundle:

- You don't want to include sourcemaps. That functionality is for local development environments. For production environments, it adds too much weight. Also, you might not want to let your code be readable by everyone, everywhere.
- You don't need to put up a local development server.
- You don't need iterations, so you have no watchers, just a simple build.

In this section, you'll create the possibility for such a production build by keeping to one key principle: never duplicate a pipeline. You don't want to generate redundant code just to satisfy two environments, as shown in figure 6.12.

You can achieve this by making the execution of certain tasks more intelligent. You should be able to optionally run your stream through the same sourcemaps plugin, without having to modify the existing pipeline. This section shows how.

6.3.1   *The noop() task*

To stop the execution of certain plugins in your pipeline, consider the opposite of executing something: not doing anything. This sounds ridiculous at first, but think about the following: assume that you have some sort of switch that allows you to steer the contents of your stream in different directions. You can make this choice for each stage, and then the stream continues to flow into the next one. Figure 6.13 gives you a visual.

You can either run the task or do nothing and just pass the contents to the next stage. This is practically a task that does "no operation," hence the name *noop*. To create it, you use streaming packages provided by NPM. The through2 package is wonderful for creating pipeline blocks. See the following code listing for details.

Listing 6.6   Gulpfile.js

```
var through = require('through2');

var noop = function() {
    return through.obj();
};
```

through2 is the package of choice if you want to create pipeline stages.

❶ through.obj creates a new stage for your stream.

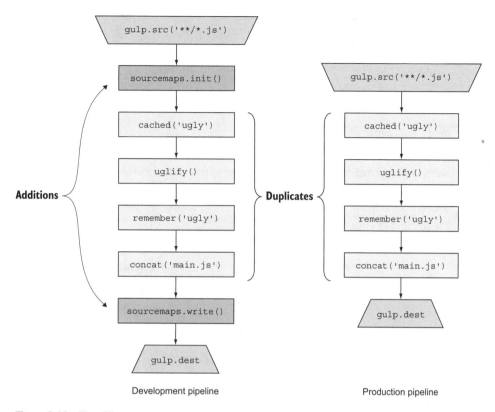

Figure 6.12 **The difference between the build pipeline for the production environment and one for the development environment. The only thing that has an impact on the outcome of both pipelines is the inclusion of sourcemaps. The addition of sourcemaps should be optional and used only in the development environment. The rest of the pipeline is the same.**

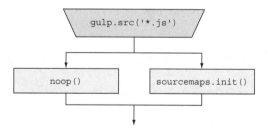

Figure 6.13 **The idea of a pipeline switch. Depending on some condition, you either steer the stream to the intended task or pass it to another one. The other one should only pass contents through to the next stage.**

Usually this function would take a transformation function as parameter, but if you leave that out, the original files will just be piped through ❶. obj indicates that you're piping objects, which is what your Vinyl files are.

This noop function works like a Gulp plugin, but instead of changing contents or processing files, you pass the contents to the next stage. With this function in place, you can move on to creating the switch.

6.3.2   *dev() and prod() selection functions*

What we call switch will be transformed into selection functions: dev() to execute tasks in the development environment and prod() to execute them in the production environment. They take one parameter—the task to execute if a certain condition is met—and activate it depending on the condition. Figure 6.14 shows how this works for the dev() function.

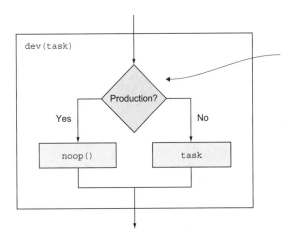

The dev() function should execute the task only if the production flag is not set. If it is set, the stream will be passed through an empty task.

Figure 6.14   The dev() function checks to see if the production switch has been set. If so, it will pass the stream through the noop function, which does practically nothing. If the switch hasn't been set, dev() will execute the passed task.

The condition is stored in a Boolean variable that's kept inside your Gulpfile. You set this isprod flag to false, indicating the development environment. The following listing contains the implementation.

Listing 6.7   Gulpfile.js

If the production flag is set to false, tasks will be executed in the development environment and vice versa.

dev takes one parameter: the plugin to execute if you're in the development environment.

```
var isprod = false;

var dev = function(task) {
    return isprod ? noop() : task;
};

var prod = function(task) {
    return isprod ? task : noop();
};
```

If this flag is set to true (the condition is not met, you're in production mode), you pass your files through noop(), doing nothing; otherwise, the task is pushed into your pipeline.

prod() does the same as dev() but the other way around.

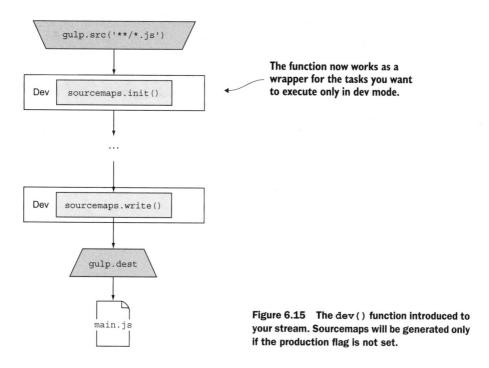

The function now works as a wrapper for the tasks you want to execute only in dev mode.

Figure 6.15 The `dev()` function introduced to your stream. Sourcemaps will be generated only if the production flag is not set.

These functions return a stream function through which you can pipe your object stream. This allows you to use them in the pipe calls from Gulp. See figure 6.15 for an illustration.

These selection functions work just like a Gulp plugin. The code equivalent looks like the following listing.

Listing 6.8 Gulpfile.js excerpt: Sourcemaps in dev mode

```
gulp.task('scripts',
  gulp.series('test', function scriptsInternal() {
    var glob = mainBowerFiles('**/*.js');
    glob.push('app/scripts/**/*.js');
    return gulp.src(glob)
      .pipe(dev(sourcemaps.init()))
      .pipe(cached('ugly'))
      .pipe(uglify())
      .pipe(remember('ugly'))
      .pipe(concat('main.min.js'))
      .pipe(dev(sourcemaps.write('.', {
      sourceRoot: 'js-source'
      })))
      .pipe(gulp.dest('dist/scripts'));
  })
);
```

The dev function allows you to execute the sourcemaps tasks only in development.

With this setup you're well prepared for both environments. You can use the same switch to turn on Browsersync and the watch processes on demand, as shown in the following listing.

Listing 6.9 Gulpfile.js excerpt: Productions switch

```
gulp.task('server', function(done) {
  if(!isprod) {                              This if-statement deactivates
    bSync({                                  the development functions
      server: { baseDir: ['dist', 'app'] }   in production mode.
    })
  }
  done();
});
```

And the same goes for the watcher process in your default task, as shown in the next listing.

Listing 6.10 Gulpfile.js / function watcher

```
function watcher(done) {
  if(!isprod) {
    var watcher = gulp.watch([...], gulp.parallel('scripts'));

    // …

    gulp.watch('app/styles/**/*.less', gulp.parallel('styles'));
    gulp.watch('dist/**/*', bSync.reload);
  }
})
```

These switches provide a good base for creating output for different environments. They also can be extended to feature even more environments. Because switching happens inside a function, you can easily check for development, staging, or various production environments. In the current setup, by changing one variable you can switch from production mode to development mode and vice versa. It would be handier, however, to direct this from the command line.

6.3.3   *Parsing command-line arguments*

Because Gulp is executed from the command line, you can pass more parameters than mere tasks to it. This allows you to extend the standard behavior with custom flags. One handy plugin in the Node.js ecosystem is yargs, which takes care of parsing parameters and assigning them to certain properties. Your goal is to add one flag, indicating the production environment. It should work like this:

```
$ gulp --env=prod
```

Parameters with two dashes are automatically parsed as flags. They're accessible by their name, as shown in the next listing.

Listing 6.11   Excerpt Gulpfile.js

```
var arguments = require('yargs').argv;
var isprod = (arguments.env === 'prod');
```

> ◁── **Require yargs and access the parsed arguments, storing them in the arguments variable.**
>
> **When adding a parameter with two dashes, you get a property with the same name in your arguments object.** ❶

This line ❶ includes the passed value. You check if it's prod, which stands for "production." If not, you're in development mode.

And that's it! You have a convenient and easy-to-use way of switching between different environments, which also allows you to control other Gulpfile internals (such as output paths) via the command line

```
$ gulp --outputFolder=dist
```

with

```
.pipe(gulp.dest(arguments.outputFolder + '/scripts/'))
```

in the Gulpfile. Use this to create packages that can be deployed on your application servers.

6.4   *Summary*

In this chapter, you learned how to prepare your output for both development and production environments:

- You learned how incremental builds work and which technologies exist to integrate those into Gulp. You created build caches to allow for quick iterations, without having to recompile previously existing intermediate results.
- The introduction of sourcemaps helps you to read the original source files in your browser's development tools while executing the compiled output. You used both the built-in solution and the accompanying plugin for more flexibility in your output.
- Finally, you created execution switches to change between production output and your local development environment. To accomplish this, you learned how to write your first plugin: a plugin that pipes the virtual file objects through to the next stage.
- You also learned how to use the yargs package to parse command-line arguments. This allows you to control switches without adding too much redundant code.

Your stream optimizations have just started. In the next chapter, you'll continue to improve your Gulpfile by learning more pipelining techniques.

Working with streams

7

This chapter covers

- Merge streams and passthrough streams for combining different sources
- Stream arrays for duplicating streams
- Stream combiners for creating stream snippets
- Stream queues for handling stream element order
- Stream filters for dynamically changing stream contents

Previously you created build pipelines for different types of assets, like CSS and JavaScript. Stylesheets and scripts are fundamentally different, so you had to treat them differently. That resulted in one build pipeline for each asset type, which you saw in chapter 2. But what if you have to handle files that are of the same type and require the same process but vary enough that you have to duplicate pipeline definitions?

Think back to our original script task from chapter 2. With this task, you built exactly one JavaScript bundle. All your sources were combined into one output file. What if you have to create more than one? Or even worse, what if you have to create bundles originating from different JavaScript preprocessor languages? CoffeeScript

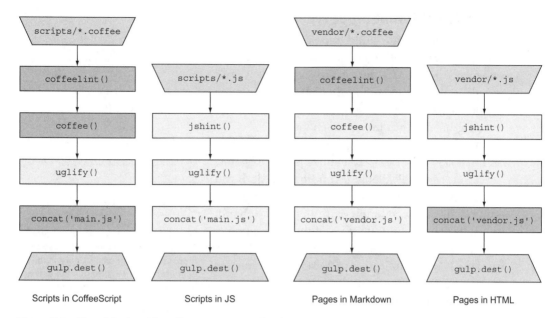

Figure 7.1 The original problem. You want to compile different JavaScript bundles. Some are written in CoffeeScript, some in JavaScript, and some bundles even need both. The process is roughly the same, but the input type has a significant effect on choices in the process. Instead of copying the same build pipeline again and again, you want to create just one that can handle all inputs and configurations.

or TypeScript both compile to plain JavaScript. Those languages need a transformation step before the main task of concatenating and minifying can take place.

To be honest, the process could easily be implemented with any build tool. But having different combinations of input formats, languages, and variations would require several configurations or code duplication. Look at figure 7.1, for example. Having two input types (CoffeeScript and JavaScript) and two output files (for vendor scripts and your own app) produces four slightly different build pipelines.

But with Gulp, you can do better. Because Gulp is based on Node.js streams, you can harness the power and ecosystem of this technology to create flexible build pipelines that can adapt to those parameters without having to duplicate too much code or configure too much. Preferring code over configuration is one of the key principles in developing Gulp build files, and in this chapter you'll see how to do this.

In this chapter, you'll tweak and restructure your original script pipeline from chapter 2 for all the different inputs that you want to serve, while retaining its original maintainability.

After this chapter, you'll be an expert in pipeline plumbing.

EXAMPLES IN THIS CHAPTER   All the examples in this chapter are not based on our original project but work on their own and are tailored to special use cases. If you want to see them in action, check out the https://github.com /frontend-tooling/chapter-7-examples project on GitHub.

7.1   *Handling different input types*

Up until now, your build pipelines were pretty straightforward. You selected a specific set of files, piped it through a series of processing steps, and saved the output to some other place on your file system. Take a look at figure 7.2 as a reminder of the original `scripts` task from chapter 2.

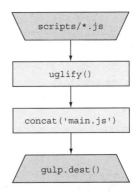

As brief and easy to comprehend as this pipeline is, it has one major flaw. It features just one distinctive input type: only filenames ending with .js. If you want to use any other input type that features the same steps but needs a few extra steps beforehand, you'll have to rebuild the steps of the original pipeline over and over again for new Gulp tasks and streams. Code duplication is never an option for good software developers, so let's look into some alternatives that harness the power of streams.

Figure 7.2   The original scripts build pipeline. You select all the JavaScript files, minify them using Uglify, and concatenate them into one file in the end. You're going to reuse this pipeline for different input types.

7.1.1   *Passthrough streams*

For the first use case, you want to create one bundle that features both CoffeeScript files and JavaScript files. Think of a project that was originally written in CoffeeScript because of some architectural decision. You want to write the new parts in plain JavaScript instead. Instead of converting all CoffeeScript files to JavaScript, you can modify your build process and compile both CoffeeScript and JavaScript into one bundle.

One way to achieve this goal is to use passthrough streams. With Gulp, you usually deal with readable streams at the beginning when selecting files and use writeable streams when you pipe them through each task and store the contents at the end. Passthrough streams allow for both being written to and being read from. It turns out that `gulp.src` is capable of creating both readable *and* writeable streams. At any time in your build pipeline, you can add (or pass through) new files to the stream that skip the early process and are piped through the tasks that follow. Figure 7.3 illustrates this.

You can achieve this by adding a parameter to `gulp.src`, telling the selection function that it should take contents from earlier on. Take the following listing, for example.

Listing 7.1   Gulpfile.js excerpt

```
gulp.task('scripts', function() {
  return gulp.src('src/scripts/**/*.coffee')
    .pipe(coffee())
    .pipe(gulp.src('src/scripts/**/*.js', {passthrough: true}))
    .pipe(concat('main.js'))
    .pipe(uglify())
    .pipe(gulp.dest('dist/scripts'));
});
```

Pipe the results from the earlier steps to another gulp.src call. ❷

Select all CoffeeScript files and pipe them through coffee. ❶

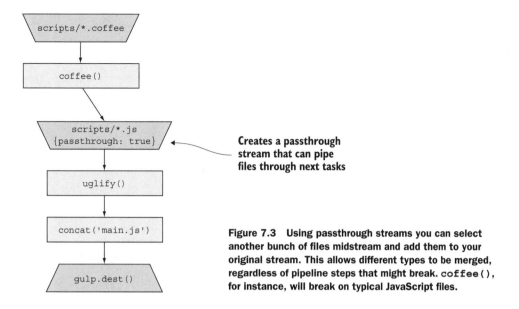

Figure 7.3 **Using passthrough streams you can select another bunch of files midstream and add them to your original stream. This allows different types to be merged, regardless of pipeline steps that might break.** `coffee()`, **for instance, will break on typical JavaScript files.**

Instead of starting with JavaScript files, you first handle your CoffeeScript files ❶. Usually, this would erase the stream and feature just the P.js files, but with `passthrough`, you add the results from the earlier steps to the new stream ❷. For this particular case, where you have to add new files anywhere in your pipe, this is the way to go.

With passthrough streams in place, you can now add different input formats to one stream and send them through the same process. Instead of dealing with lots of configuration or redundancy, you have everything neatly in one place. Should one step in your pipeline change, you can maintain it in one place. If you have another input format to add, you can pipe it through the same stream.

7.1.2   Merge streams

Passthrough streams work fine for the previous case, but they lack one feature: the second batch of source files merged into the original stream can't be processed separately. Think of adding a linting process to your pipe for both JavaScript and CoffeeScript files. Because CoffeeScript is a completely different language (more like Ruby), you can't use the JavaScript linter. And once it's processed, a JavaScript linter would fail because the output wouldn't match your coding standards.

You can test CoffeeScript using a piece of software called CoffeeLint. But this tool can only tackle CoffeeScript and can't be used with plain JavaScript files. You're in a situation where you'd actually need to have two separate streams, process them according to their input type, and then merge them into one stream once the distinctive operations have finished.

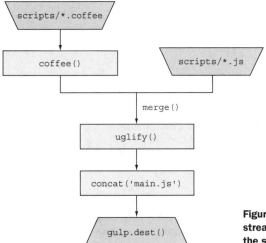

Figure 7.4   The pipeline using merge streams does exactly the same as using the standard passthrough stream.

You can do this using merge streams. Merge streams execute two separate streams in parallel and then merge the results into one stream that's processed by the subsequent tasks. This parallel streams can feature any kind of process.

Let's re-create the example from the section 7.1.1 by using merge streams instead of passthrough streams. Check out figure 7.4 for details.

What you see in figure 7.4 is the same process as in figure 7.3. Passthrough streams in Gulp are realized using a merge stream package. You're re-creating the same behavior but making it more extensible for your needs. In having two separate streams, you can add as many tasks as you like to each one of those streams, as shown in figure 7.5.

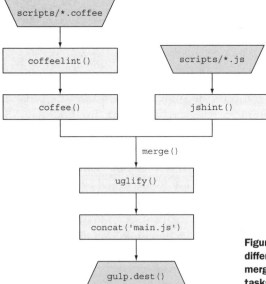

Figure 7.5   With merge streams you can execute different tasks on different sources, before merging them into one stream and executing the tasks that affect both.

To implement this, you use the popular `merge2` package, as shown in the following listing. This is capable of passing object streams like the ones created by Gulp.

Listing 7.2   Gulpfile.js (excerpt)

```
var coffeelint = require('gulp-coffeelint');
var coffee     = require('gulp-coffee');
var merge      = require('merge2');

...

gulp.task('scripts', function() {
  var coffeeStream = gulp.src('src/scripts/**/*.coffee')      ❶ The stream
    .pipe(coffeelint())                                          taking care
    .pipe(coffeelint.reporter())                                 of CoffeeScript
    .pipe(coffeelint.reporter('fail'))                           files
    .pipe(coffee());

  var jsStream = gulp.src('src/scripts/**/*.js')              ❷ Select all the plain
    .pipe(jshint())                                              JavaScript files in that
    .pipe(jshint.reporter('default'))                           directory and run them
    .pipe(jshint.reporter('fail'));                             through JSHint.

  return merge(coffeeStream, jsStream)                       ❸ Merge both
    .pipe(concat('main.js'))                                     streams into one.
    .pipe(uglify())
    .pipe(gulp.dest('dist/scripts'));                        ❹ Pipe them through the
});                                                             usual stuff: minification,
                                                               concatenation.
```

You select the files as usual, pipe them through the CoffeeLint plugin, and convert them to JavaScript ❶. You handle reporters the way you know from JSHint, which was discussed in chapter 2. You already know this code snippet ❷ from chapter 2. The magic happens here ❸. After this step, you have one stream containing both the converted CoffeeScript files and your JavaScript files, just as you'd have using passthrough streams. You're used to the next step ❹.

Although passthrough streams offer a great way of adding sources to your stream as you go on processing, merge streams are the way to go if you have more and different processing steps in your build pipeline for each of the source streams. Stick to the built-in passthrough streams for merely adding new source files. If it gets more complex, rely on merge streams.

7.2   *Handling variations in output*

With passthrough streams and merge streams you're able to use different input types for one specific output. This means that no matter how many distinctive inputs you have, you get one result in the end. This is mostly because one step in your build process has the unique task of bundling everything into one file: `gulp-concat` takes all the processed script files and concatenates them into one.

For the previous use cases, this was exactly what you wanted. But how do you move forward if you want to create multiple JavaScript bundles with your build scripts? For example, you might want separate output files for all the vendor-specific JavaScript as well as your own application. How can you reuse the streams that you already defined but make sure that both input and output are handled separately and don't interfere with other bundling processes? This section shows you some ways to handle this issue.

7.2.1   *Parameterized streams on a task level*

Let's make the carefully crafted combination stream from section 7.1 reusable for multiple bundles. Think of having several components at hand that you want to build separately, because they may be used in different places in your app. Think also of a project that has been developed over time or even builds on an old project where you want to reuse certain parts. You might have written a core in CoffeeScript that you want to build separately from the actual UI layer that's new and was written in, say, the next version of JavaScript.

> **The next version of JavaScript**
>
> The ECMAScript standard for JavaScript is defined on a yearly basis nowadays. The TC39 committee decides each year which language features are developed and specified enough to be implemented in the wild (browsers and the Node.js platform). Because the development of the standard is always ahead of certain browsers, developers are invited to use transpilers to compile the applications written in the current ECMAScript standard (titled ES2015, ES2016, and so on, based on the year it was finalized) into something browsers can understand. Those transpilers transform syntactic sugar into executable code and polyfill (that is, provide code that a browser is expected to run natively) features that aren't yet available.
>
> In doing so, developers are able to use the newest features of the language without having to wait for a release of the compatible runtime. With the fragmentation of browsers and operating systems, developers rarely can be sure that their application is run in a browser that features everything necessary.

For both parts of your application—the core and your UI layer—the process is the same:

1 Make code style checks.
2 Run your files through the transpiler (or preprocessor).
3 Combine it with possible plain JavaScript files.
4 Create a minified bundle.

The last two steps are the same for any JavaScript bundle that you've created so far, but the code style checks and the transpiler part are different depending on the technology that you use. They even require different Gulp plugins to work.

With Gulp, you have a natural way of achieving reusability even though certain parts of your process change. Think back to the first chapter of this book, where we listed the benefits of Gulp as a build system. It's basic JavaScript—no strings or

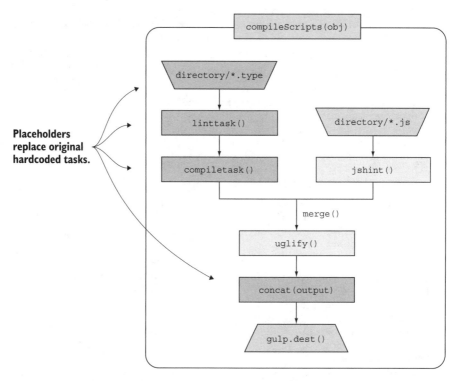

Figure 7.6 By removing hardcoded tasks and replacing them with placeholders (shown in italics), you can reuse a build pipeline for various streams. When it's refactored into a function, you can use it for multiple streams and even tasks.

occluded APIs attached. Sure, you have your set of task definition and streaming functions provided by Gulp, but the rest is any code that you like to add.

With this in mind, you can rework your original pipeline to a parametrized stream using placeholders instead of the original tasks and replace those by passing parameters to a function. Check out figure 7.6 for an illustration.

This function can then be called by any task that you have at hand. The following implementation features two tasks, one for the core and one for the UI layer, with a different code transpiler attached to each. Check out listing 7.3 for more information.

EXAMPLES ON GITHUB The samples for ECMAScript 6 require numerous additional plugins and resource files that would be too much to explain in the scope of this chapter. Please check out the listings and package.json at https://github.com/frontend-tooling/chapter-7-examples if you want to know more.

Listing 7.3   Gulpfile.js (excerpt)

```
/** new plugins **/
var eslint = require('gulp-eslint');
var babel  = require('gulp-babel');

function compileScripts(param) {
  var transpileStream = gulp.src(param.directory + '**/*.' + param.type)
    .pipe(param.linttask())
    .pipe(param.fail)
    .pipe(param.compiletask());
  var jsStream = gulp.src(param.directory + '**/*.js')
    .pipe(jshint())
    .pipe(jshint.reporter('fail'));

  return merge(transpileStream, jsStream)
    .pipe(concat(param.bundle))
    .pipe(uglify())
    .pipe(gulp.dest('dist'));
}
gulp.task('core', function() {
  return compileScripts({
    linttask: coffeelint,
    fail: coffeelint.reporter('fail'),
    compiletask: coffee,
    directory: 'core/',
    type: 'coffee',
    bundle: 'core.js'
  });
});
gulp.task('ui', function() {
  return compileScripts({
    linttask: eslint,
    fail: eslint.failAfterError(),
    compiletask: babel,
    directory: 'ui/',
    type: 'es',
    bundle: 'ui.js'
  });
});
```

compileScripts is the ❶ stream originally defined in a previous task.

Build the stream dynamically for CoffeeScript files.

Build it again for ES2015/ES2016 language features using a transpiler called Babel.

The parts where you compile your files to be transpiled have been replaced with params that you pass to that function ❶. The major benefit of this setup is to have the process specified and defined in one place and replace just the flexible elements through configuration objects.

7.2.2   Stream arrays

Let's expand on the idea of having a set of similar configured stream properties and trying to reuse the same stream over and over again. Although the setup in section 7.2.1 works well, it has one drawback: it requires you to instantiate the stream for each of your configuration objects manually. Also, in the setup just shown you place each stream in a separate task.

Wouldn't it be much more convenient if you had one `scripts` task executing any script stream that you can think of—one task that instantiates all the bundles for you based on a set of configurations?

An idea that helps you fulfill this wish is stream arrays. Stream arrays are, as the name might suggest, arrays of different streams, all executed at once. They make heavy use of standard array functions, most prominently the `map` function of the JavaScript Array object.

The `map` function of an array is used to transform a given array into a different array. It iterates over every element and applies a certain mapping function to this element. The result is stored in the same place in a new array. The following code listing showcases this functionality.

Listing 7.4   Map function substitute

```
Array.prototype.map = function(mapFunction) {
  var result = [];
  for(var i = 0; i < this.length) {
    result.push(mapFunction(this[i]));
  }
  return result;
}

[1, 2, 3].map(function(el) {
  return el * 2;
});
```

This function is usually already implemented by browsers and Node. ❶

map iterates over all elements of an array. ❷

This result is returned. ❸

You map an array of numbers to a function that calculates each element times two. ❹

If this function ❶ isn't already implemented, this snippet can be applied here. The `map` function from an array takes one parameter: the mapping function that should be applied on each element. `map` applies the `map` function to this element and stores the result in a new array ❷. You get an array of the same size and a set of elements that's deducible from the original ❸. The result is an array with the values [2, 4, 6] ❹.

`Array.prototype.map` is convenient if you want to batch-transform your elements. Think about it. Maybe you want to transform a set of configuration objects to a set of streams. This is exactly what stream arrays are about. Take figure 7.7, for example.

From an array of configurations, you get an array of streams. Using the `merge` package discussed earlier, you can combine them into one stream for execution. Figure 7.7 showcases two variations being mapped to the `compileScripts` stream. Because your variations are now an array, you can add as many elements to it as you like, as shown in figure 7.8.

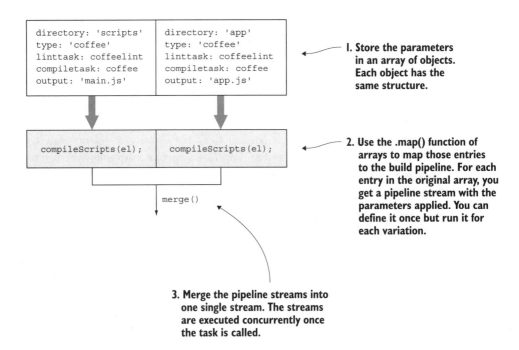

1. Store the parameters in an array of objects. Each object has the same structure.

2. Use the .map() function of arrays to map those entries to the build pipeline. For each entry in the original array, you get a pipeline stream with the parameters applied. You can define it once but run it for each variation.

3. Merge the pipeline streams into one single stream. The streams are executed concurrently once the task is called.

Figure 7.7   Using the `Array.map` function, you can create a multitude of streams for a set of configuration objects. Using `merge` at the end of the process, you can bundle all streams into one and turn it back into a task.

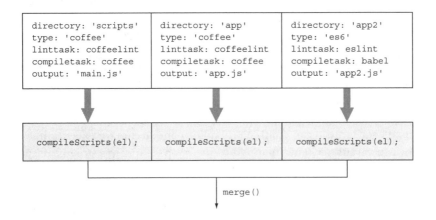

Figure 7.8   The same principle but different tasks. You can now compile multiple CoffeeScript bundles as well as JavaScript written in ECMAScript 6. The process stays the same and you can modify it in one place.

The following code listing gives an example of how this could be implemented in Gulp.

Listing 7.5 Gulpfile.js (excerpt)

```
var variations = [{                          ①  The variations array
  linttask: coffeelint,
  fail: coffeelint.reporter('fail'),
  compiletask: coffee,
  directory: 'core/',
  type: 'coffee',
  bundle: 'core.js'
},{
  linttask: coffeelint,
  fail: coffeelint.reporter('fail'),
  compiletask: coffee,
  directory: 'vendor/',
  type: 'coffee',
  bundle: 'vendor.js'
},{
  linttask: eslint,
  fail: eslint.failAfterError(),
  compiletask: babel,
  directory: 'ui/',
  type: 'es',                           ②  With the map functions
  bundle: 'ui.js'                           you create a stream for
}];                                         each configuration object.
gulp.task('scripts', function() {
  var streams = variations.map(function(el) {
    return compileScripts(el);             Once you have all the
  });                                      streams, merge them into
  return merge(streams);                   one to be executed by Gulp.
});
```

You can put as many configuration objects into your `variations` array as you see fit ①. For this example, you compile the known core and UI scripts as well as all vendor scripts that might be written in JavaScript or CoffeeScript. You use the same `compileScripts` function as you did in section 7.2.1 ②.

Stream arrays are a great way of combining variations of the same task without needing to repeat yourself. You can define and maintain the compilation process in one place and roll out all changes to your different bundles.

7.3 *Additional streaming techniques*

In the last two sections you learned how to handle different input formats when creating one bundle and also how to handle different input variations when creating multiple bundles with the same stream. With merge streams, passthrough streams, and stream arrays you can handle most situations where you want reuse certain code or create complex streams that are usable by Gulp. Even though you can handle the majority of them now, you might run into situations where you need a little more. This section aims to complete the list of the most common streaming techniques that you can apply to your Gulp streams.

7.3.1 *Avoiding repetition with stream snippets*

We've talked a great deal about avoiding repetition in this chapter. But sometimes it's impossible to use one of the techniques described earlier. Maybe you have too many variations in your streams and can't handle them anymore by using configurations in a sane way. Or the streams are entirely different and have just a few tasks in common. But there are still ways to avoid repetition once you run in such a situation. Take JavaScript bundles again, for example. In every example you've seen so far, minification happened and was followed by concatenating the output files into a bundle. We could even say that concatenation never happens unless the output has been minified first. Let's make sure these two tasks always happen together.

Maybe you could use a combination task or a stream snippet that you include in your pipeline and execute multiple tasks instead of one. This snippet should work like any other plugin but execute a series of plugins instead of a defined function. To create such a snippet, you can use one of the packages from the Node.js stream ecosystem: `stream-combiner2`.

> **streams2**
>
> By now you've probably realized that all the stream-related packages that we use feature the 2 suffix: `merge2`, `through2`, and `stream-combiner2`. Although stream functionality is integrated into the Node.js core, those packages are provided by the community. They work as sequels to the original stream APIs, creating an API that's easier to use than the original and subject to change.

The straightforward API takes any task and pipes the contents through. Let's create a snippet and use it for a task that handles vendor scripts (not using JSHint) and create another one that builds your own scripts (using JSHint). The following listing shows how this is done.

Listing 7.6 Gulpfile.js (excerpt)

```
var combiner = require('stream-combiner2');

function combine(output) {
  return combiner.obj(              ◁——❶ The stream combiner call
    uglify(),
    concat(output)
  );
}

gulp.task('vendor', function() {
  return gulp.src('vendor/**/*.js')
    .pipe(combine('vendor.js'))     ◁——❷ Use the snippet you defined
    .pipe(gulp.dest('dist'));             earlier like any other task.
});

gulp.task('scripts', function() {
  return gulp.src('src/**/*.js')
    .pipe(jshint())
```

```
    .pipe(jshint.reporter('fail'))
    .pipe(combine('bundle.js'))
    .pipe(gulp.dest('dist'));
});
```

You use the stream combiner call in object mode (because Gulp stream chunks are objects) and add all the tasks you need ❶. You don't need to pipe them. The stream combiner makes sure the contents are piped through every step ❷.

Should you want to add another step to your pipeline, you can do it in your snippet, and it rolls out to all the tasks that you defined earlier.

7.3.2 *Handling flow with stream queues*

When merging streams into one, you used the `merge2` package. This particular package is helpful because it keeps the asynchronicity of Gulp intact and executes all the streams in parallel. But sometimes you don't want that. Think of creating a CSS file from several resources:

- One features file from Bower components.
- Then there's some library code you've reused from another project. This library code might include CSS `@import` rules pointing to even more files you want to include in your package.
- And last, there's the new code you've written in LESS.

In CSS, keeping the order intact is absolutely necessary. The Cascade (what the *C* stands for in CSS) allows statements that come later to override certain rules. With `merge2`, however, there might be a chance that this order gets messed up because some tasks take longer than others. You can help yourself by using stream queues. Stream queues make sure that outputs of the streams that are in the queue are still in the right order for the subsequent processes. Check out the following listing that uses the `streamqueue` package.

Listing 7.7 Gulpfile.js (excerpt)

```
var queue      = require('streamqueue').obj;
var cssimport  = require('gulp-cssimport');

gulp.task('styles', function() {
  return queue(gulp.src(mainBowerFiles('*.css')),
    gulp.src('lib/lib.css')
      .pipe(cssimport()),
    gulp.src('styles/main.less')
      .pipe(less())
  ).pipe(autoprefixer())
  .pipe(concat('main.css'))
  .pipe(gulp.dest('dist'));
});
```

❶ Use the streamqueue package and directly use the obj method.

❷ The first element in your stream queue is all CSS files installed via Bower components.

❸ Second, add your own library code.

Finally, you have the application styles compiled with LESS.

❹ streamqueue assures the results of every stream are still in order.

As with other stream-related modules from the Node.js ecosystem, you have an object mode that's suitable for Gulp streams ❶. This ❷ is library code that should be handled first. You point to one file that includes every other file from this library with `@import` rules ❸. The `cssimport` task includes all those files into the main file and replace the `@import` statements with the contents. This allows you to append a few other tasks, among them concat: a plugin that concatenates all the files top to bottom ❹. This will create your final file.

Like merge streams, stream queues are a good way of dealing with different input types when creating one bundle. Whereas merge streams allow for maximum concurrency, stream queues keep the execution order, and thus the stream order, intact. When order is relevant to your application's code or styles, go with stream queues instead of merge streams.

7.3.3 *Changing stream contents with Gulp filters*

Stream queues, passthrough streams, merge streams—all great techniques for adding different sources into one continuous Gulp stream. But what about removing elements again from that stream? Let's look at an example. You have a folder of both ES2015 and ES2016 files that you want to compile with Babel, as well as some old JavaScript files that don't require transpiling. Because ES2015/ES2016 is in fact JavaScript, you might want to use the js extension instead of es, as discussed in section 7.2.1. It makes even more sense, because the eslint linting plugin can deal with any version of JavaScript as long as it *is* JavaScript (CoffeeScript, for instance, won't work). So there may be no use for more than one plugin. There's a problem, however. You don't want to run the `babel` compilation step over files that don't need to be compiled. Although it won't break, it will slow down your process.

You can use a package called gulp-filter to change the contents of the stream you're currently processing. Based on file path patterns, you can filter some of file objects that you want to pipe through certain tasks. For later steps, you can restore that filter and add all the elements back into the original stream. Assume that all your ES2015/ES2016 code is stored in a separate folder or has some annotation in its filename; you can use this to specifically say which files you want to pass along. The following code listing shows how this is done.

Listing 7.8 Gulpfile.js (excerpt)

```
var filter = require('gulp-filter');

gulp.task('scripts', function() {
  const babelFilter = filter('*.babel.js', { restore: true });
  return gulp.src('scripts/**/*.js')
    .pipe(babelFilter)
    .pipe(eslint())
    .pipe(eslint.failAfterError())
    .pipe(babel())
```

❶ You annotate all files that should be transpiled by adding "babel" before the JavaScript extension.

❷ Select all the JavaScript files in your scripts directory.

```
   .pipe(babelFilter.restore)
   .pipe(uglify())
   .pipe(concat('main.js'))
   .pipe(gulp.dest('dist'));
});
```

When finished with the compilation, ❸ restore your filter.

Using the Gulp filter you can leave out any file that doesn't match this pattern for the next steps in your pipeline ❶. There are plain-old JavaScript files and files to transpile mixed in one folder ❷. All those files can be linted using ESLint. This means that you add the previously filtered objects back into the stream ❸.

You can add multiple filters to one stream. Assume that you also have all your vendor scripts in that directory, and you don't want to pass them through ESLint. Your stream might look like the next listing.

Listing 7.9   Gulpfile.js (excerpt)

```
var filter = require('gulp-filter');

gulp.task('scripts', function() {
  const babelFilter = filter('*.babel.js', { restore: true });
  const vendorFilter = filter('!vendor/**/*.js', { restore: true });
  return gulp.src('scripts/**/*.js')
    .pipe(vendorFilter)
    .pipe(eslint())
    .pipe(eslint.failAfterError())
    .pipe(babelFilter)
    .pipe(babel())
    .pipe(babelFilter.restore)
    .pipe(vendorFilter.restore)
    .pipe(uglify())
    .pipe(concat('main.js'))
    .pipe(gulp.dest('dist'));
});
```

Select all JavaScript files in your scripts ❶ directory.

❷ Filter all vendor files.

When you restore your filter, you add back all files from the ❸ previous filter steps.

Vendor files are also now included ❶. You don't want to run them through ESLint ❷. This means that vendor scripts, plain JavaScript files, and ES2015/ES2016 files are back in the stream ❸.

Gulp filters are a nice way of changing the contents again midstream. But we encourage you to be pickier about the contents in the first place, because reading operations are involved with the selection of your files. So it's better to add constantly than to select all and then remove what you don't need. If you don't need to restore the filter before the end of your file, you probably can use a good selection pattern instead.

7.4   Summary

In this chapter you harnessed the wonderful power of streams to create complex sequences of contents and operations:

- Passthrough streams allow you to add new sources to y pipeline midstream. This allows great scenarios where you can execute compilation and transpiling steps before going to the common tasks.

- Merge streams take this concept even further by allowing you not only to add as many different source types as you like but also to execute distinctive processes for every stream part before combining them into one.

- Stream arrays and parameterized streams take this idea even further. Instead of just creating one bundle, you can create multiple bundles with variations by using just one stream definition. This stream can be initialized as many times as you like and executed in one task.

- Stream snippets allow you to bundle common tasks into a function that can be added like any other Gulp task to your streaming pipeline. This ensures that you avoid repeating yourself when you see that certain tasks have to be used together multiple times.

- Stream queues are useful for keeping the order of output files intact. This is helpful if your code requires you to hold onto a certain sequence and execution of some stream parts take longer than others.

- After adding new files into a stream, you learned how to remove files again if they're not needed in subsequent tasks. For that, you use gulp filters.

- Now that you know how to use streams in all possible variations, let's look at the most confusing part of Gulp: its vast plugin ecosystem.

Extending Gulp

8

This chapter covers

- The well-maintained Gulp plugin ecosystem
- How to deal with Gulp-unfriendly plugins
- Stream-based tools and how to combine them with Gulp
- Promises and their integration into the Gulp build system

JavaScript build tools usually provide just a core of basic functionality and API. The rest is handled by using a broad variety of plugins that use the existing functionality of other tools and wrap them to be compatible with the build software.

Gulp is no exception, as you've seen in the various examples in the previous chapters: the CSS preprocessor LESS has a Gulp relative called gulp-less, and the JavaScript minification tool Uglify is wrapped by gulp-uglify. For the creators of Gulp, having such a plugin system makes a lot of sense. Instead of having the burden of providing all the software to make all edge cases work, plugins offer a quick and easy way of integrating new tools and content transformers for the community.

With this great extensibility also comes a huge downside: the easier it gets to write new plugins, the more redundant software and duplicates are to be found.

The Gulp plugin directory counts over 1,900 plugins at the time of this writing, and more are being added day by day. This is a problem for developers who have to choose between similar-sounding alternatives. Imagine if you want to minify your CSS: you have the choice to use gulp-minify-css, gulp-cssmin, gulp-css, or fd-gulp-cssmin. Which one would you pick, and what criteria back your choice?

To make it easier for developers, the creators of Gulp have a strong standard for what makes a good and a not-so-good Gulp plugin. In short, their credo states that the fewer plugins you have to use, the better it is for you and the ecosystem in general. Having too many plugins makes it harder to find the right one for your needs. There are likely to be redundancies and more than one plugin for the same problem. Depending on how specific the plugin's name is, you might even end up with a plugin that doesn't solve your problem but is good for only one special case.

The uncertainty of a plugin's extent and the vast amount of duplicates and redundancies are issues Gulp competitors have to deal with constantly. Also, some plugins might be not in the vein of Gulp's underlying architecture (for example, ignoring the contents of the readable stream created by `gulp.src`). Those plugins are considered Gulp-unfriendly by the community.

The creators of Gulp even urge you not to use certain plugins in favor of a more direct approach, meaning that the Node.js ecosystem features packages that both solve your problems and integrate with Gulp seamlessly, without the need for any plugin.

In this chapter, we establish four rules that help you keep to the direct approach:

- If the plugin doesn't transform the file (either its contents or its place inside the stream), it can be done another way.
- If the plugin does more than one task, the task should be done by more than one plugin.
- If the tool you want to use is stream-based, you don't need a Gulp plugin but rather use the tool directly.
- If the tool you want to use returns a Promise,[1] you might not need a Gulp plugin but rather use the tool directly.

Living by those four rules will make your Gulpfiles a lot clearer and the search for the right tool or plugin much, much easier. Ready? Let's start by finding out what Gulp-unfriendly plugins are out there and how to spot them.

8.1   The Gulp plugin blacklist

One term that often pops up when talking about Gulp plugins is the tag name *gulp-friendly*. Developers can tag their extensions with this name, and Gulp will list them on the plugin page.[2] This tag can include not only Gulp plugins but also software and Node.js packages that work with Gulp and are close to its architecture. This tag isn't

---

[1] A concept for asynchronous JavaScript. We'll get to that concept in section 8.3
[2] http://gulpjs.com/plugins/

some credit or award given by the original Gulp crew but something an extension provider can add on their own. This means that plugins that aren't good for the ecosystem at all (because they break some of the rules we defined earlier) can also be tagged gulp-friendly. That's an issue! On the one hand, you can spot packages that work with Gulp, even though they're not classified as a plugin, but on the other hand, the careless addition of this tag to every package possible makes it more or less useless.

This is why the Gulp team maintains a list of gulp-unfriendly plugins at GitHub. This blacklist is used to filter wrongly marked Gulp plugins that you shouldn't use. It includes duplicates, deprecated plugins, and also software that might have been written with the best intentions but fails at executing some of Gulp's core principles. The Gulp team maintains this list by issuing a short statement about each of those plugins and why it shouldn't be used. The statement feels like a verdict passed by the maintainers. They can be manifold, depending on the situation, but three of the verdicts are quite common.

8.1.1 Verdict: not a Gulp plugin

One verdict you see often in this blacklist is the phrase "not a Gulp plugin." This phrase seems pretty generic, but it can be summed up with our first rule: "If it does not change a file (either its contents or its place in the stream), it is not a Gulp plugin." Let's look at one plugin on the blacklist that's "not a Gulp plugin" per se: gulp-compass.

Compass is an extension to Sass, a CSS preprocessor. You've seen that Sass is pretty much like LESS so far, but is Ruby/C++-based and has some syntax and feature differences. Compass is an extension that features some extra project management and functionality. Some developers created a plugin for Gulp that wraps around that functionality, but it fails to hit on some core principles. Let's look at some sample code in the following listing that shows how to use the gulp-compass plugin.

Listing 8.1   Excerpt of Gulpfile.js—Compass task

```
gulp.task('compass', function()              ◁——  Caution: do not try at home
  return gulp.src('./src/*.scss')
    .pipe(compass({
      css: 'app/assets/css',                      These lines of code
      sass: 'app/assets/sass',                    indicate the problem.
      image: 'app/assets/images'
    }))
    .pipe(gulp.dest('app/assets/temp'));
});
```

The two lines marked in the example show the problem. According to the documentation, these lines tell the plugin its input directory (the `sass` property in the configuration object) as well as the output directory (`css` in the same configuration object). Wait a minute. Why do we have to tell Compass file input and file output? Isn't this something Gulp can do by default? As it turns out, this plugin only cares about being inside a stream, not the content of the stream. That's why the Gulp core team flagged this plugin as "not a Gulp plugin."

A correct and more Gulp-friendly way of handling Compass would be using the gulp-ruby-sass plugin directly and activating the Compass extension there, as shown in the following listing.

Listing 8.2   Excerpt of Gulpfile.js—Compass without Compass plugin

```
var sass = require('gulp-ruby-sass');

gulp.task('compass', function() {
  return sass('./src/*.scss', { compass: true})
    .pipe(gulp.dest('app/assets/css'));
});
```

> **sass returns a stream of virtual file objects, much like anything with gulp.src would do.**

The `compass` flag activates everything from Compass that's needed. gulp-ruby-sass is in tune with the Gulp ecosystem, returning a set of virtual file objects that can be modified, transformed, and saved. Note that this plugin doesn't require files to be loaded via `gulp.src`. This is because nothing previously transformed can by piped into this plugin, due to gulp-ruby-sass being a tiny wrapper around Ruby software. So although it's not writeable, it still creates a readable stream and thus is perfectly gulp-friendly.

8.1.2   *Verdict: use something else instead*

You'll often see something like "Use XY instead" or "Use XY directly" in the blacklist. This is again connected to rule 1, where plugins that don't transform files or don't transform the stream should be reconsidered. Or there may be a more direct way of dealing with the task at hand.

Some plugins, like gulp-shell, make it obvious that they execute shell commands, as you can see in the following example.

Listing 8.3   Excerpt of Gulpfile.js

```
gulp.task('execute-shell', function() {
  return gulp.src('', {read: false})
    .pipe(shell('ls'));
});
```

> **This plugin is meant to execute code on the shell, but it doesn't need any file objects to do so.**

Actually, the plugin's author recommends not "reading" files. The plugin doesn't need any file objects and is completely oblivious to the readable stream that originates from `gulp.src`. This breaks rule 1.

You can easily see that this plugin doesn't quite fit the Gulp guidelines. Where is the stream needed? Which files should you transform? The answer is none. Fortunately, the Gulp blacklist shows a few tools that can do that same task, without needing a stream or plugin.

Listing 8.4   Another excerpt of Gulpfile.js

```
var exec = require('child_process').exec;  ◁———  This is from the Node.js core modules.

gulp.task('execute-shell', function (done) {
  exec('ls', function (err, stdout, stderr) {            ◁─┐  You can execute shell
    console.log(stdout);                                    commands with the right
    console.log(stderr);                                    module directly; no need
    done(err);                          ◁─┐  Tell Gulp that you're     for the stream or for files.
  });                                       finished with your task.
});
```

So think twice about whether you really need that plugin. Sometimes it's just a wrapper around functionality that's already usable with Gulp, which is a more direct way. Other examples include the tools we cover in the next two sections.

8.1.3 *Verdict: does too much*

One line you also see constantly in the blacklist is the verdict "Does too much." This particularly goes for plugins that try to resolve more than one task. With Gulp, the single-responsibility principle applies: a Gulp plugin should just do one thing and one thing well. There are many reasons behind this philosophy. Let's look at it using the example of minifying resources like HTML, CSS, and JavaScript.

NO NEED FOR CONFIGURATION

Gulp streams shouldn't be overconfigured. It's preferable to use a set of tools that know what to do with the input without any configuration if possible. For example, the minifyCSS plugin you used in chapter 2 doesn't take any arguments when minifying the CSS output.

LITTLE TO NO DEPENDENCIES

If a plugin does more than one thing, let's say minifying both CSS and JavaScript, it will most likely wrap the tasks around some other API—maybe even around Uglify and MinifyCSS, the tools you already used. If one of those tools gets bug fixes or adds new functionality, the vendor of a plugin that combines those processes has to update their dependencies alongside the tools they're using. This might result in a lot of work, and most likely some of the work will be delayed getting to the actual releases. At some point, the vendor will no longer be up to date with the dependencies. By splitting the task into two different plugins, the onus of "keeping up to date" is on the end user.

LOOSE COUPLING OF SUBTASKS

Again, if you have a plugin that minifies both CSS and JavaScript, should you remove the plugin accidentally when removing one subtask, the other task that uses it might fail. It's not clear whether a plugin belongs to a certain task alone, especially with minifying CSS and minifying JavaScript technically being specific tasks.

One plugin that's blacklisted is gulp-minifier, which does exactly the things stated earlier: it does more than one thing, it has a lot of dependencies to other tools, and it's used by more than one input type that you would usually create subtasks for. Look at the code that you'd have to use.

Listing 8.5   Excerpt of Gulpfile.js

```
gulp.task('example', function() {
  return gulp.src('example/src/**/*').pipe(minify({      ◁┐    The plugin has lots of
    minify: true,                                          │    configuration to set for
    collapseWhitespace: true,                         ❶   │    the task to finally work.
    conservativeCollapse: true,
    minifyJS: true,
    minifyCSS: true
  })).pipe(gulp.dest('example/dest'));
});
```

This goes against the Gulp philosophy of code overconfiguration ❶. Also, it's not clear if you're dealing with CSS, JavaScript files, or both. You can see that code like this is way too convoluted and isn't as elegant as the samples you looked at earlier. So if a plugin does more than one thing, consider using a couple of plugins that each do just one of those tasks.

8.2   *Integrating other stream-based tools*

On to the next rule: If the original tool is stream-based, you don't need a plug-in. Streams are integral to Gulp. The whole idea of the streaming build system is to pipe virtual file objects in a stream through a series of operations. But the concept of streams goes even further, as you'll see in this section.

8.2.1   *Streams, buffers, and Vinyl file objects*

Within Gulp, streams are a fundamental concept that we explained thoroughly in chapter 2. Remember, a stream is a continuous flow of data, delivered in chunks, originating from an input, and finally leading to some output. Think of each keypress on your keyboard as adding a new key event to a stream, with the contents being piped to a text file.

But with Gulp, you mostly deal with object streams, with each chunk of data that you access being a virtual file object (or vinyl file object, with *vinyl* being the name of the virtual file system). Virtual file objects are a representation of real files on your hard disk, containing various properties necessary to identify an item. Take a look at figure 8.1.

The properties base and path represent the filename you dealt so often in the previous chapters. Every time you change the output's filename—either through concatenation, by renaming, or by a transformation to another type—these properties must be changed. The base property contains the file's name without the path, allowing for quick renames of the file itself, and the path will most likely be changed once you save the file back from the virtual file system to the real one (with gulp.dest).

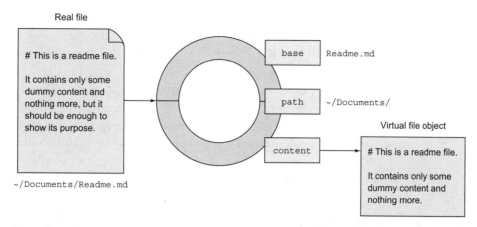

Figure 8.1   On the left side is a real file; it contains some content, has a filename, and is stored in a directory. This physical file on the hard disk can be transformed into a virtual file object or vinyl file object. Vinyl file objects are lightweight wrappers around file contents, which allow for quick access to the content and in-memory storage. Additionally, vinyl file objects offer easy access to paths and filenames.

The other property, `content`, is even more interesting. It can take two types—a buffer or a Node.js stream—both of which allow for different types of transformation.

STREAMS

In general, a stream in Node.js is a continuous stream of data. This data can be accessed chunk by chunk (with the size of the chunk depending on which stream you're dealing with).

Gulp.js streams are object-based, each chunk representing one file in the stream (the previously mentioned virtual file objects). The contents of such a virtual file object can also be of the type stream. This time, however, we're talking about a readable text stream. The concept underneath is still the same: you're accessing data chunk by chunk, transforming each chunk, and piping the results to the next stage. Take a look at figure 8.2.

This permits very fast operations on the data because you can digest each bit on its own (usually you deal with lines inside a file) and can easily make room for the next bit to come. But it comes with one downside: once the data is processed and you move

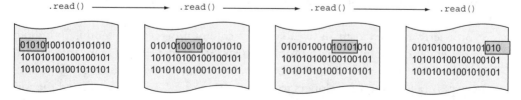

Figure 8.2   If the contents of a vinyl file object are stored as a stream, you have an easy way to access the data of this stream chunk by chunk. You take a piece, transform it, and go to the next one. But although this is very fast and memory-friendly, it only allows movement in one direction.

on, you can no longer access it. Think of a Gulp plugin that transforms all contents of a file to uppercase. After transforming one character to uppercase, you don't care anymore about the state of this character and can move on to the next one.

BUFFER

This is why you can also use buffers in virtual file objects. A buffer is some reserved space in your computer's memory, which can be filled with a certain amount of data. This data can be accessed freely inside the memory's space, with a pointer moving around and giving you the desired bit if you need it. See figure 8.3 for an illustration.

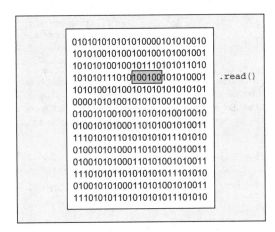

Figure 8.3   A buffer is also a way of accessing the file's contents. The whole file needs to be loaded, but once this is done, you can freely move inside the content and transform parts of any size in any place. For plugins that have to incorporate results from later on in their process to earlier parts, this is crucial.

This process isn't as fast as using streams because you can't discard any intermediate results you might no longer need. But you have the ability to change your results as much as you like at any given point inside your buffer. This is particularly helpful when dealing with tools like Uglify, because they have to maintain a table of compressed and altered variable and function names throughout the compilation process, thus needing the ability to move to multiple points in the buffer at any given time.

With that knowledge, you can now start integrating other stream-based tools to Gulp.

8.2.2   *Integrating Browserify*

With your knowledge of streams and buffers, you can now add stream-based tools to your Gulp setup. One tool that has been a prime example of this kind of integration is Browserify.

Browserify created a stir in the developer community recently. Module bundling and dependency resolution are a problem in JavaScript that spawns many solutions in the community. Browserify found a completely tool-based way of dealing with it without requiring JavaScript developers to learn anything new. It merely adapted the way modules are handled in Node.js to something browsers can also use.

So Browserify makes a pattern available for developers dealing with client-side applications that's as easy as requiring something in Node.js. This pattern, which you already know from Node.js, should be familiar to you by now. The following code is even usable by both Node.js and Browserify.

Listing 8.6 sum.js

```
module.exports = function(arr) {
  return arr.reduce(function(prev, curr) {
    return prev + curr;
  }, 0);
}
```

❶ CommonJS-able environments allow you to define modules by adding module.exports to the global namespace.

❷ sum.js creates a sum by using the Array function of reduce.

With this ❶, the developer can define which parts of their module are exposed to the public once this module is required by another module. You can export values, objects, or functions. The reduce function iterates over all elements of the array and executes the function defined, in this case adding the current value to the sum of the existing ones ❷.

Listing 8.7 main.js

```
var sum = require('./sum');
console.log(sum[1, 2, 3, 4, 5]);
```

You require the module you defined earlier and use the exported function in your code.

The browser doesn't feature methods like require or objects like module in its global namespace. The browser also can't load modules from the file system as Node.js would.

This is where Browserify comes in. Browserify not only adds the necessary require and module additions to the global namespace; it also creates a bundle where each required module will be added, to have it available inside the browser directly after loading. This removes the necessity of loading files on demand from the disk (or from a server). See figure 8.4 for an illustration.

NOTE Not only does Browserify add easy-to-use module capabilities to your client-side scripts through a preprocessing step, it also lets you load dependencies from NPM (built-in) and Bower (through the debowerify plugin) directly into your bundles. Check out their documentation at http://browserify.org.

Browserify comes with a command-line tool but also features an API. This API, as it turns out, emits a stream. What you're dealing with now is a tool—Browserify—that emits streams of compiled content, and a build system—Gulp—that relies heavily on streams. This sounds like something you might combine.

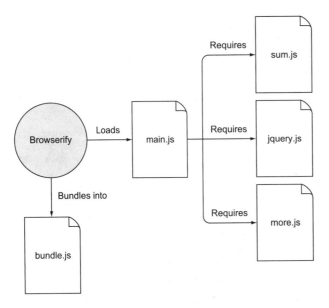

Figure 8.4   How Browserify works. All JavaScript modules are allowed to use `require` and `module.exports` statements. Those are recognized by Browserify, which knows which modules to add to the bundle. It bundles everything, resolves dependency graphs, and adds the required functionality of `require` and `module.exports` to the browser.

The only problem is that the streams are of different types. Whereas Browserify emits a text stream, Gulp uses a stream of virtual file objects as described in section 8.2.1 and chapter 2. But if you remind yourself what a virtual file object looks like and see that the content property of a virtual file object is basically also a text stream, you'll see the similarity.

The Browserify stream is similar to the content stream of a virtual file object. The things missing now are the name of the file and an optional path name to make the virtual file object complete. To create one, you can use a Node.js module called vinyl-source-stream. Take a look at figure 8.5 for an illustration of this pipeline.

The accompanying code is pretty straightforward, as the next listing shows.

Listing 8.8   Excerpt of Gulpfile.js

```
var browserify = require('browserify');
var source     = require('vinyl-source-stream');

var bundle = browserify({
  entries: ['app/scripts/main.js']
});

gulp.task('scripts', function() {
  return bundle.bundle()
    .pipe(source('main.min.js'))
    .pipe(gulp.dest('dist/scripts'));
});
```

The bundle call creates a new stream of compiled contents.

The Browserify API allows you to define new bundle information.

It takes the entries you want to compile as parameters, similar to the gulp.src in the previous examples.

❶ Because it's a stream, you have full piping functionality.

Here you pipe it through the vinyl-source-stream node module ❶. This module moves the text stream to the contents of a virtual file object and adds the necessary

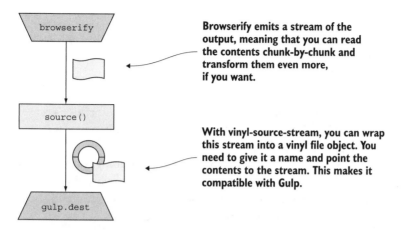

Browserify emits a stream of the output, meaning that you can read the contents chunk-by-chunk and transform them even more, if you want.

With vinyl-source-stream, you can wrap this stream into a vinyl file object. You need to give it a name and point the contents to the stream. This makes it compatible with Gulp.

Figure 8.5   Browserify is a processor to handle JavaScript modules, and its API emits a stream that can be further used. This stream contains just the contents of the file to save. With the vinyl-source-stream package you can wrap it into a vinyl file object to be used with Gulp.

filename information you give as a parameter. With that, you have the ability to transform the results of any stream-emitting tool to a file you can store on your hard disk—and more! Because the Gulp task system requires you to return a stream, you can execute any stream-based tool with Gulp, even if it doesn't create files in the end.

8.2.3   *Transforming contents*

With Browserify now dealing with the bundling of your JavaScript, you should grab the chance and actually do something with your newly created application bundles. Even if Browserify takes care of all the bundling, it still has some rather verbose contents, because all your JavaScript stays as you wrote it. You still want to Uglify the scripts to have optimal content for your browsers. But the content's type after a source transformation is still a stream, and Uglify can only deal with buffers, as you saw in section 8.2.1. Fortunately, with vinyl-buffer you can also use a module from the ecosystem of your virtual file system. vinyl-buffer converts the contents that are stored in a stream into a buffer, as shown in figure 8.6.

The accompanying code looks like the following listing.

Listing 8.9   Gulpfile.js

```
var browserify = require('browserify');
var source     = require('vinyl-source-stream');
var buffer     = require('vinyl-buffer');

var bundle = browserify({
  entries: ['app/scripts/main.js']
});

gulp.task('scripts', function() {
```

```
    return bundle.bundle()
      .pipe(source('main.min.js'))
      .pipe(buffer())
      .pipe(uglify())
      .pipe(gulp.dest('dist/scripts'));
});
```

> The vinyl buffer plugin transforms the content property from a stream to a buffer so it can be used with Uglify

Both vinyl-source-stream and vinyl-buffer are tools that transform or create a virtual file object for the virtual file system. vinyl-source-stream creates a new file object. vinyl-buffer changes the content property. By knowing the parts of one file object that well, you can do even more. Think back to chapter 6 with the integration of sourcemaps. Sourcemaps are just another property that gets added to the virtual file object. If your stream-based tool also allows the creation of sourcemaps, you can add those to your file object once you're ready, as shown in the following listing.

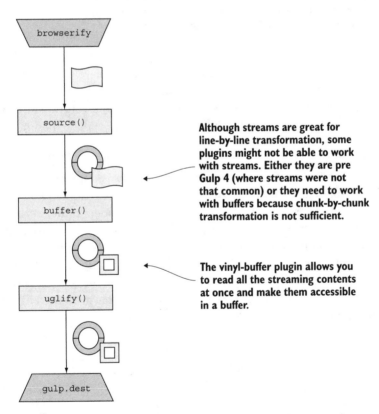

Although streams are great for line-by-line transformation, some plugins might not be able to work with streams. Either they are pre Gulp 4 (where streams were not that common) or they need to work with buffers because chunk-by-chunk transformation is not sufficient.

The vinyl-buffer plugin allows you to read all the streaming contents at once and make them accessible in a buffer.

Figure 8.6   gulp-uglify, the plugin you use to minify JavaScript, has to change code throughout the file, which requires the plugin to operate on multiple parts of the document. Therefore, gulp-uglify needs a buffer to operate on. With the vinyl-buffer plugin you change the contents of the vinyl file object from stream to buffer to make it compatible with this sort of plugin.

Listing 8.10   Gulpfile.js

```
var bundle = browserify({
  entries: ['main.js'],
  debug: true
});

gulp.task('scripts', function() {
  return bundle.bundle()
    .pipe(source('main.min.js'))
    .pipe(buffer())
    .pipe(sourcemaps.init({loadMaps: true}))
    .pipe(uglify())
    .pipe(sourcemaps.write('.'))
    .pipe(gulp.dest('dist'));
});
```

⟵ debug tells Browserify to create a sourcemap; it will also be emitted from the stream after the bundling.

⟵ With the gulp-sourcemap plugin and the loadMaps option, it will transform the emitted sourcemap into a property that gets added to the virtual file system.

With vinyl-source-stream wrappers, you can transform standard readable text streams into object-based virtual file streams. In doing so, you make them compatible with Gulp and some Gulp plugins. The stream you create is entirely new; its contents are from the original text stream of its original tool (in this example Browserify). But Gulp plugins have the ability to deal with either streamable contents or buffered contents or both. vinyl-buffer is a great way provided by the Vinyl file system to deal with such plugins.

Browserify is a prime example of how different stream-based tools can be integrated into Gulp. Browserify works with streams, as does Gulp, so these tools share a huge similarity in how they work with their contents. If there's already a tool dealing with streams, use it and wrap it to the Gulp ecosystem with those handy vinyl modules.

8.3   Integrate Promise-based tools

The last rule in our list, "If the original tool returns a Promise, you might not need a plug-in," requires some more explanation, because you haven't heard from Promises yet. Generally speaking, Promises are a way of dealing with asynchronous and concurrent operations while still having a synchronous way of handling results. Sound confusing? Well, it can be. Just a quick spoiler ahead: Promises are well integrated into the Gulp task system. You'll find out in this section what Promises are and how they work.

8.3.1   How Promises work

In JavaScript, asynchronous computations and methods are common. Think of dealing with events or loading scripts and other resources asynchronously from a web server. Those computations have one thing in common: the results aren't available yet but will be at some later point.

Promises are a construct in JavaScript that allows for handling such data that you don't have yet. A Promise is quite literally a "promise" that this data will be available eventually. In this case, the Promise is *resolved* or *fulfilled*. But it's also a promise that

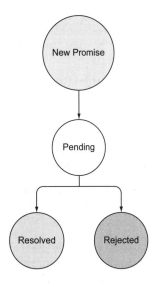

Figure 8.7   The states a Promise can take. When one is created, the state of the Promise is pending, which means that the value of your asynchronous computation is not yet available. Once the value is available, the Promise is resolved. If an error occurs, the Promise is rejected.

you'll be notified if an error occurs and you can't get your data at all. In that case, you *reject* the Promise (see figure 8.7).

Let's see how you can use Promises to make some asynchronous code "thenable." *Thenable* means that you can chain a multitude of functions, each of those handling the result from the previous one, preferably asynchronously. Think of a function that sums up all the elements in an array. The native array method reduce is a good way to, well, reduce all the elements to a single value. But this code is synchronous and blocking. Putting it in a setTimeout call allows you to make it asynchronous, but then you need some callbacks to deal with the results. This is a great case for Promises, as shown in the next listing.

Listing 8.11   An example Promise

```
function sum(arr) {
  return new Promise(function(resolve, reject) {          ①  Create a new Promise.
    setTimeout(function() {
      try {                                                   Wrap your execution
        var sum = arr.reduce(function(prev, curr) {       ②  in a setTimeout.
          return prev + curr;
        }, 0);
        resolve(sum);                                      Once your sum is ready, resolve it with
      } catch(err) {                                       the value; the status is now resolved.
        reject(err);
      }
    }, 0);                             Should an error occur, you
  });                                  can catch this error and set
}                                      the state to rejected.
```

The idea is to have a sum function that works asynchronously **❶**. The Promise takes one callback function as a parameter. This function has two other functions as parameters: `resolve` and `reject`. Once you create this Promise, the status of the Promise is pending. Wrapping your execution in a `setTimout` makes it run asynchronously **❷**. You invoke this timeout immediately, though. This ensures that the main thread, which called `sum` to begin with, can continue running.

sum now returns a Promise, which means you can continue working without the result. The thread calling the Promise knows that at some point you'll have your result, and `then` you want to do something with it. Figure 8.8 shows how the execution of this works in the form of a timeline.

Let's stay in the terminology of keeping Promises with the previous example. The `sum` function gives you a Promise that you will eventually get the sum; `then` you want to do something with the result. The next listing is pretty much the code you need to handle this type of execution.

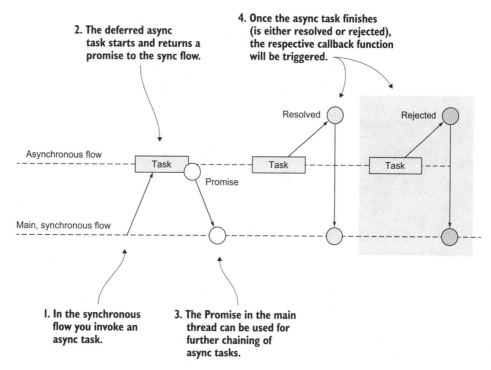

2. The deferred async task starts and returns a promise to the sync flow.

4. Once the async task finishes (is either resolved or rejected), the respective callback function will be triggered.

Resolved

Rejected

Asynchronous flow

Task   Task   Task

Promise

Main, synchronous flow

1. In the synchronous flow you invoke an async task.

3. The Promise in the main thread can be used for further chaining of async tasks.

Figure 8.8 How Promises are executed in time. The main, synchronous flow calls a function that returns a Promise (1–2). While this function keeps executing (2), you already have a construct ready in your synchronous flow to handle the results (3), so you do something with those results. At some point (4) you either reject or resolve the Promise, which either causes an error or causes the next step in the execution to be called.

**You want to sum up this array; the
function returns a Promise.**

**Assuming the Promise resolves, then you
want to do something with the result, in
this case printing it on the console.**

```
sum([1,2,3,4])
  .then(function(result) {
    console.log(result);
  })
  .catch(function(err) {
    console.error('There has been a problem');
  });
```

**Assuming the Promise is
rejected, you want to catch
this rejection and deal with it.**

Promises allow you to chain a series of execution steps and pass the results from asynchronous tasks over to the next function. This chaining of tasks should be familiar to you. It's close to piping data in streams through functions, something you do all the time!

8.3.2   *Promises in the Gulp task system*

The nature of Promises—having the ability to chain asynchronously executed tasks and continue working with the results—make them perfectly suited to the Gulp task system. It turns out that Promises are fully supported by the `gulp.task` function. Even better, you've already used it in your Gulpfile! In chapter 3 you got acquainted with the del module. Not only does del delete files; it also returns a Promise that will resolve eventually, as shown in the next listing.

```
gulp.task('clean', function() {
  return del('dist');
});
```

Instead of requiring a stream, the Gulp task system can also handle Promises. The orchestration of task execution works the same way: either the stream ends or it runs into an error, much as a Promise resolves or rejects.

For which tasks are Promises better than streams? Gulp streams deal with all things file-related really well, so Promises are a good alternative if you don't necessarily have files and file transformations or have tools already available that feature Promises. One example is the following task: you want to check if the Gulp plugins we've saved in your dependencies and devDependencies are actually in the feared and dreaded blacklist.

Gulp stores all blacklisted plugins in a file on GitHub. With the raw subdomain you can retrieve the raw contents from that file from anywhere on the web. With an implementation of the fetch standard, you can create a response with the contents of this file using Promises. From there on, you can process these contents and compare them to the entries in your package.json file. Figure 8.9 illustrates this.

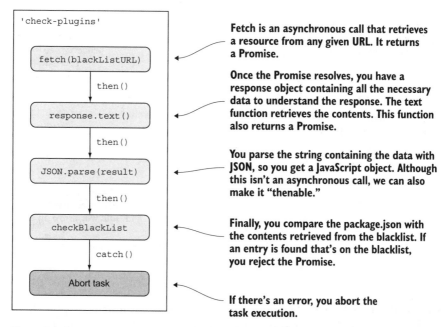

Figure 8.9 The process in Promises and then-abled functions. A task like this is similar to a standard stream-based task.

The implementation is shown in the following listing. You use node-fetch as the fetch implementation. The Promise standard is in Node.js with version 4.0.

Listing 8.14   Excerpt of Gulpfile.js

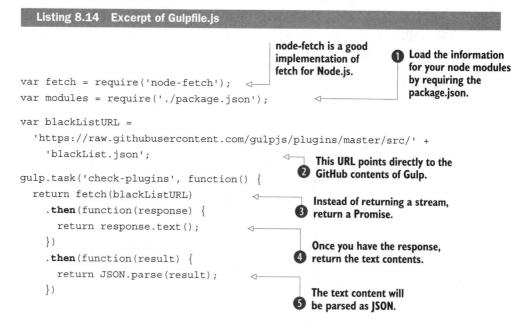

Once you have the text as a plain JavaScript object, check if your plugins are in the blacklist and create a new Promise.

Create an Array of ⑥ properties to look up in your package.json.

```
.then(function(blackList) {
    return new Promise(function(resolve, reject) {
        ['dependencies', 'devDependencies'].forEach(function(el) {
            Object.keys(modules[el]).forEach(function(key){
                if(!!blackList[key]) {
                    reject(`You are using ${key}. Not good!`);
                }
            });
        });
        resolve('Everything okay!');
    });
});
```

Retrieve all keys from the underlying property, which are the package names that are stored either in devDependencies or dependencies.

Should you find an entry in the blacklist, reject the Promise, and Gulp will throw an error.

Otherwise, move on.

Because this is JSON, you'll get a plain JavaScript object once you've loaded it ❶. This file ❷ contains all blacklisted plugins. In this case, the Promise is that you'll have the response for fetching this URL at some point ❸. This function ❹ also returns a Promise. This call ❺ is synchronous, but once you're in a then chain, you can create each step as something that requires input from the previous step and gives output to the next step. You want to see if any dependencies or devDependencies contain entries in the blacklist ❻.

Quite some code! Still, we don't need any Gulp plugin and can easily create new tasks with Promise-based tools. If you want to deal with files and save and transform them, it might be easier to find something stream-related.

8.4   *Summary*

In this chapter, you learned about the Gulp blacklist and about different ways to handle Gulp tasks without plugins:

- Some plugins are not in tune with Gulp's core principles. Those plugins are listed on the Gulp plugin blacklist. The Gulp core team maintains this list and updates it regularly.
- Other Gulp plugins don't alter the stream or the files inside the stream. Those plugins are often not necessary, and the task can be done more directly. The Gulp blacklist offers alternatives.
- You can easily integrate other stream-based tools like Browserify in your Gulp build pipelines with a few extra lines of code, making the text stream compliant to the virtual file system.
- Parts of a virtual file object can be altered from a text stream to a text buffer to work with other plugins.

- Promises are a way of asynchronously dealing with operations. Promises are fully compatible with the Gulp task system, so you can use computations and operations handled in Promises as well.

This concludes your study of Gulp. Now that you can basically build everything in the most efficient manner, you'll see how to refactor existing codebases to be used over and over again, by creating reusable components.

Creating modules and Bower components

This chapter covers

- Asynchronous module definitions
- CommonJS module system
- Universal module definitions
- Exposure of module functionality
- Deployment of private and public components

When developing, we usually try to encapsulate specific functionality into reusable patterns, be it functions that have defined output on various input or objects and classes that combine state and behavior in a broader sense. The idea is to reuse the provided functionality and rely on the trustworthiness of a thoroughly specified and tested module.

Modules wrap functionality and provide an API to the outside program code. Other modules can consume this module's API and use its functionality, without knowing the inner workings of this particular subprogram. Whereas modules structure functionality on a code level, components do so at an organizational level.

Components are self-contained collections of modules, meaning that they provide functionality independent of their surrounding program code. As modules, they too offer a sense of reusability, this time between different projects. Developers should be able to add a component into their project in the form of a dependency and use this functionality without any substantial setup.

Take a common UI pattern on the web, for example. Clicking a toggle menu button shows or hides the menu element on a website. Clicking an accordion header opens the hidden content below it. Another click hides this content again. Even though the widgets or UI elements are totally different, the underlying behavior is the same: you click a trigger element, and it shows/hides other elements on the website. This sounds like something that you'd want to encapsulate in a module and provide for all your upcoming projects in the form of a component; see figure 9.1.

In this chapter, you'll refactor this toggle UI pattern into a module and make it reusable as a Bower component. This helps not only to bring structure to your projects but also to separate clutter and standard functionality from the core. Individual tasks your software must solve are combined into one graspable unit. You'll learn how to define modules in JavaScript and what information is necessary to treat these modules like dependencies you know from chapter 4: redistributable, installable pieces of software that you can add to a multitude of projects.

> **On module patterns**
>
> The following two sections describe the most common JavaScript module patterns. Using modules isn't necessarily required to create Bower components, but it allows you to better structure your code and integrate it well with existing applications. Because the focus of this chapter is to make the reuse of your JavaScript code as easy as possible, module patterns are not only a recommendation but a must.

9.1 Asynchronous module definition

Unlike other programming languages, JavaScript lacked a module definition syntax and loading mechanism for quite a long time. This was because JavaScript was executed in the browser, and the loading mechanism was a simple script tag that pointed to the resource. With JavaScript's arrival on the servers with Node.js and the huge popularity of rich client-side applications, the demand for a well-defined and robust module system in JavaScript has risen.

There are now specifications on how modules should be defined in JavaScript, but as with everything new on the web, the adoption rate for the various platforms can vary. At the time of this writing, no platform has fully implemented the module specification. This doesn't mean that you can't use modules. JavaScript standards often come from a close inspection of popular libraries and ideas that are already out there.

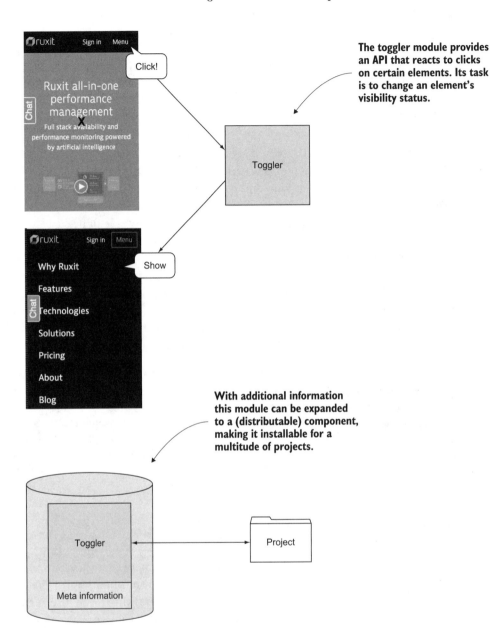

Figure 9.1   The toggler module encapsulates functionality that reacts on click events and thus changes the visibility status of certain parts on the website. The API takes different parameters (the element status that has to be changed) but works completely independent from the rest of the application. With added meta information, we can extend this module to a redistributable component.

The two most common ways to define modules are AMD and CommonJS. We'll look into both AMD and CommonJS and the combining UMD pattern.

Let's start with AMD, because it's not only one of the oldest ways, it was also specifically designed for our platform of choice: the browser.

9.1.1   *AMD—module definitions for the browser*

Asynchronous module definitions (AMD) are one of the two most common ways modules can be defined for JavaScript. AMD is defined by the Group for AMD JS Module APII,[1] a group of software developers from different companies, working in the public domain and open source. As the name states, the AMD standard allows you to define modules and dependencies for use with asynchronous loading techniques. This is particularly suited to browser environments, where asynchronous loading is built in with HTTP requests and AJAX calls. It allows for several patterns, like conditionally loading modules that might only be required on certain occasions, while the rest of the code is already running. This transfers only the files and code needed by the application, only at the time where they're needed, instead of carrying along lots of unused JavaScript.

AMD provides two methods for defining and loading modules. Let's look at both of them.

THE DEFINE METHOD

The `define` method is used—as the name suggests—to define modules. It allows you to pass along dependencies that are to be loaded along with the module. The only parameter required is the factory function, which holds the module's code. The `define` method uses the following signature:

```
define(
    'moduleId',
    ['list', 'of', 'dependencies'],
    function(list, of, dependencies) {
        ...
    }
);
```

❶ The first parameter is the optional module ID (as string).

❷ The second parameter is an optional list of dependencies.

❸ The factory function

If the ID is defined, the module is from then known by this name ❶. Otherwise, module loaders use the file path. It's an array with strings, each pointing to the file that should be loaded (without the JS suffix) ❷. The factory function ❸ holds the module's code. A return statement exposes the functionality for other modules. The function's parameters are a list of the dependency module's exposed APIs, in the order stated in parameter 2.

So a module that's defined via AMD requires at least a factory function that exposes the API that should be used by other modules. The list of dependencies triggers asynchronous module loading along the dependency tree, as shown in figure 9.2.

---

[1] https://github.com/amdjs

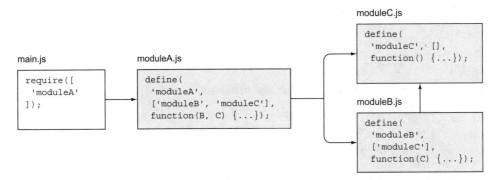

Figure 9.2   A schematic flow of asynchronous module definitions and loading. Each arrow depicts a loading process. In your main JavaScript file you load one module: moduleA. It has two modules as dependencies: moduleB and moduleC. moduleB also has moduleC as a dependency. The definition through functions and callbacks allows for asynchronous loading of files over the network. The callback then makes the exposed functionality accessible by the respective parameters.

Loading a module is done via an HTTP request from a client (browser) to a server. This transmission is costly and requires a certain amount of time. If a module has already been transmitted, it won't be loaded a second time because its contents are already available.

AMD has the possibility of defining both named and unnamed modules. Named modules can be loaded using the name given to them by the developer; unnamed modules are implicitly named based on the filename.

THE REQUIRE METHOD

The `require` method is the counterpart of the `define` method. Whereas the `define` method allows you to define modules and dependencies, the `require` module allows you explicitly load modules when you need them. This can be used as an entry point for an application, where you load all the necessary modules, but also in mid-application, if you need to load even more functionality. Figure 9.3 shows how conditional module loading works using `require`.

Because loading works asynchronously, the newly required functionality is only available in a callback function:

```
require(['jquery', 'toggler'],        ◁——— The required modules
    function($, tog) {             ◁—
        ....                          ┌─────────────────────
    }                              │ The callback function,
);                                 │ where both required
                                   │ modules are available
```

`define` and `require` aren't available in JavaScript runtimes. They need to be provided by AMD loading implementations: module loaders. One of the most popular ones is require.js. It requires some setup, but it also has excellent documentation at http://requirejs.org that leads you through a full project definition.

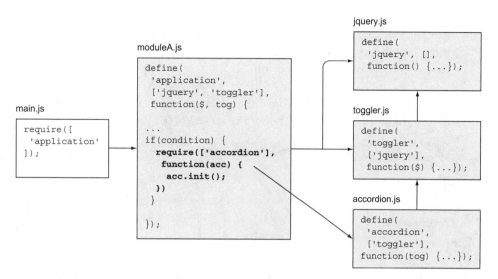

Figure 9.3 Conditional loading of more modules. You can use the `require` statement at any time in your code to load another module. This call creates a new request to download the module. Because this happens asynchronously, you need the callback to access the exposed functionality.

9.1.2 Refactoring to AMD

Let's see how you can refactor a concrete example of standard jQuery code into an AMD module. You want to create reusable functionality of changing the state of certain elements in your HTML markup. Think about a website using a menu button to show and hide the menu items. Or imagine having expandable elements throughout your website, where you click headlines to show and hide content underneath. Although menus and expandables have different UI features, their behavior is the same: click something to show it; click again to hide it. Once you've written the code, you most likely end up with functionality like that shown in listings 9.1 and 9.2.

The component you're creating has jQuery as a dependency, and it scans for all occurrences of `data-toggle` attributes in your markup. The `data-toggle` attribute points to another element in your document, which should be shown or hidden depending on its state.

Listing 9.1   Sample HTML markup

```
<button data-toggle="#menu">
  Menu
</button>
<nav id="menu" hidden>
  <ul>
    <li><a href="/">Home</a></li>
    <li><a href="/about">About</a></li>
    <li><a href="/products">Products</a></li>
  </ul>
</nav>
```

① The button has the bespoke data-toggle attribute.

② Navigation with the ID menu has an initial state of hidden.

This attribute ❶ points to an ID in your document. This can be any selector that's compatible with jQuery. The hidden attribute is an HTML5-specified attribute that hides certain parts of the document if added ❷. You remove and add this attribute based on clicks of the menu button.

The example markup shows a menu button. You now want to add behavior to this button. Clicking it should remove the hidden attribute on the element connected to it. The following listing gives the implementation for that behavior.

Listing 9.2 Toggler.js

Calling this function will initialize the behavior.

❶ The jQuery selector for all your toggle buttons listens for the data-toggle attribute you provided in the markup.

```
function init() {
  $('[data-toggle]').each(function(idx, el) {
    var $el = $(el);
    var $target = $($el.data('toggle'));
    $el.on('click', function(e) {
      e.preventDefault();
      if($target.attr('hidden')) {
        $target.removeAttr('hidden');
      } else {
        $target.attr('hidden', true);
      }
    });
  });
}
```

Each element has to be wrapped again for jQuery use.

The target element (the one with the hidden attribute") is specified via a ❷ selector in the data-toggle attribute.

The click handler on the original button checks if the hidden attribute is set on the target, and if not, sets it, and vice versa.

This ❶ will return a collection of jQuery elements that you can iterate over with the each function. You can access this selector ❷ using the jQuery data function, and because it returns a string, you can use this as a new selector for a jQuery element.

This script is a perfect showcase for creating modules, because it features many of the requirements mentioned earlier:

- An init function, which is exposed by an API that's called by the developer.
- A dependency, in this case jQuery.
- Its functionality is self-contained and reusable.

You want to modify this script into a module compliant with AMD principles. As shown in section 9.1.1, AMD introduces two concepts for that: a define method for facilitating module definitions and a require method that handles module loading. You need the first method—define—to encapsulate the scripts functionality. See the next listing for more details.

Listing 9.3 toggler.js as a module

```
define(
  'toggler',
  ['jQuery'],
```

Explicitly define your module as toggler, which is how it is now known by the module loader.

It has one dependency, jQuery; it's the module loader's job to know where jQuery is to be found.

```
function($) {
    function init() {
        ...
    }

    return { init: init };
}
);
```

❶ The jQuery dependency is passed with a variable name you can decide.

The code from your original JavaScript file

❷ Expose the functionality for other modules.

Because you used the $ sign for jQuery all the way through, it's fitting to use it here again ❶. When developers require the toggler module, they have to call the `init` function to start it ❷.

With an AMD module, you created a way of encapsulating functionality and making it reusable throughout your project. Defining and loading modules can be done asynchronously, relying on tools like RequireJS to execute this task. The next listing shows the basic setup with RequireJS.

Listing 9.4   main.js

```
requirejs(['toggler'])
```

The main.js file contains nothing more than a loading instruction to the toggler module you defined earlier. RequireJS does the rest: loading the JS file and loading the jQuery dependency. To avoid naming collisions, require.js uses `requirejs` instead of `require` as a loading function name. This can be changed in the configuration.

Included in the HTML is a pointer to the require.js library with another pointer to the file to be loaded. It looks like this:

```
<script data-main="scripts/main.js" src="scripts/require.js"></script>
```

This kicks off a chain of asynchronous loading calls. Require.js loads main.js, which loads toggler.js, which loads jquery, just like in figure 9.3. Asynchronicity, however, is sometimes hard to wrap your head around. A more synchronous manner is provided by the module definition types in the next section.

9.2   *CommonJS and Universal Module Definition*

Although AMD was specifically designed for use with the browser, its complicated loading mechanisms distracted some users. This allowed for the rise of a much easier format: CommonJS. It's different in that it doesn't require you to think in asynchronous loading patterns. Requiring a module is just a call away. The groundwork for that is a compile step that creates bigger bundles of combined functionality, including everything that you need to run the application. The big downside compared to AMD is that you can't load specific functionality on demand.

With the popularity of both module definition types, a developer would have to serve both to make a component widely available. This led to a unifying format called Universal Module Definition (UMD). Let's look at both module definition types.

9.2.1 *CommonJS modules*

CommonJS modules are the second most popular module definition choice, with increasing popularity in recent times because of efficient tooling and a much easier syntax. Originally, CommonJS modules were known as JavaScript server modules. This should ring a bell: it's the well-known `module.exports/require` combination you've used in your Gulpfiles and with Browserify in chapter 8. The usage of this pattern should be familiar to you already:

```
var $ = require('jquery');        ◁┐   Dependencies are loaded
                                   │   by requiring them into
function init() {                  │   the current file.
   ...
}                                 ┌─  The module export object gets a new property:
module.exports.init = init;    ◁──┘  a pointer to your initialization function.
```

The module is now usable much like in the previous example, but without callbacks, in a synchronous manner. There's no need for dependency tree definitions because they're resolved on the fly when needed. With the omission of callbacks and dependency definitions, the code becomes much clearer and more understandable, especially for people unfamiliar with the asynchronicity of JavaScript. This also led to CommonJS slowly becoming the preferred way of defining and loading modules.

I must say a word about loading, though. CommonJS is a truly synchronous loading mechanism, meaning that each `require` statement stalls the execution and waits until the module is loaded. Figure 9.4 illustrates this.

This is no problem for systems like Node.js, where file access is quick and fast, or Browserify, where all necessary modules are already in the bundled JavaScript file. This means, however, that native loading of CommonJS modules isn't suitable for browsers, because the loading mechanism couldn't be done synchronously (the first A in AJAX stands for "asynchronous," after all). The only way to make CommonJS modules workable in the browser is by bundling them into a single JavaScript file with tools like Browserify.

9.2.2 *Universal Module Definition*

AMD and CommonJS modules are used equally by the community and throughout different projects. The choice often depends on the requirements of a project and your application's architecture. Is it reasonable to split the application into several smaller bundles that can be loaded on occasion? Or would you rather deploy the whole JavaScript app and use modules as a way of maintaining the codebase? In other cases, you might drop module definitions altogether and use the JavaScript engine's global namespace. These decisions differ from project to project, so you can't exclude any of these ways. Because both module definition types have their place, the community thought of a way to combine both approaches into the Universal Module Definition.

The idea is to use a so-called factory function to normalize the commonalities between the different module approaches: all module definition types need to pass

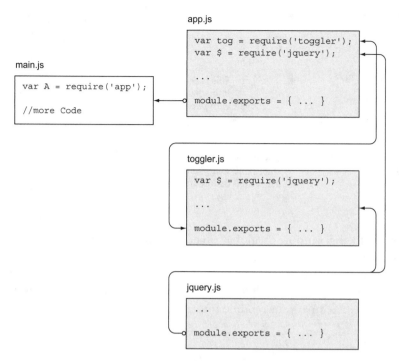

Figure 9.4 Contrary to the asynchronous nature of AMD, CommonJS modules directly provide the exposed functionality from a module, allowing developers to use them in a synchronous manner. Each arrow can be read as a load but not over the network, more from memory or the file system. This access is quick and rarely stalls.

dependency modules along, and all module definition types expect an exported object to be used by other modules. The `factory` function provides exactly that: each parameter is one dependency module; the return value of the `factory` function is the module object. Some initialization code checks which module system is available and uses the `factory` function as needed. Figure 9.5 illustrates this process.

Translated in code, the UMD version of the toggler module looks like this:

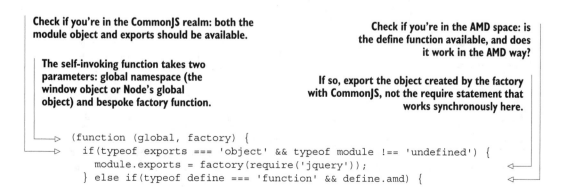

```
        define('toggler', ['jQuery'], factory);
    } else {
        global.toggler = factory(global.jQuery);
    }
}) (this, function($) {

    function init() {

        ...

    }

    return {
        init: init
    }

});
```

If so, call the factory function as usually done in AMD.

The last way: create a new object in the global namespace.

This function is immediately called ❶ with two parameters.

The init function that you carry along

Export it with the return statement, just like the usual AMD definition way.

This ❶ refers to the window or global object of your JavaScript engine. The next parameter is the `factory` function that you define. The `factory` function also takes parameters, namely your dependency modules, in this case jQuery. With this in place, you can now use your toggler module with any module definition system you like—or none at all! Next step: turn your module into a component.

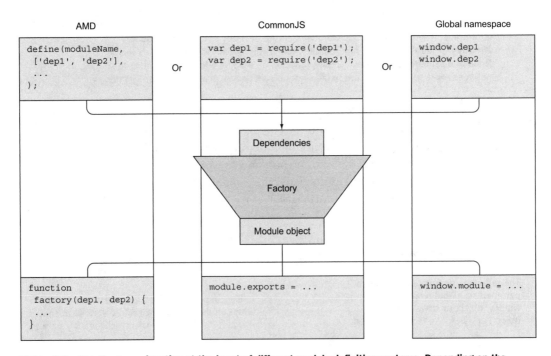

Figure 9.5 The `factory` function at the heart of different module definition systems. Depending on the availability of different module definition types, you call the factory in different ways: either the AMD way or the CommonJS way. If both are unavailable, you add your module to the global namespace of your JavaScript engine.

> **A note on ES2015 modules**
>
> The ECMAScript committee has created a specification on how modules should be defined in JavaScript. It adds additional syntax by way of `export` and `import` keywords and tries to be syntactically independent of the module loader underneath. At the time of this writing, no browser supports this new syntax. There are, however, tools like rollup.js that allow you to compile this syntax to AMD, CommonJS, and UMD.

9.3 Defining and deploying Bower components

Modules and components have similar features. Both enclose a set of functionality into a self-contained and reusable unit. The goals of both are different, however: a module aims to create a unit that's maintainable and reusable on a code-level base. This means that inside your project you constantly refer to its functionality from different pieces of code. But those pieces are just consumers of an API, so the file structure should not be of concern if you think in terms of modules.

A component, on the other hand, wants to gain this reusability at the organizational level of a project. This means that a component can consist of several modules and even feature a greater set of functionality than a module, as long as it retains its key features: self-containment, clear API, and a clear list of dependencies. Take jQuery, for an example: the part where jQuery deals with event handling is organized in a module. The whole jQuery bundle can be seen as a component.

The toggling script is already a module, which means you can consume its API throughout your project. If you want to distribute this piece of code throughout several projects, you have to enhance it to make it a component. Let's do that with Bower.

9.3.1 Bower.json specification

Let's prepare your component for Bower. For this example, you only wrap the module you created previously into a redistributable package. Depending on the components you want to create and distribute, this can include multiple modules and assets.

Put the toggler.js file in a new, empty directory where you can add all the necessary files that enhance the lonesome JavaScript file to make it a full-fledged component. Bower needs nothing more than some metadata that it can use to populate the registry. This will make the component findable and thus installable. Necessary metadata are as follows:

- The component's name
- The component's version
- The Git endpoint where the component can be found

Sound familiar? It should. You've come across these properties already when installing components with Bower or installing your tools with NPM. The metadata is saved in JSON format in a file in the component's directory. This is the very same JSON file it also uses to store dependencies: bower.json. You came across this file back in chapter 4, when you installed the first components for your sample project. Back then, you used it to store your dependencies; now you'll use bower.json to store more information.

To start, enter

```
$ bower init
```

in your new directory that contains your JavaScript module. But this time, you'll pay attention to the questionnaire:

- The *name* is the only required entry in the bower.json file. Enter a suiting one, or let Bower see for itself.
- A *description* is brief information on what the component is about. It helps others understand what you want to achieve with your component. Enter one, or leave it blank to be omitted.
- The *main file* is list of files that should be referenced when used with main-bower-files or other tools you got to know in chapter 4. Setting this field is highly recommended. In this case, Bower will suggest a pointer to toggler.js. This list can be longer. If your component has more than one main file, or if you have JS and CSS files you want to include in your bundles, add as many paths as you like.
- The *type of module* you want to expose is a list of module definition systems you learned before. You can select more than one by pressing the spacebar in front of each name. AMD is obvious; *globals* means that you're exposing everything in the global namespace. CommonJS modules are known as *Node* in this list. If you're already working with ES2015 modules, select ES6.
- You can enter some *keywords* if you want your component to be more findable, enter the *author*'s name and mail address for development credit, define an optional open source *license*, and point to the component's *website*.
- If you already have *dependencies* installed, you can add them to the list of dependencies. In this case, you'll do that later.
- Bower will also ask you to add a list of *common ignore patterns*. Usually, this includes files that start with a dot (common for hidden files in Unix/Linux systems), all other Bower components or node modules (you don't want to transfer them with the component but rather install them again with bower install), and test directories. If you want to add more files that should be ignored, add them here.

After the final question, if you want to set it all private, Bower will show you the outcome once more for proofreading. If you accept, you will get something like the next listing.

```
Listing 9.5  Bower.json
{
  "name": "toggler",
  "authors": [
    "Stefan Baumgartner"
  ],
  "main": "toggler.js",
  "moduleType": [
    "amd",
    "node",
    "globals"
  ],
  "license": "MIT",
  "ignore": [
    "**/.*",
    "node_modules",
    "bower_components",
    "test",
    "tests"
  ]
}
```

Right now, you're missing one important piece: the jQuery dependency. You install jQuery using Bower and add the `--save` parameter to make sure it will be added to bower.json.

```
$ bower install --save jquery
```

With this final piece, your component's meta information is ready. Still, you're missing two important pieces: the version number and the Git endpoint. Both are done via Git and shown in the next section.

9.3.2 Deploying and registering components

You still need two properties before you can register your components with Bower: a Git endpoint and a version number. Bower requires you to deploy your components with Git. They have to be reachable by a public Git version control repository, so do this on GitHub, on Bitbucket, or on any other publicly available Git hosting service.

> **NOTE** Git is a topic far too big to be covered extensively in this book. This section will show you the basic steps. For more information on Git and versioning, a book like *Git in Practice* by Mike McQuaid (Manning, 2014) is recommended reading.

For this example, we'll assume you already have a repository created on GitHub and an endpoint URL available where you can deploy your files. Go to your folder, and initialize your local repository:

```
$ git init
```

Now, add all the files you've created and commit them:

```
$ git add .
$ git commit -am "initial commit"
```

Add your new endpoint as a remote to your Git repository, and push all your files up to that remote:

```
$ git remote add origin https://path-to-your-github-repository
$ git push origin master
```

Your files are now publicly available, and you have a Git endpoint. The version number is also realized with Git, in the form of a version tag:

```
$ git tag -a v1.0.0 -m "version 1.0"
$ git push origin --tags
```

This will create version 1.0 on GitHub. Refer to the appendix for more information on semantic versioning and correct version numbers. With both the version number and Git endpoint ready, you're now able to add your component to the registry. The Bower registry is a globally available registry server that features a list of components with additional metadata (in the form of a transmitted bower.json) and an Git endpoint to retrieve the available versions as well as the necessary files. When you install a component with Bower, Bower will query the registry for available components (based on the name), and the registry in turn will tell Bower where to query for versions and download files. Figure 9.6 shows this process.

With your deployment ready, you need to tell the Bower registry where your component will be found. You can do this with the following call:

```
$ bower register <component-name> <git-endpoint>
```

In this case it's toggler and the path to the GitHub repository that you got earlier. And that's about it! With each new version tag that you deploy, Bower will be able to download and install a new version of your component!

9.3.3   *Private registries and components*

Bower's architecture is geared toward being completely open source. The registry as well as most of the components are publicly available. Even the documentation states that Bower components should be available for everybody—meaning not in hidden or private Git repositories—once you put them in Bower's public registry. This might not always be the best place for your components. Your company's policy might prohibit publishing them in the wild, or your component might contain confidential data that nobody else is allowed to see.

Bower also has a solution to that problem. First, you're not limited to installing components from the Bower registry. Next to component names, Bower takes a URL as a parameter during the installation call:

```
$ bower install --save http://example.org/main.js
```

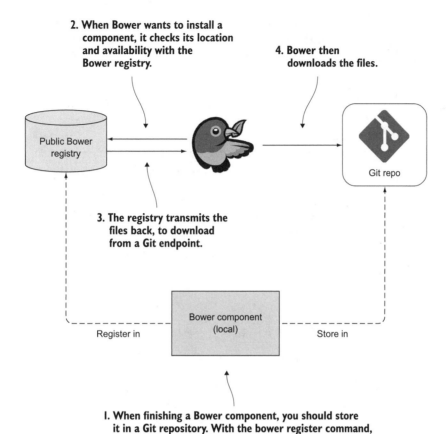

2. **When Bower wants to install a component, it checks its location and availability with the Bower registry.**

4. **Bower then downloads the files.**

Public Bower registry

Git repo

3. **The registry transmits the files back, to download from a Git endpoint.**

Bower component (local)

Register in   Store in

1. **When finishing a Bower component, you should store it in a Git repository. With the bower register command, you can transmit the information from bower.json to the registry. Then Bower knows which files to download and from where.**

Figure 9.6   Once a component is ready to deploy and be stored in a Git repository, you can tell the (public) Bower registry where to find the component and which files should be transmitted. Bower will ask the registry for this information during installation and download the defined files from the Git repo.

This will download and install the file accessible via that URL into your folder of Bower components. This can be any file—CSS, JavaScript, you name it. If you point it to a Zip or TAR file, it will download the file and extract all contents. This way, you can use Bower without needing the registry. We lose some capabilities, however: versioning is done with Git, so you no longer have any versions. Also, you can't conveniently search for components anymore. You have to know where to find them.

Bower allows not only for common URLs but also for Git endpoint URLs to be directly installed:

```
$ bower install --save-dev https://github.com/polymerelements/paper-toggle-
    button
```

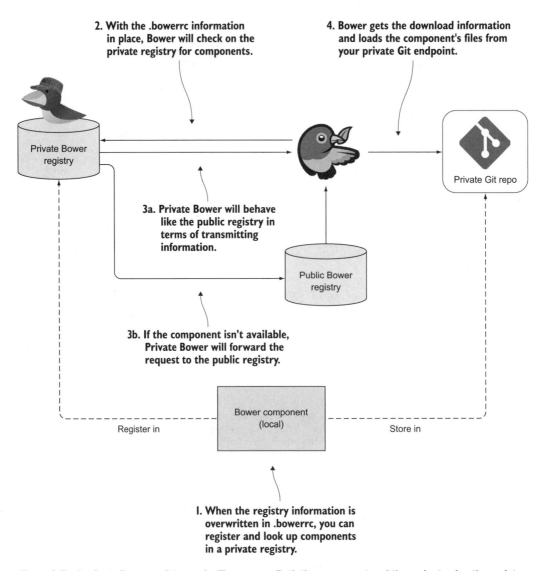

**2. With the .bowerrc information
in place, Bower will check on the
private registry for components.**

**4. Bower gets the download information
and loads the component's files from
your private Git endpoint.**

Private Bower
registry

Private Git repo

**3a. Private Bower will behave
like the public registry in
terms of transmitting
information.**

Public Bower
registry

**3b. If the component isn't available,
Private Bower will forward the
request to the public registry.**

Register in

Bower component
(local)

Store in

**1. When the registry information is
overwritten in .bowerrc, you can
register and look up components
in a private registry.**

Figure 9.7   A private Bower registry works like a proxy. Both the component and the project using the registry
have to specify the registry's address in their .bowerrc file. The private Bower registry answers all calls by
Bower and forwards the calls to the public registry should a component not be available in the private registry.

This will treat the Git repository just as it would be downloaded with Bower. You also
retain versioning, because version tags are maintained via Git. Still, you lose the ability
to search for and find packages.

If you're dealing with lots of private components, you might opt for a private
Bower registry. Bower is written in open source, which means that the Bower registry
app is openly available. You might download and deploy by yourself, or you might
want to use a conveniently packaged solution like Private Bower.

Private Bower functions not only as a private Bower registry but also as a registry proxy. This means that Private Bower will first look at your privately registered components before forwarding that request to the public repository. See figure 9.7 for more details.

Private Bower can be installed and run on any Node.js capable server with

```
$ npm install -g private-bower
$ private-bower
```

After that, the server will be available by your server's hostname or address and port 5678. All you have to do now is tell Bower that you want to use your own registry rather than the public one. For this, you create a Bower configuration file in both your component and the project in which you want to install private Bower components; one file is for registering, and one is for installing. The file is called .bowerrc and should feature the entries shown in the following listing.

> **Listing 9.6   .bowerrc**

```
{
  "registry": "http://path.to.your.registry:5678",
  "timeout": 30000
}
```

If you try out Private Bower on your local machine, point it to http://127.0.0.1:5678 after starting the server. This will allow you to play around with it.

With that, you're able to create not only modules but also components suitable for public and private distribution.

9.4   Summary

This chapter was all about modules and components:

- Asynchronous module definitions, or AMD, allow you to define modules that can be loaded in an asynchronous manner, which is perfect for browsers. They feature two methods called `define` and `require` that have to be provided by a module-loading library like require.js.
- CommonJS modules work in a synchronous manner, stalling execution and needing fast access to memory or the file system. They were created for Node.js but have been adapted using tools like Browserify.
- The Universal Module Definition format, or UMD, combines AMD, CommonJS, and the global namespace using factory functions.
- After creating modules, you promoted them to components. For this, you took a closer look at the contents of the bower.json file. You deployed your components using Git and registered them with the public Bower registry. This makes your components searchable and versioned.

- If for some reason you're restricted from publicly deploying your components, you can use Git endpoints, Zip files, or plain files to install the component without a registry. This also means that you don't retain the benefits of a search for versioning.
- If you're using lots of private components, you have the option to use a private Bower registry or registry proxy using Private Bower. You define a pointer to that registry using the .bowerrc file.

Having a pointer to a company's private Bower registry is something that can be perfectly scaffolded with Yeoman. It's time to pay that tool a visit again.

Advanced
Yeoman generators

10

This chapter covers

- Sub-generators
- Yeoman's file system utilities
- User configurations
- Generator composition

So far you've created a good setup to scaffold new projects. You optimized the build tools for rapid development cycles and created your own components to add to the project. But creating a new project isn't something you do on a daily basis. Depending on the kind of project you're developing, you'll spend weeks, months, or even years expanding, maintaining, and creating new features for it.

And even if your projects start out the same, over the course of time, they're going to differ heavily from each other, both in content and in the structure you're going to use. Think of deciding on one module definition system (UMD, AMD, or CommonJS) at the start of your project. With the addition of each new module, the structural similarities between projects get fewer and fewer. As you switch between projects, or newcomers join the development phase over time, adding new modules or files correctly to your existing project will be subject to friction.

In this chapter you'll learn how to overcome possible friction and inconsistencies for ongoing projects by improving your Yeoman generators. Yeoman generators allow you to set consistently defined project standards across all projects and for every member of your team, by making project templates easy to scaffold. With Yeoman sub-generators you'll be able to maintain the same level of consistency for new project parts, adding new files that correspond to a defined template. This will make Yeoman an important part of your tool chain even after you've rolled out new projects.

10.1 Adding new files to existing projects

The longer a project is running, the more files and modules you'll add to it. Although your current Yeoman generator gives you a good head start to kick off a new project, you won't use it as you expand the codebase. Let's change that.

In the previous chapter you learned about modules. Modules are encapsulated and reusable pieces of code. In JavaScript, they need to follow a certain pattern: AMD, UMD, or CommonJS. The longer you work on a JavaScript app, the more modules you will add to it—modules you create over time. For each module you have to do the following:

- Create a new file.
- Add module boilerplate code to this file (see AMD, UMD, or CommonJS from chapter 9).
- Include this module in your main application file (either a main.js file or the index.html file).

As you can see, there's a list of tasks for each module that you could easily automate, saving you time and reducing possible copy/paste or typing errors. This makes for a great example of one of Yeoman's advanced features: sub-generators. You can use sub-generators to add new modules to your project and edit existing files. Let's take a look.

10.1.1 The concept of sub-generators

Sub-generators are part of the Yeoman generator package and deal with smaller things accompanying the bigger, more complete app generator. They're meant to supplement the app generator with additional scaffolding or to scaffold additional material to an existing project that has been generated with Yeoman. Think of having an app generator that creates a new project (like the one you created in chapter 5). This provides you with the necessary scaffolding for a new project. Sub-generators add files and templates to the existing project; for example, new CommonJS or AMD modules.

Technically, a sub-generator is constructed like a normal generator: it contains a set of templates and assembly instructions to fill those templates with the appropriate content. You learned that already in chapter 5.

It's more the mindset on how to use it that qualifies it as a sub-generator instead of a full app generator. An app generator creates full projects; sub-generators work on a more granular level, adding little pieces to the project created by the app generator—CommonJS modules (via a sub-generator) to your Browserify/LESS-based web application (app generator).

The sub-generator's structure is based on conventions. Whereas the app generator, which is called by `yo generatorname`, is inside the app folder, your sub-generator folder is a direct sibling of this folder, with the sub-generator's name as folder name. See figure 10.1 for an example.

As you can see in figure 10.1, you call a sub-generator by putting its name after a colon, separating it from its app generator. In this example, the name is *module*, because you want to add new modules to your project. Yeoman will then, by convention, call the right assembly instructions from the specific folder. Let's create one for your project's generator.

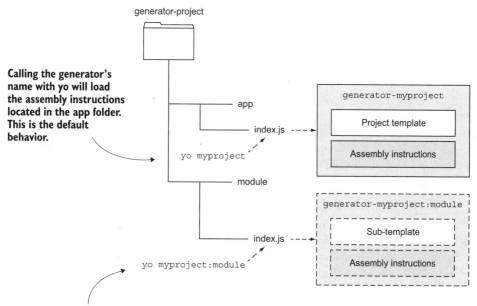

Figure 10.1 How sub-generators are structured inside a Yeoman generator. The full project generator is inside the app folder. The sub-generator's folder is adjacent to it and holds the name of the sub-generator itself. Inside are its own assembly instructions and templates.

In chapter 5, you created a new generator with the generator-generator package. Turns out, this generator also has a sub-generator for...well...sub-generators! Navigate to your myproject generator sample from chapter 5. Inside, you'll call the following:

```
$ yo generator:subgenerator module
```

The structure of this call is as follows:

- `yo generator` will call the generator package called generator-generator.
- `:subgenerator` refers to the subgenerator folder inside the generator-generator package.
- `module` is a required parameter that will name your sub-generator folder.

After calling these instructions, you get the following files:

- A new folder called module in the generators directory
- An index.js with dummy assembly instructions inside this folder
- A template folder inside with some dummy JavaScript file to scaffold
- Some tests that check if all files are scaffolded as planned

With everything in place, let's build your assembly instructions! Note that you can test your sub-generator the same way you did back in chapter 5, by calling `npm link` to make the package available anywhere on your file system.

10.1.2 Assembly instructions for a sub-generator

Your assembly instructions should do the following:

- Create a new file with the module's name inside a modules folder
- Use one of the three module definition systems from chapter 9 for structuring: AMD, UMD, or CommonJS

To create your assembly instructions, open the index.js file in your newly generated modules folder in your favorite text editor. Again, you see some predefined functionality and a generator object, including phases for the Yeoman assembly line. Compared to the app generator, you'll notice some differences.

NO INSTALLATION PHASE
Sub-generators should add only small pieces to an existing project (preferably built by the same app generator). Thus, large installations of dependencies usually don't occur here, which means that the installation phase is usually dropped compared to full-fledged app generators. Add the dependency installation phase only if you really need to.

NO PROMPTING PHASE
Sub-generators should try to use the least amount of prompting (a questionnaire asking for details) possible. Therefore, the generator for sub-generators doesn't include a prompting phase by default. In this example, however, you need a prompting phase to

choose from AMD, UMD, or CommonJS modules. That's why you have to add it yourself. The next listing shows how to add the `prompting` function to your generator object.

Listing 10.1 prompting() function in module/index.js

```
prompting: function () {
  var done = this.async();

  var prompts = [{
    type: 'list',
    name: 'moduletype',
    message: 'Which module type do you want to include',
    choices: [
      'UMD',
      'AMD',
      'CommonJS'
    ],
    default: 'UMD'
  }];

  this.prompt(prompts, function (props) {
    this.props = props;
    done();
  }.bind(this));
},
```

Select from a list of choices by creating a prompt based on the type list.

Save the result in the property named moduletype.

Keep in mind that this is suboptimal. Prompting leads to an interrupted flow because it requires your user to select additional options. A sub-generator, which is meant to be called multiple times a day, should offer the most seamless way of using it. Call it, and it's done. Although you keep the prompting phase in your generator, you'll get rid of the interruption in section 10.2.2.

ADDITIONAL INITIALIZING PHASE

Instead of a prompting phase, the standard sub-generator handles command-line arguments in the initializing phase. Instead of filling out a questionnaire, the user can directly name the required parameters on the command line while calling the generator. The created sub-generator already has an argument in place that you'll use, as shown in the following listing.

Listing 10.2 Excerpt of module/index.js

```
initializing: function () {
  this.argument('name', {
    required: true,
    type: String,
    desc: 'The module name'
  });
},
...
```

Define command-line arguments by using the call to this.argument and giving it a name. ❶

The parameter's behavior is defined by a configuration object. ❷

In this example, you want to store the name of the newly created module ❶. You can set it to required (the Yeoman generator will fail if it's not provided), select one of the JavaScript data types, and give it a description ❷.

It's called via

```
$ yo mygenerator:module newModuleName
```

This will set the parameter name to newModuleName. When you create your sub-generator with the generator:subgenerator by Yeoman, you'll have this piece of code already in place. You don't want to change this because a name parameter is exactly what you need for this example. The next phase should be familiar to you.

THE WRITING PHASE

Writing is still the same as it was in your app generator. Based on the inputs from the previous phases, you're going to copy files from your template directory to the project's directory. Based on the selection in the prompting phase, you choose one of the module templates and create a file based on the argument from the initialization phase.

> **SAMPLE TEMPLATES AT GITHUB**   Please find the necessary files for the template folder on GitHub. Follow this URL https://github.com/frontend-tooling /sub-generator-template and add the JavaScript files to your templates folder.

See the following listing for a sample implementation.

Listing 10.3   Writing phase in module/index.js

```
writing: function () {
    var fromFile = this.props.moduletype.toLowerCase();
    var toFile = this.name;
    this.props.moduleName = this.name;
    this.fs.copyTpl(
        this.templatePath(fromFile + '.js'),
        this.destinationPath('modules/' + toFile + '.js'),
        this.props
    );
}
```

This object will be passed to the copyTpl function, where you copy the selected template to the destination folder.

The new module is named after the argument passed in the initialization phase.

The props field is expanded by the module's name.

The module templates are named just like the options in listing 10.1; using toLowerCase makes sure the file system finds the right template file.

With a few lines of code, you can add new modules on the fly. In the next section, you'll refine the generator for better usability.

10.2 Improving the interface

Creating new modules based on existing templates is all very well, but you still have more steps to automate:

- The new module has to be referenced in a main JavaScript file; otherwise it won't be loaded. Why not automatically add it to the list of modules to load?
- Usually you don't mix different module styles in your projects. Once you've decided on a module definition system, you want to use that throughout the project. You can automate the step of choosing the right module definition system after you decide for the first time.

With those additions, you'll get a much leaner user interface for the developers using the generator. The steps to adding new modules and files to a project are reduced even more. Let's go!

10.2.1 Editing existing files

Every time you create a new module, you want to refer to it in one of your JavaScript files. That can be on demand in other modules or in one main file that loads all the important modules. Let's take CommonJS, for example, where you want to add the newly created module to a list of `require` statements in a main.js file. The main.js file is shown in the next listing.

Listing 10.4   main.js

```
var jquery = require('jquery');
var moduleX = require('./modules/moduleX');
// Add more modules
```

You want to add each newly created module before the comment in line 3. The process can—again—be tedious. Open the main.js file, find the right spot, type in the correct path, and try to avoid any mistakes! Sounds like something you can easily automate with Yeoman. To do so, you need to open the existing main.js file and add some new lines, before writing it back to the hard disk. You can do that with the Node.js file system API or use one of the more convenient shortcuts Yeoman provides. Yeoman includes an `fs` property with file system utilities. You already used that back when you were copying templates from your template directory to the destination path. But these file system utilities include even more: methods to read and write files from and to the hard drive:

- `this.fs.read` takes a file system path and returns a string to work with. This function works synchronously and is thus a little easier to handle than its Node.js counterpart. The `this.fs.readJSON` method does the same but reads a JSON file and returns a JavaScript object.

- `this.fs.write` also takes a file system path as a parameter and saves a string to this file. It overwrites all contents but asks if it is allowed to do so beforehand. The `this.fs.writeJSON` file is the equivalent for JavaScript objects and JSON files.

Let's try it out on some code. The following listing shows how to add a new `require` statement for the CommonJS modules.

Listing 10.5   Excerpt of module/index.js writing phase

destinationPath gives the location of a certain file in the directory where the generator is called—here main.js.

```
writing: function () {
    var moduleType = this.props.moduletype.toLowerCase();
    var toFile = this.name;
    this.props.moduleName = this.name;
    this.fs.copyTpl(
        this.templatePath(moduleType + '.js'),
        this.destinationPath('modules/' + toFile + '.js'),
        this.props
    );

    if(moduleType === 'commonjs') {
        var destPath = this.destinationPath('main.js');
        var contents = this.fs.read(destPath);
        var index = contents.indexOf('// Add more modules');
        contents = contents.substring(0, index) +
            "var " + toFile + " = require('./modules/" + toFile + "')\n"
            + contents.substring(index, contents.length);
        this.fs.write(destPath, contents);
    }
}
```

The require statement for the new module has to be added before the comment line (line 3 in the example); you get the start index of this line…

… and add a new statement before; the substring method from JavaScript helps.

Read all the contents from this file.

Save the contents back to the file. ❶

This will overwrite the whole main.js file ❶. To make sure that nothing goes wrong, the user has to accept overwriting this file. This will cause a small prompt.

Now you not only add new modules to your project but also load them directly. You can do the same with UMD and AMD modules. This allows your developers to immediately start coding, without thinking about getting everything wired up. One call on the command line, and everything is included.

10.2.2 *Dealing with user configurations*

In your sub-generator for modules, you included a prompting phase to let your users decide which module definition system to use. This causes some interruption, because the user has to fill out this questionnaire every time they create a new module. This sometimes happens multiple times a day. But if the users decide once, they most likely won't change their selection. Why not preselect this choice on each new call?

Yeoman has a technique for that called *user configurations*. It's a JSON resource file stored with each project, containing information the generator can read to set the right switches. It's also writeable, which means you can store as many configuration parameters as you like. The user configuration file is called .yo-rc.json and could look like the following listing.

Listing 10.6 .yo-rc.json example

```
{
  "generator-myproject": {
    "moduletype": "amd"
  }
}
```

❶ Yeoman resource files are JSON files, where the first level depicts a list of generators used in this project.

❷ The next level is a property list with configurations for that generator.

In the previous example, you used only the myproject generator ❶. In this example, you preselect the generator ❷.

This file can be read from and written to by an API Yeoman provides. Let's see this in action by directly looking at an example. Imagine the prompting situation from earlier. You prompt the users to select their preferred type of module definition system. Once the choice is made, you store this preference for any further selection. See figure 10.2 for more information.

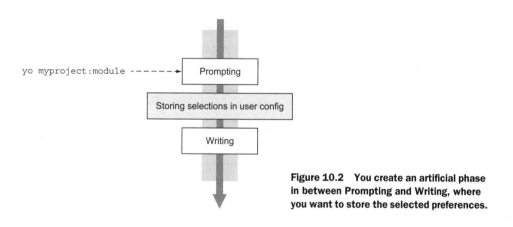

```
yo myproject:module ─ ─ ─ ─ ─▶  Prompting

                               Storing selections in user config

                                Writing
```

Figure 10.2 You create an artificial phase in between Prompting and Writing, where you want to store the selected preferences.

The following listing shows how to implement this with Yeoman's configuration API.

Listing 10.7 Excerpt of module/index.js

```
...
this.prompt(prompts, function (props) {
  this.props = props;
  this.config.set(props);
  done();
}.bind(this));
...
```

❶ The config object is inside the current Yeoman generator.

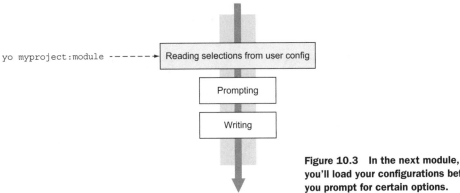

yo myproject:module - - - - - - → Reading selections from user config

Prompting

Writing

Figure 10.3 In the next module, you'll load your configurations before you prompt for certain options.

With set you can pass a whole object of property/value pairs or set each key individually ❶. As you can see in the listing, you can use the this.config.set interface to pass your prompting properties directly into a file. So you've stored the configuration.

Let's move on to the next module. You stored your configuration (whether it's AMD, UMD, or CommonJS) and want to preselect this choice when creating the next module. For that, you need to create a new phase where you do a configuration check before the prompting phase. If you have the necessary configuration in place, you move on directly to writing. See figure 10.3 for a visualization.

Where you set your configuration in the first step, you're going to get your configuration with this step. Take a look at the code in the following listing.

Listing 10.8 Excerpt of module/index.js

Check for a certain condition: is the property you want to prompt for already saved inside your configuration file?

❶ **If so, load all the saved properties and store them in the props object.**

```
if(this.config.get('moduletype')) {
    this.props = this.config.getAll();
    done();
} else {
    this.prompt(prompts, function (props) {
        this.props = props;
        this.config.set(props);
        done();
    }.bind(this));
}
```

Call it done. ❷

If you don't have any properties stored, prompt for them.

Here you simulate the prompting call we'd usually do, saving the right properties to the right field in your Yeoman generator ❶. This is usually for asynchronous callbacks, but you also can call it in synchronous code to state the moment you finish the function ❷.

In this example you used the `get` method to check for specific properties and the `getAll` method to load a whole set of properties. The last method is `delete`, by which you can specifically delete properties that you've saved in your configuration. You can use this for any reset call on your generator, as shown here.

Listing 10.9 module/index.js—initialization phase

```
this.option('reset');                              ①  Define a reset option.
if(this.options.reset) {
  this.config.delete('moduletype');                   Then check if this
}                                                   ②  option has passed.
```

With this call, we enable the generator to parse "-reset" options from the command line ①. Once this option passes, you delete your preferred preset configuration for `moduletype`. With these lines of code, you can call your generator with `yo myproject :module moduleName --reset`. You reset your set configuration and create a new module called moduleName.

With user configurations your submodule generator got even more efficient. Each time you create a new module, you already know the type it should have and are able to produce it without having the user interrupted by the prompting phase.

10.3 Composing generators

Sub-generators extend your generator's features tremendously. Now you're able to not only set up a new project but also create new modules for it or extend the codebase otherwise. But there are still some issues you need to address:

- Sub-generators can tend to be too big for what they're supposed to be. Think of your module sub-generator again: it's handling three different types of modules! Wouldn't it be better if there were three different generators but one interface, separating your concerns accordingly?
- Generators can be redundant. Think of your generator wanting to set up the popular UI framework Bootstrap. There is already an existing `generator-bootstrap`, but it allows your users too much freedom, like selecting the preprocessor framework. You want to streamline that for your project standards, so you might end up creating your own.

Yeoman provides a feature for both issues: generator composition. It allows you to call generators from within a generator and pass certain options and arguments over to it. Let's have a look.

10.3.1 Generator composition with global generators

Let's take the sub-generator issue for a first step. You want to split AMD, UMD, and CommonJS into separate sub-generators and use the myproject:module generator as a common interface for one of the other three. This allows separation of concerns. You can do different things with your sub-generators and call them individually if you need to. The module sub-generator still helps you with preselection but doesn't actually contain template files anymore. Those are stored within other generators. Figure 10.4 shows what to do.

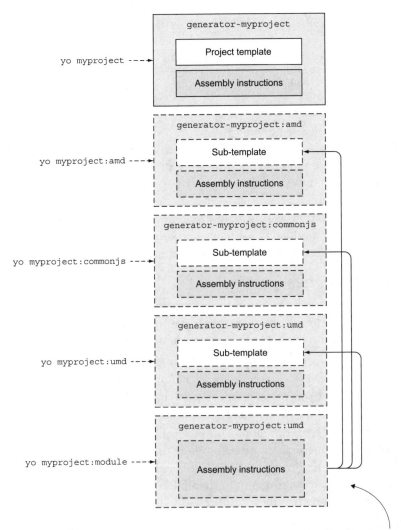

Figure 10.4   Generator composition allows you to use generators within generators. This allows for shortcuts (like myproject:module forwarding to the desired module generator) and for separating writing phases. Each line shows a different command executing a different generator. But within the module generator, you can decide if you want to run one of the others (amd, commonjs, umd).

Let's do that directly in code. First, you refactor your module generators into three similar-looking sub-generators for AMD, UMD, and CommonJS, as shown in the following listing.

Listing 10.10   amd/index.js

```
'use strict';
var yeoman = require('yeoman-generator');

module.exports = yeoman.generators.Base.extend({
  initializing: function () {
    this.argument('name', {
      required: true,
      type: String,
      desc: 'The AMD name'
    });
    this.log('You called the AMD with the argument ' + this.name + '.');
  },

  writing: function () {
    var toFile = this.name;
    this.props = {};
    this.props.moduleName = this.name;
    this.fs.copyTpl(
      this.templatePath('amd.js'),
      this.destinationPath('modules/' + toFile + '.js'),
      this.props
    );
  }
});
```

❶ The AMD generator skips the prompting phase because you don't need any selections.

Fill it with the only parameter possible, the name.

Then copy the specific template to your desired directory. ❷

We want to create AMD modules ❶. That's it! Since we skip the prompting phase, we still have to pass the props Array, so we create it here. This generator pattern is the same for UMD and Common.js ❷.

With that, you now have three separate generators that can be called completely on their own. None of them features a prompting phase, just as sub-generators are intended to do.

The module generator then has a new writing phase, shown in the next listing, where you select the correct sub-generator. Because your myproject generator is globally installed, Yeoman knows where to find the sub-generators you intend to call.

Listing 10.11   module/index.js—writing phase

```
...
writing: function () {
  var name = this.name;
  var module = this.props.moduletype.toLowerCase();
  this.composeWith('myproject:' + module, {
    args: [ name ]
  })
}
...
```

Instead of selecting the correct file, call the respective sub-generator.

Calling a generator with composeWith takes two arguments: the generator's name and an object with options and arguments. ❶

Here you pipe the name you passed as a command-line argument over to the other generator ❶. When compositing generators, you can pass two parameters: arguments and options.

An argument is an array. It consists of a list of values that have been passed to the generator on the command line. In this case, that's the module's name. An option is an object. This contains a list of property and values that will be interpreted by Yeoman as command-line options (think of the reset flag).

Your developers now get one interface, and depending on their selections, they already call one of the three sub-generators. But you can expand each writing phase based on your needs.

10.3.2 *Generator composition with dependencies*

Back to our Bootstrap example: you want to set up the popular UI framework Bootstrap from within your generator. You want to restrain your users from installing Bootstrap in any preprocessor language other than LESS, because your whole project is set up that way. But the original `generator-bootstrap` that you'd use opens up that option. What should you do? Create your own way of installing Bootstrap, or harness the abilities of generator composition to preselect the intended way? Doing it your own way would mean that you'd also have to maintain this project yourself. Using the original Bootstrap generator in your generator means that the Bootstrap generator team will maintain that project for you. I say, let's go for the latter.

The setup is as follows. Instead of loading one of your global generators, which are located in the global node modules directory, you install one of the generators as a dependency and load it from there. See figure 10.5.

To achieve this, you install `generator-bootstrap` locally to your own generator:

```
$ npm install –save generator-boostrap
```

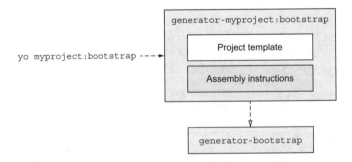

Figure 10.5 generator-bootstrap is included as a dependency of your generator, so it's included in its node_modules. By resolving the path to this generator, you can call it and its sub-generators from within your own Yeoman generator. There's no need to install it globally.

In doing so, the generator will be installed alongside your generator but will only be available locally from within generator-myproject, not globally. That's why you have to resolve the path to it when passing on the options. See the next listing.

Listing 10.12 bootstrap/index.js

```
'use strict';
var yeoman = require('yeoman-generator');

module.exports = yeoman.generators.Base.extend({

  writing: function () {
    this.composeWith('bootstrap', {
      options: {
        format: 'less'
      }
    }, {
      local: require.resolve('generator-bootstrap/app/index.js')
    });
  }
});
```

> The bootstrap sub-generator has a writing phase, where you call the generator-bootstrap app generator by calling the composeWith function.

> **1** Pass the options restraining users from using any other pre-processor.

> **2** You can't rely on your users to install the generator-bootstrap globally, so you install it locally as dependency.

In this case you use less **1**. You can determine how the parameters are called by inspecting the generator-bootstrap documentation. This requires Yeoman to know where to find the generator files **2**. Therefore, you use require.resolve to find the path to the right generator file.

This will bridge the prompting phase of generator-bootstrap and preselect the less flag for you. You can extend this even more. Because generator-bootstrap does little more than install some Bower components, you can later add the appropriate reference to your main.less file, as shown in the following listing.

Listing 10.13 bootstrap/index.js

```
'use strict';
var yeoman = require('yeoman-generator');

module.exports = yeoman.generators.Base.extend({

  writing: function () {
    this.composeWith('bootstrap', {
      options: {
        format: 'less'
      }
    }, {
      local: require.resolve('generator-bootstrap/app/index.js');
    });

      var dpath = this.destinationPath('styles/main.less');
      var contents = this.fs.read(dpath);
      contents += '\n@import "../bower_components/"' +
```

> **1** With the Yeoman path tools, you can easily spot your main.less files in the destination directory.

> Load the contents of this file using the read function of your file system utilities.

> **2** The utilities return a string, so you can add a line as you please.

```
        'components-bootstrap/less/bootstrap";'
   this.fs.write(dpath, contents);
  }
});
```

Then, we write the contents
back again to the file system.

This one was created using the app generator ❶. In this case, just move it to the bottom ❷.

With the last step your generator has become a multicolored beast: you can call different module generators, have an interface to all of them, and even call other generators that might provide additional help for your developers.

10.4 Summary

The second part of this book dealt with reusing certain patterns both in building and in developing. The last chapter brought this to Yeoman generators:

- Sub-generators allow you to modify already scaffolded projects. You add new parts (modules) to existing software, which automates even more tasks usually done by your developers. You implemented different sub-generators for UMD, AMD, and CommonJS modules.
- The Yeoman file system API is comfortable for reading and writing both text and JSON files from and to the hard disk. You can use this and the built-in safety mechanism of an overwriting prompt to change existing files. This is convenient for adding new modules to a main file.
- User configurations save preferences taken by the user, which can help in multiple ways. You can prefill prompts and make your scaffolding even faster, or you can save certain user settings that are important if you want to add new modules later on. Yeoman's user configuration API is a convenient way of loading and saving these configurations.
- Generator composition allows you to use other (sub-)generators to avoid repetition. You can use them to add your own little touch to an existing generator or to create shortcuts that would require user input.

With sub-generators and their APIs, you created a powerful tool that will help you during your development cycle. With it, Yeoman becomes an important part that's used not only at the start of a project but over and over again.

appendix
Introduction to Node.js

This appendix covers

- The Node.js ecosystem for JavaScript-based tools
- NPM as a way to install new Node.js-based modules
- The difference between local installation and global installation
- The contents of a package.json file
- The proper way to handle version numbers

Back in 2009 some clever people at a company called Joyent released Node.js, a standalone implementation of Google's V8 JavaScript engine. Its original goal was to provide an environment for fast network applications. Little did Joyent know that years later and long after the initial hype, developers would be using Node.js for all sorts of things: servers, command-line applications, and even webcam-driven quadcopter steering.

Even though it has become popular because of its primary use of server-side JavaScript, there's much, much more to Node.js. It removes the restrictions caused by the browser environment (which is bound to a platform that's made for display only) and offers developers access to the operating system via a language they already know. The ability for people to have a premier scripting language available for literally any task they want to achieve has contributed to Node's success.

This appendix aims to give you a general introduction to Node.js and the Node.js ecosystem by example.

A.1 Meet Node.js

Node.js is a platform designed to run on every popular operating system, be it Linux, Windows, or Mac OSX. With that said, *run* doesn't necessarily mean "behave the same way across all platforms." There are some differences here and there, mostly when reading file paths because of their different natures, but you'll most likely never encounter them.

For this chapter, and the rest of the book, we expect you to be familiar with your operating system's command-line interface (Terminal on Mac, command prompt on Windows, shell on Linux). You don't have to know all the tricks, but you should have a knack for navigating around the file system and entering simple commands.[1]

Ready? Let's go!

A.1.1 Node.js installation

You have many ways to install Node.js, and the easiest one is to open the website,[2] download the installation bundle for your operating system, and run through the installation wizard. This should work perfectly for Windows and Mac OS X.

On Linux, you probably have Node.js available through your distribution's package manager. The packages found there are made to fit nicely with your operating system's environment, so it's always a better call to use them rather than installing them from the web.

On Windows, make sure that you check the options shown in figure A.1, adding Node and the NPM package manager as well as NPM modules to your PATH environment variable. The NPM package manager is important because it allows you to install Node.js modules for your software. This ensures that you can access the command-line interfaces for those tools wherever you are on your system. Should you miss one of those options in your installation, run the installer again and select them.

Once you've finished the installation, you should make sure the Node.js commands are available in your command-line interface (CLI). Open your CLI and type in the following command:

```
$ node --version
```

---

[1] A good resource for command-line commands for Mac/Linux is available at http://cli.learncodethehardway .org/book/; for Windows use this: http://www.cs.princeton.edu/courses/archive/spr05/cos126/cmd-prompt.html

[2] http://nodejs.org

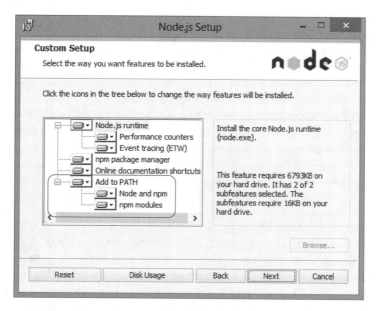

Figure A.1   You must check all of these install options to make sure the environment is intact.

If everything goes right, you'll see output indicating the version of Node.js you've installed. If you enter

```
$ node
```

into your command line, a console prompt will open that's similar to the Console tab in your browser's developer tools, allowing you to write inline JavaScript. See figure A.2 for a quick example. On Windows, you even have a new shortcut to that console in your Start menu.

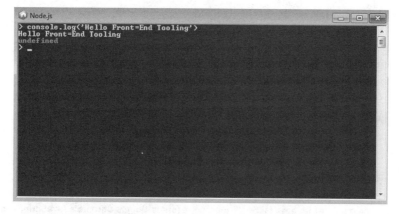

Figure A.2   A simple JavaScript example on the Node.js console

A.1.2   *The Node.js ecosystem*

If you pay attention to the installation, you'll notice that Node.js doesn't come by itself. Rather, you get a package of various parts next to the runtime that build up the Node.js ecosystem, as shown in figure A.3.

THE V8 RUNTIME

Originally a fork of Google Chrome's JavaScript engine, V8 was extracted to run without any reference to the browser. This also means that you don't have things typically available in browser environments (for example, the DOM) available here; you have no navigator or window object. This takes care of the basic syntax. Any JavaScript code you write gets parsed and executed by this runtime.

THE NODE.JS CORE

With Node.js being the JavaScript engine without the rest of the browser, you might guess that you don't have a browser-specific API available, and rightfully so. All HTML-related functionality has been dropped. But to develop software with Node, you need at least some kind of API. The Node.js core consists of such functionality, tailored to work on the server side. This includes file system access, networking protocols, and streaming—briefly speaking, everything that has to do with input and output and thus everything that requires functionality from the operating system. The core is meant to

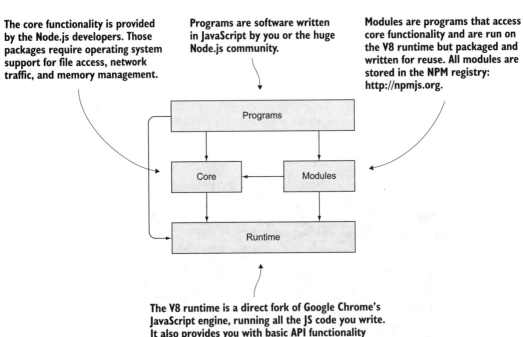

The core functionality is provided by the Node.js developers. Those packages require operating system support for file access, network traffic, and memory management.

Programs are software written in JavaScript by you or the huge Node.js community.

Modules are programs that access core functionality and are run on the V8 runtime but packaged and written for reuse. All modules are stored in the NPM registry: http://npmjs.org.

The V8 runtime is a direct fork of Google Chrome's JavaScript engine, running all the JS code you write. It also provides you with basic API functionality available in the browser, excluding everything that was written for the DOM.

Figure A.3   The Node.js ecosystem. At its base is the V8 runtime, a fork of Google Chrome's JavaScript engine. The Node.js developers provided the core functionality, which allows you to access parts of the operating system. On top of those are programs and modules (programs bundled for reuse).

be as lightweight as possible, which means that only things that are impossible to write in JavaScript are included there.

PROGRAMS

These are any JavaScript that can be written and run using Node.js, either software you write or software provided by third-party developers. You can require functionality from the core and write JavaScript as you're used to doing from the browser. Pack everything into a .js file and run it by calling it on the command line. One simple example would be packing

```
console.log("Hello JavaScript from not the browser! ");
```

into an index.js file and running `node index.js` on the command line afterward. You might already know the output of this little program. `console` in this case is provided by the Node.js core. The rest is simple JavaScript run and executed by the V8 engine.

On Unix-based systems (such as OS X or Linux), adding the line

```
#! /usr/bin/env node
```

to the beginning of a script makes those files executable without calling them as parameters of the `node` command. On Windows, you need a wrapper for that, which is automatically provided by the Node.js package manager (more on that later). This allows you to create and use the command-line tools that are used throughout this book.

MODULES

Finally, there are modules. Modules are a concept of Node.js that assures the reusability of code. Every program that you write can be bundled into a module and packaged for distribution. Modules provide encapsulated functionality that you can use and reuse in your new programs; every JavaScript file is considered a module. To provide functionality from your modules to other programs, Node allows you to export functions and JavaScript objects through a global object called module; with the `exports` property you can define either objects or functions that are visible to the outside, which can look somewhat like this:

```
var LN10 = 2.302585092994046;           ◄——  Define a constant, holding the
                                              logarithmic constant you need
                                              for the base 10 logarithm.

module.exports = function(x) {          ◄——  module.exports is a key symbol in Node.
  return Math.log(x) / LN10;            ◄——  Use basic JavaScript functionality from the
}                                             Math library (not necessary to load).
```

Put the previous code in a log10.js file and you have a function ready for base 10 logarithmic calculations. To use this function, you have to `require` it from another module or program. When you `require` a module (by its filename, for instance), you load the functionality you exposed via `module.exports`:

```
var log10 = require('./log10');         ◄——  require is the opposite of module.exports.
console.log(log10(Math.random()));      ◄——  You can now use this
                                              functionality in your software.
```

NODE MODULES   Note the missing .js suffix. Modules are distributed either by NPM, which is a global module repository, or via endpoints from a version control system like SVN or Git.

A.2   *Global and local node modules via NPM*

Once you install Node, you get not only the whole core and runtime installation but also a way to install Node modules from a centralized server: NPM. NPM *could* be an acronym for "Node package manager," but the developers jokingly distance themselves from thinking of this as an acronym.[3] But we still refer to it as the package manager for Node, because it does exactly that.

A.2.1   *Global versus local installation*

In Node.js there are two ways in which modules can be installed: globally or locally, as shown in figure A.4. Global installation is necessary if you want to install a tool that can run on its own from the command line. Those modules come with an executable file that will be put into your execution path. Take Gulp, for example: installing it globally allows you to execute it with the command gulp wherever you are in your file system. The global modules are stored in a module space, which Node.js links to in your environment variables.

Local installation is the way to go if you want to use those modules for your own software. The modules provide functionality in library code that can be required from your own JavaScript files. You need this functionality in Gulp, where everything that transforms your files is stored in a plugin and therefore library code.

One of the core principles when creating software in Node is that functionality that can be bundled into a module should be bundled into a module. This is also why Node doesn't provide basic runtime functionality like other programming languages that aren't related to operating system functionality. If it can be written in JavaScript, it should be written in JavaScript.

A.2.2   *An example of global installation: LESS*

To understand the concepts behind Node.js in the context of this book, we're setting up an example using LESS, a CSS preprocessor. CSS preprocessors help you author CSS files by adding concepts like variables or mixins (reusable code snippets) to the language. There are plenty of CSS preprocessors available, but LESS runs entirely in JavaScript and subsequently on Node, and it's also one of the most installed tools from the Node.js package repository. You want to install LESS to compile files written for this preprocessor to CSS, which you also use in chapter 2. LESS is written in Node.js, but as an end user you won't notice the technology underneath. It behaves like any other command-line tool. A very basic LESS file looks like this:

---

[3]   See https://docs.npmjs.com/misc/faq#if-npm-is-an-acronym-why-is-it-never-capitalized

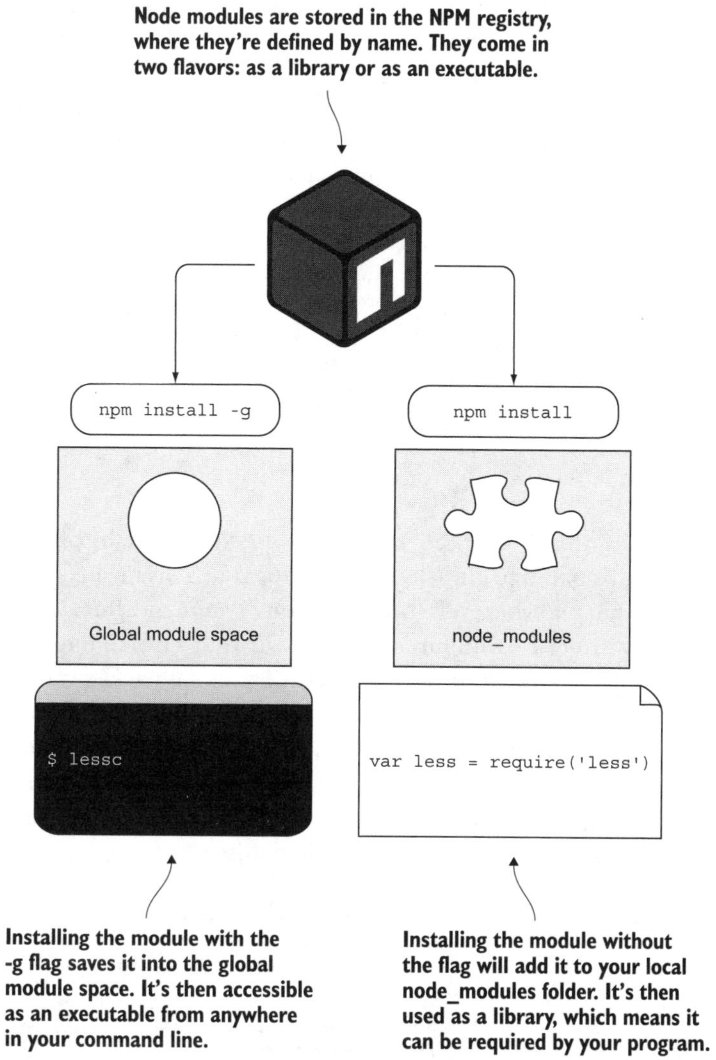

Node modules are stored in the **NPM** registry,
where they're defined by name. They come in
two flavors: as a library or as an executable.

```
npm install -g
```

```
npm install
```

Global module space

node_modules

```
$ lessc
```

```
var less = require('less')
```

Installing the module with the
-g flag saves it into the global
module space. It's then accessible
as an executable from anywhere
in your command line.

Installing the module without
the flag will add it to your local
node_modules folder. It's then
used as a library, which means it
can be required by your program.

Figure A.4 Global vs. local installation. Your goal is to create executable
applications. Global node modules already provide you with executable
programs; local node modules are used as libraries for your own applications.

```
@import (less) "normalize.css";        ◁———❶ The @import rule exists in CSS too.

@firstVariable: blue;                  ◁———❷ Define your first variable.
@secondVariable: red;

body {
  background-color: @secondVariable;   ◁———┐  Instead of using the value
  color: @firstVariable;                  ❸ directly, use your variable.
}
```

With the new (less) annotation you can promote any CSS file that follows to a LESS file ❶. It behaves totally the same, but the import occurs in place, meaning that the entire file is included. You also use a rule starting with @, but the name is totally up to you ❷. Then you can set any value to your new property. You can reuse this variable ❸ throughout the file and change its value in just one place: where you defined it.

The code is very readable, and you probably guess the outcome. You're importing the external CSS file normalize.css (the less parameter makes sure the contents are included in the output file; without it, this command would appear in the output as-is), and the two variables are substituted wherever they appear. You might also recognize that you won't win prizes for outstanding design and aesthetics, but then again, this is just a demo.

Let's compile it. You need the LESS command line for that too, and luckily, it's available on NPM. Boot up your terminal and enter the following:

```
$ npm install -g less
```

This command will download the LESS package from NPM, and by adding the -g parameter, you make this package globally available for you. This means that you have the less command available wherever you're on your command line. This is also a good test to see if everything is configured correctly. If your environment is in tune, you'll see a short spinning animation, followed by a list of subpackages downloaded (in a tree view) on which your tool depends, and the place where it has been installed.

You'll see that some packages LESS depends on have other package names written next to them within braces. Those are dependencies but are needed by your submodule. Although the command-line output shows you all packages and the first level of your dependency tree, the actual tree looks more like this:

```
less@2.4.0                          ◁——————┐    The LESS package you
├?? graceful-fs@3.0.5     ◁─────────┐      │    installed, with the version
├?? mime@1.3.4                      │      │    number after the @ sign
├?? image-size@0.3.5                │
├?? promise@6.1.0                   │
?    ??? asap@1.0.0                 │           A package used by LESS
├?? errno@0.1.1                     │           directly (via require),
?    ??? prr@0.0.0                  │           with the noted version
├?? source-map@0.2.0 ()             │           in its code
?    ??? amdefine@0.1.0
├?? mkdirp@0.5.0 ()
?    ??? minimist@0.0.8        ◁─────────┐      Packages used by LESS also
??? request@2.53.0                       │      might need packages to
    ├?? caseless@0.9.0                   │      work; mkdirp requires this
    ├?? json-stringify-safe@5.0.0        │      version of minimist.
    ├?? forever-agent@0.5.2
    ├?? aws-sign2@0.5.0
    ├?? stringstream@0.0.4
    ├?? oauth-sign@0.6.0
    ├?? tunnel-agent@0.4.0
    ├?? isstream@0.1.2
```

```
├?? node-uuid@1.4.3
├?? qs@2.3.3
├?? combined-stream@0.0.7
├?? mime-types@2.0.9
├?? tough-cookie@0.12.1
├?? http-signature@0.10.1
├?? form-data@0.2.0
├?? bl@0.9.4
???? hawk@2.3.1
```

So although LESS is built upon just a few dependencies, those packages use other modules. This tree can be a lot deeper than two levels, depending on how split-up the other Node modules are. It's even possible that packages are installed twice in different version numbers, just because their dependencies require it. But NPM is clever enough to know when a certain module with a correct version number is available elsewhere and won't download it more than once.

Let's get back to LESS. If your environment is configured correctly, entering

```
$ lessc --help
```

will show you the help output of your downloaded tool. The command

```
$ lessc main.less > main.css
```

takes your main.less file you've written as input and stores the text output in a CSS file. Voila, you've compiled your very first LESS file.

A.2.3 *An example of local installation: Autoprefixer*

In the previous example you installed a tool in your global execution space, available anywhere you need it. Most of those tools not only come with their own command-line interface but also provide a library that you can use in your own projects, which LESS does.

Let's assume that you have some CSS properties in use. You have to apply vendor prefixes to make them runnable on your targeted browsers, but you don't know which prefixes are still in use by current-generation browsers and where they're just code bloat:

❶ This is the official specification of linear gradients.

This feature has been experimental for a long time. ❷

```
header {
    background-image: linear-gradient(to bottom,black,white);
    background-image: -webkit-linear-gradient(top,black,white);
    background-image: -moz-linear-gradient(top,black,white);
}
```

This was also true for older Firefox browsers. ❸

This ❶ gives a direction (to bottom) and defines two colors the gradient should flow from and to. Some WebKit-based browsers (mostly mobile ones) need a vendor prefix (in this case -webkit) to activate this feature. Adding this line ❷ will make gradients available there. Autoprefixer should add this line. Firefox quickly adapted the syntax described previously, and older Firefox browsers that still need a prefix are almost extinct. You wouldn't include the last line of code ❸ because it most likely would get interpreted. Autoprefixer should remove it.

> ### Vendor prefixes
>
> Vendor prefixes are used by browser vendors to denote experimental features, where syntax or functionality is subject to change. Browser vendors use a specific abbreviation that's put before JavaScript methods and CSS properties to differentiate among other browser vendors' implementations, their own, and the final specification. For instance, -webkit-animation is the vendor-prefixed version of the CSS animation property, found in browsers using the WebKit rendering engine.

To achieve this, you can run a tool called Autoprefixer. Autoprefixer catches vendor prefix data from a platform called CanIUse[4] and adds needed prefixes to your CSS properties and values. It also deletes unnecessary prefixes from your code if they aren't used anymore, which keeps your output nice and clean.

Autoprefixer is also a Node.js tool that comes both as an executable from the command line (if you install it globally) and as a library, when installed locally.

If you want to process your LESS code with Autoprefixer, you first have to compile LESS code to CSS and take this output to the Autoprefixer tool. That works with some command-line magic (or LESS's plugin system), but you can also write a little program on your own for this task.

To install both libraries, go to the folder where your project is, and type the following:

```
$ npm install less autoprefixer
```

Note two things: first, the -g parameter is missing, indicating a local installation. A local installation is—compared to a global one—not available anywhere on your file system but exclusively related to the project where you've installed it. Second, you have not one but two more parameters after install, showing that you can install as many libraries as you want with one command. Once you've installed them, you'll notice that you suddenly have a node_modules folder in your directory, containing both packages.

The following listing contains the LESS code you want to process. Save it as a file somewhere on your file system.

---

[4] http://caniuse.com

Listing A.1   main.less

```less
@fore-color: blue;
@back-color: red;

body {
  background-color: @fore-color;

  header {
    background-image: linear-gradient(to bottom,@fore-color,@back-color);
  }
}
```

You have two variables and want to substitute their occurrences with the correct values. The selector body header also has a linear-gradient, which doesn't work on some current-generation mobile platforms. This has to be prefixed.

To create your program, in the library where you've installed your modules, create a new index.js file with the following contents.

Listing A.2   index.js

Use strict mode to not run in any EcmaScript 3 traps.

One of the libraries from the Node.js core used to access the file system

These two lines are the modules you installed earlier.

process.argv holds command-line parameters. ❶

```javascript
'use strict';

var fs       = require('fs'),
    less     = require('less'),
    prefixer = require('autoprefixer');

var filename = (process.argv.length > 2) ? process.argv[2] : undefined;

filename && fs.readFile(filename, function(err, data) {
  if(err) throw err;
  less.render(data.toString(), function(err, output) {
    if(err) {
      console.log(err);
      throw err;
    }
    console.log(prefixer.process(output.css).css);
  });
});
```

If you provided a filename, read the file.

Should an error occur, quit.

Data is available as binary. ❷

Parsing is complete ❸ **and successful.**

You want the third parameter ❶. You run your tool with node index.js main.less; starting from 0, main.less is the third parameter on position 2. toString() gets the string contents, which you pass to the render function from LESS ❷. You parse your LESS code. You then take the compiled CSS code and pass it through to Autoprefixer ❸. Finally, you output your prefixed CSS code.

The program is rather short, and even without further Node.js knowledge, you can pretty much guess what every line of code does. It's JavaScript, after all. Moving away from actually calling methods, I want to guide you to the very first lines, where you require node modules from your installation:

```
var fs       = require('fs'),
    less     = require('less'),
    prefixer = require('autoprefixer');
```

Compared to the example in section A.1.3 where you required your own log10.js module, there's a significant difference between the parameters, a leading dot and a slash:

```
var log10 = require('./log10');
```

The dot with the slash indicates the current directory, which makes this string a path assignment, equal to paths on your file system. If you have any of those characters in the passing string, Node.js will automatically assume that your module is located somewhere on the file system and will try to load it from there. If you don't have any path characters, Node.js will instantly take it for a module and search for the path, as described in figure A.5.

The search process is as follows:

- Is this a module provided by the Node.js core, like fs or http?
- Is this a JavaScript file contained in the node_modules folder?
- Is this a folder with an index.js file contained in node_modules?
- Is this a folder with a package definition file, pointing to the main file of the module?

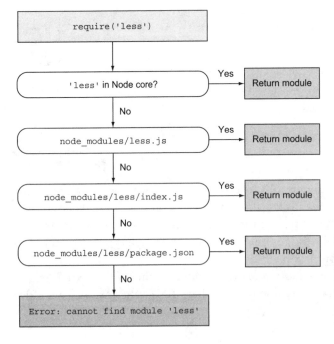

Figure A.5   A flow diagram depicting Node.js's search algorithm for packages. Once a module is required, Node.js runs through a chain of different conditions to check for the right JavaScript file.

If none of those rules apply, Node shoots an error. If Node.js can find the JavaScript files based on those rules, it will load the respective file and expose the API of this JavaScript file to the caller. The last bullet point is special, because you haven't heard from package definition files yet. Those are covered in section A.3.

A.2.4 *Temporarily replacing the global installation with a local one*

Whether you install a package globally or locally, the module, which is downloaded, is always the same. This means that even if you install it locally, the executables are installed too, even if they're not available in your execution path. They're still accessible and executable, though. You can use this fact to your advantage. What if you want to compile LESS files from a legacy project with an earlier version? Perhaps some breaking changes were introduced that would ruin the output of your preprocessor code.

At the time of this writing, LESS is in version 2.6.1. One version that was used for practically ages was version 1.3.3, which was released at the end of 2012. Some of your old, legacy LESS files still might need this version to work. Luckily, you can easily specify the version that you want to download:

```
$ npm install less@1.3.3
```

You can now access the executable directly from the point where you installed it:

```
 ./node_modules/less/bin/lessc —version
util.puts: Use console.log instead
lessc 1.3.3 (LESS Compiler) [JavaScript]
```

Even if you've installed the modern 2.4.0 LESS globally and made it accessible throughout your file system, you still have a way to run a separate and contained legacy version of the same program locally to run your legacy LESS code. You access the whole functionality but without interference from the global version you'd run otherwise. This is a great way to ensure that you still can use your old projects without risking serious breaks. You also can use different versions of your tool safely without updating your whole environment.

A.3 *Distribution and versioning of modules*

In the previous section you saw that the last spot where Node looks for a module to load is the package definition file, or package.json, as we'll call it from now on. Although we didn't cover this file at all until now, it's by far one of the most important pieces when dealing with modules, because it contains all the necessary data to keep your module running.

A.3.1 *The contents of a package.json file*

A package.json files serve two purposes:

- Defining all the necessary metadata so the NPM module registry can work with your package

- Saving information for dependencies and development dependencies, so NPM knows which submodules it has to install for your module

Let's look at the package.json from your LESS module. I suggest you open the file on GitHub,[5] where additional metadata, which is added by publishing your module to the NPM registry, is missing. This makes it a lot more readable for you:

```
{
    "name": "less",
    "version": "2.4.0",                          ❶ name, version, description
    "description": "Leaner CSS",
    "homepage": "http://lesscss.org",
    "author": { "name": "Alexis Sellier", "email": "self@cloudhead.net"},
    "contributors": [ "The Core Less Team" ],
    "bugs": { "url": "https://github.com/less/less.js/issues" },   homepage, author, ❷
    "repository": {                                                contributors
        "type": "git",
        "url": "https://github.com/less/less.js.git"
    },
    "bin": { "lessc": "./bin/lessc" },           ◄──── ❹ bin
    "main": "index",                             ◄──── ❺ main
    "engines": { "node": ">=0.10.0" },           ◄──── ❻ engines
    "scripts": { "test": "grunt test" },         ◄──── ❼ scripts
    "dependencies": { ... }                      ◄──── ❽ dependencies
    "optionalDependencies": {                    ◄──── ❾ optionalDependencies
        "errno": "^0.1.1",
        "graceful-fs": "^3.0.5",
        ...
    },
    "devDependencies": {                         ◄──── ❿ devDependencies
        "diff": "^1.0",
        "grunt": "^0.4.5"
        ...
    },
    "keywords": [ ... ]
}
```

repository, bugs ❸

Here you define the name and version with which your package will be recognized in the NPM registry ❶. You can update the version number manually when designing your own modules. The NPM registry stores older versions. As shown before, you can install them with npm install <packagename>@<versionnumber>. This ❷ is the place where you can proudly shine. And this ❸ is the place for your users to go if you didn't shine. Here you can find information, usually GitHub addresses, where you can give feedback or look at the source code. You can also point to internal bug tracker projects and source repositories. If you have a tool that can be run from the command line, you can define the symbolic link or CMD (a.k.a the executable file) as well as the file it should point to ❹. You can also define more than one executable pointing to a

---

[5] https://github.com/less/less.js/blob/master/package.json

different file. Node will create both executables for you. All commands you want to install globally will have to be defined here.

When working with the module locally, you can define the main file of your library ❺. Usually it's index.js, but you can point to any JavaScript file you like. Other than the bin property, this one can't be an object with multiple entries and has to point to a single instance. The engines field allows you to specify the minimal version of your Node engine, where you know your software will work ❻. Here ❼ you can define some command-line shortcuts that you can run via npm. In this example, you defined test to point to grunt test, which can be executed through npm run test. This might not look like much of an efficiency gain at first, but it wasn't defined solely to have shortcuts but also to have specified entry points for software using your module to run defined commands. In this case, you know that you can run unit tests by calling this command, but you don't care how those unit tests are executed. Continuous integration platforms like Travis[6] make use of this.

Simple and straightforward, your software depends on those Node modules, and it won't run without them ❽. NPM will install them. If it can't find a module, the installation process will fail and your module will be marked as incomplete. Install them with npm install --save underscore. You get extra benefits if you use these modules, but your software won't break if NPM can't find the packages ❾. NPM will install them, but should they no longer be available, NPM will continue with success anyway. Install them with npm install --save-dev grunt. You'll need these dependencies if you want to develop on the module itself, like a build system, or tests, or something similar ❿. These won't be installed unless you tell NPM to do so. Install them with npm install --save-optional errno.

Because the package.json file stores all dependencies, you don't have to save your node_modules folder if you commit your modules to source code repositories or if you publish them to the NPM registry.

A simple $ npm install command in a folder where a package.json is available reinstalls all dependencies that have been defined in the correct version number. This is also helpful if you tried to update one of your dependencies (by using npm update <packagename>), and you found out that the update didn't work out with your previously installed modules. Just delete node_module and reinstall everything using this simple command.

Also notice that the version numbers are noted next to the package name in the package.json definition file. You might also recognize the symbol right before them, the caret (^):

```
"devDependencies": {
  "diff": "^1.0",
  "grunt": "^0.4.5"
  ...
},
```

This, of course, has a special meaning.

---

[6] http://travis-ci.org

A.3.2   *NPM version handling*

When you install a dependency or module for the first time and store it in your package.json, NPM adds the caret symbol (^) before your version number. This caret tells NPM that this was the version you installed originally, but you can use one with a higher version if it fits the definition of compatibility. To understand how this compatibility is defined, we have to make a short excursion to a versioning system created by people at GitHub, called SemVer,[7] shown in figure A.6.

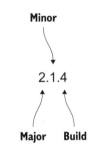

Minor

2.1.4

Major   Build

Figure A.6   Versioning system

Version numbers usually consist of three parts: the version major (the first number), the version minor (the middle number), and the build number (the last number). Having version numbers with those three parts is common, but SemVer has a system behind it.

This system has a lot of rules, but to sum it up in three key concepts, we can define it as follows:

- The major version gets incremented if you introduce breaking changes to your software, which means that your API has functionality that's incompatible with previous versions.
- The minor version gets incremented if you introduce new functionality but in a backward-compatible manner. Your API is still intact, but internally it works differently. Here you can also introduce deprecations of functionality you want to remove with the increment of the next major version.
- The build number is incremented if you introduce bug fixes to your existing API. Nothing significant changes here.

This means a build change is mandatory to update, a minor change is good to update, and if you're going full major, you probably won't take on any other tasks for the upcoming weeks.

NPM thinks the same way; that's why they introduced some steering symbols where you can automate the decision as to which version to use.

Adding a tilde symbol (~) says "Install a package *reasonably close* to the defined version." So for ~1.2.3, NPM takes any build number into account starting from 1.2.3 up to (and excluding) 1.3.0. A caret symbol (^) says "Install a package *compatible with* the defined version." This takes the minor number into account. So for ^1.2.3, you get any package up to the next major version, which would 2.0 (excluding that one).

If you've already downloaded a package, type `npm install`, and if a newer one is available, NPM will still use the installed one.

---

[7] Short for Semantic Versioning: http://semver.org

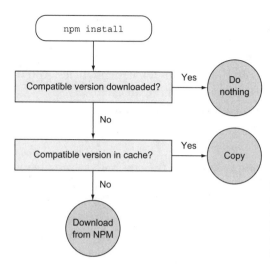

**Figure A.7   How NPM handles downloads.
A call to npm install checks to see if a
compatible version is already installed. If not,
it checks for a compatible version in the
download cache. If it's still not available, it
checks the NPM registry.**

The process illustrated in figure A.7 is similar if you've already installed a package. If
you reduce the version number afterward but have a higher version installed, NPM will
also keep that one in your project:

$$1.2.0 <= {\sim}\mathbf{1.2.4} < 1.3.0$$
$$1.0.0 <= {\wedge}\mathbf{1.2.4} < 2.0.0$$

SemVer works incredibly well in the context of Node.js, but it has one pitfall to keep in
mind: if your major version is zero, the software is in beta, and your API is considered
unstable. This is a sign for developers using that package that functionality as well as
interfaces are subject to change and might be considerably different once the module
reaches version 1.0.

A.3.3   *Creating modules and publishing*

If you want to bundle your software as a module of its own, you need to do two things:

1 Provide a package.json.
2 Make it publicly available.

So you want to create your own package.json for storing dependencies and take credit
for your awesome new module. You can do that in different ways:

- Create one from scratch and type everything on your own.
- Adapt from an existing one.
- Use the tool provided by NPM.

If you type

```
$ npm init
```

you'll get a short command-line questionnaire. This questionnaire is pretty clever. If you already specified a Git endpoint, it will add this information on its own. If you specified a main file in the root of your project, it will also add its name (if you haven't, it will assume that you created an index.js file at some point). It also stores all your downloaded and installed Node modules under dependencies. You'd have to edit it afterward if you wanted to put them somewhere different.

If you already have a package.json available, it will read that first and prompt for the options you haven't specified yet.

PUBLISHING

Now it's time to publish it. The easiest way is using the npm publish command in your command line. Provided your module's name is free to use, your code will be available on the NPM module registry[8] and thus searchable and installable.

There's another way, which is the preferred one if you might have some confidential company information inside your JavaScript (which you shouldn't): you can leave your module on your Git repository. You can use npm install with a Git URL as a parameter, making all the other commands (except search) available to you without a registry.

The package.json file is the key to all features of a Node.js module. It stores version numbers, handles installation and dependencies, and takes care of pointing to the correct files developers need when working with the modules. With the insights you gained in the previous sections, there's nothing keeping you from developing Node.js software.

A.4   *Summary*

In this appendix, you learned how the basic concepts behind Node.js work in the context of the book:

- The Node.js ecosystem consists of the runtime, the core, the modules, and your own written programs.
- Node.js modules are published and distributed via NPM, the Node.js module registry.
- Modules can be installed globally or locally. If installed globally, they're used as a tool; installed locally, they're used as a library.
- When installed locally and used as a library, the package must feature an index.js file or specific meta information for a main file in the package.json. This makes it possible to require the package in your own code.
- Node modules must provide a package.json file. Package.json files contain necessary metadata for your module as well as their various kinds of dependencies.

---

[8] http://www.npmjs.org

index

Angular 2 Development with TypeScript
by Yakov Fain and Anton Moiseev

ISBN: 9781617293122
325 pages
$44.99
November 2016

Secrets of the JavaScript Ninja,
Second Edition
by John Resig, Bear Bibeault, and Josip Maras

ISBN: 9781617292859
464 pages
$44.99
August 2016

Getting MEAN with Mongo, Express,
Angular, and Node
by Simon Holmes

ISBN: 9781617292033
440 pages
$44.99
November 2015

For ordering information go to www.manning.com

MORE TITLES FROM MANNING

JavaScript Application Design
A Build First approach
by Nicolas G. Bevacqua

ISBN: 9781617291951
344 pages
$39.99
January 2015

Building the Web of Things
With examples in Node.js and Raspberry Pi
by Dominique D. Guinard and Vlad M. Trifa

ISBN: 9781617292682
344 pages
$34.99
June 2016

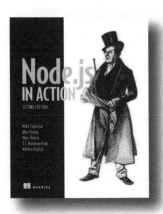

Node.js in Action, Second Edition
by Mike Cantelon, Alex Young, Marc Harter,
   T.J. Holowaychuk, and Nathan Rajlich

ISBN: 9781617292576
450 pages
$49.99
May 2017

For ordering information go to www.manning.com